PAUL RICOEUR

PHILOSOPHY & SOCIAL CRITICISM

Series Editor: David M. Rasmussen, Boston College

This series presents an interdisciplinary range of theory and critique emphasizing the interrelation of continental and Anglo-American scholarship as it affects contemporary discourses. Books in the series are aimed at an international audience, focusing on contemporary debates in philosophy and ethics, politics and social theory, feminism, law, critical theory, postmodernism and hermeneutics.

PAUL RICOEUR

The Hermeneutics of Action

EDITED BY

Richard Kearney

SAGE Publications

London • Thousand Oaks • New Delhi

This edition first published 1996

Previously published as a Special Issue of the journal
Philosophy and Social Criticism, volume 21 (1995),
number 5/6.

 SAGE Publications Ltd
6 Bonhill Street
London EC2A 4PU

SAGE Publications Inc
2455 Teller Road
Thousand Oaks, California 91320

SAGE Publications India Pvt Ltd
32, M-Block Market
Greater Kailash - I
New Delhi 110 048

British Library Cataloguing in Publication data

A catalogue record for this book
is available from the British Library

ISBN 0 7619 5138 5
ISBN 0 7619 5139 3 (pbk)

Library of Congress catalog record available

Typeset by Type Study, Scarborough, North Yorkshire
Printed in Great Britain by The Cromwell Press Ltd,
Broughton Gifford, Melksham, Wiltshire

Contents

Richard Kearney

Introduction

The shortest route from self to self is through the other. This dictum of Paul Ricoeur expresses his central conviction that the self is never enough, is never sufficient unto itself, but constantly seeks out signs and signals of meaning in the other.

Hence Ricoeur's resolute refusal of the idealist temptation – extending from Hegel to Husserl and Sartre – to reduce being to being-for-consciousness. Hence also his renunciation of the 'short route' to being, advanced by Heidegger, out of commitment to the 'long route' of multiple hermeneutic detours through the exteriorities of sense, instantiated in culture, society, politics, religion and the human sciences. This brave, and often arduous, option is further exemplified in Ricoeur's resolve to keep existential understanding (*Verstehen*) in dialogue with scientific explanation (*erklären*) – by way of deepening science and delimiting ontology. No approach to meaning can dispense with detour. Consciousness must pass through the unconscious (the semantics of desire); intuition through critical interpretation (hermeneutics of suspicion); reason through language (linguistics); and reflection through imagination (poetics).

Ricoeur's hermeneutic detours arise ultimately out of a fidelity to an ontology which, in the final analysis, must always remain 'truncated' – provisional, tentative, a task rather than a fait accompli, a wager rather than a possession. This is why Ricoeur compares ontology to a promised land which can only be glimpsed before dying, but never occupied as such. The way of appropriation must always go through the way of disappropriation. There is no belonging except through distantiation. The self can only retrieve itself through the exodus of oneself-as-another. But this return of self (*moi*) to itself (*soi-même*) also carries with it an additional charge: a call to *action*. This final answerability of self to other is registered in Ricoeur's work

Introduction

as both a poetic responsibility to the alterity of sense and an ethical responsibility to other sufferers and supplicants. Both forms of summons, poetical and ethical, extend along the asymptotic lines of an interminable horizon, that of an ontology of action.

In the heel of the hunt, it is probably true to say that the fundamental *désir à être* sketched in Ricoeur's phenomenology of will, finds its term in an *ontologie d'agir*, where the hermeneutic subject returns from text to action.

The current collection opens with three recent essays by Paul Ricoeur, each epitomizing his concern to apply hermeneutics to the practical field of justice, responsibility and politics. The subsequent essays in this *Festschrift* are drawn largely from a conference marking Ricoeur's 80th birthday held in Naples in May 1993. The review essays in the final section pay tribute by way of critical commentaries on a number of recent Ricoeur publications, most of which are not yet available in English. Finally, I would like to thank David Rasmussen for kindly inviting me to serve as guest editor of this issue, Debra Matteson for her expert editorial assistance, and of course the various contributors to this volume. The fact that these contributors hail from nine different countries (Canada, Denmark, France, Germany, Great Britain, Ireland, Italy, Luxembourg and the United States) is, I believe, a telling indicator of the international import and influence of Ricoeur's work.

University College Dublin, Ireland

Paul Ricoeur

Reflections on a new ethos for Europe

It is no extravagance to formulate the problem of the future of Europe in terms of imagination. The political organization of Europe poses the unprecedented problem of how to get beyond the form of the nation-state at the institutional level, without repeating its well-known structures at a higher level of 'supranationality'. Furthermore, the invention of new institutions cannot be fashioned after any of the existing federal states (Switzerland, Germany, the United States of America) which are holders of the same symbols of sovereignty (currency, army, diplomacy) as the less complex nation-states. The expression 'post-national state' meets these two requirements, insofar as it leaves open – precisely to the imagination – the question of knowing what new institutions can respond to a political situation which is itself without precedent.

I should like to say here how a reflection which focuses on the ethical and spiritual activities of individuals, intellectuals and cultivated persons, and also of intellectual communities, churches and other religious denominations, can contribute to this political imagination.

Indeed, it would be a mistake to believe that transfers of sovereignty in support of a political entity which is entirely unrealized can be successful at the formal level of political and juridical institutions without the will to implement these transfers deriving its initiative from changes of attitude in the ethos of individuals, groups and peoples.

The problem is familiar enough. Taken as a whole it is a matter of combining 'identity' and 'alterity' at numerous levels that will need to be distinguished. What we most desperately lack are models of integration between these two poles. For the moment, I refer to these poles in highly abstract terms, not unlike the supercategories of Plato's *Dialogues*! However, in order to shatter this impression of disconcerting abstraction I propose to classify models for the integration of identity and alterity according to an increasing order of spiritual density.

I The model of translation

The first model which is presented for consideration is that of the translation of one language into another. This first model is perfectly appropriate for the situation of Europe which, from the linguistic point of view, displays an irreducible pluralism which it is infinitely desirable to protect. Of course, it is not the dream of giving another chance to Esperanto which threatens us most, nor even the triumph of one great cultural language as the sole instrument of communication; rather it is the danger of incommunicability through a protective withdrawal of each culture into its own linguistic tradition that threatens us. But Europe is and will remain ineluctably polyglot. It is here that the model of translation entails requirements and assurances which extend all the way to the heart of the ethical and spiritual life of both individuals and peoples.

In order to understand this model, a turning-back to the most fundamental conditions of the workings of language is required. It is necessary to begin with the fact that language (*le langage*) exists nowhere else than in languages (*des langues*). It realizes its universal potentialities only in systems differentiated on phonological, lexical, syntactic and stylistic levels, etc. And yet languages do not form closed systems which exclude communication. If that were the case there would be differences between linguistic groups similar to those which exist on the biological level between living species. If there is only one human race, it is because transferences of meaning are possible from one language to another; in short, because we can translate.

But what does it mean to be able to translate? This possibility, or rather this capacity, is not ascertained solely by the fact that we actually succeed in translating speech and texts from one language to another without totally prejudicial and, above all, entirely irreparable semantic loss. The possibility of translating is postulated more fundamentally as an a priori of communication. In this sense, I will speak of 'the principle of universal translatability'. Translation is de facto; translatability is de jure. It is this presupposition which has reinforced the courage and stimulated the ingenuity of the decipherers of hieroglyphics and of other systems of signs, some of which still remain undisclosed. But let us look closely at the translation process itself. First, it presupposes bilingual translators, thus flesh and blood mediators; then it consists of the search for optimum commensurability between the distinctive resources of the receiving language and those of the original language. In this respect, the arrogant model of the 'remains of the Egyptians', which we find at one point in St Augustine, is not a worthy one. The model to be preferred is the more modest one proposed by von Humboldt, i.e. that of raising the distinctive spirit of his own language to the level of that of the foreign language, particularly when it is a matter of original productions which constitute a challenge for the receiving language. It is really a matter of living with the other in order to take that other to one's home as a guest.

We see immediately how translation constitutes a model which is suited to the specific problem that the construction of Europe poses. First, at the institutional level, it leads us to encourage the teaching of at least two living languages throughout the whole of Europe in order to secure an audience for each of the languages which is not in a dominant position at the level of communication. But, above all, at a truly spiritual level, it leads us to extend the spirit of translation to the relationship between the cultures themselves, that is to say, to the content of meaning conveyed by the translation. It is here that there is need of translators from culture to culture, of cultural bilingualists capable of attending to this process of transference to the mental universe of the other culture, having taken account of its customs, fundamental beliefs and deepest convictions; in short, of the totality of its significant features. In this sense we can speak of a *translation ethos* whose goal would be to repeat at the cultural and spiritual level the gesture of linguistic hospitality mentioned above.

II The model of the exchange of memories

I call the second model that of the exchange of memories. We see immediately how it links up with the preceding model: to translate a foreign culture into the categories peculiar to one's own presupposes, as we have said, a preliminary transference to the cultural milieu governed by the ethical and spiritual categories of the other. Now the first difference which calls for transference and hospitality is a difference of memory, precisely at the level of the customs, rules, norms, beliefs and convictions which constitute the identity of a culture. But to speak of memory is not only to evoke a psycho-physiological faculty which has something to do with the preservation and recollection of traces of the past; it is to put forward the 'narrative' function through which this primary capacity of preservation and recollection is exercised at the public level of language. Even at the individual level, it is through stories revolving around others and around ourselves that we articulate and shape our own temporality. Two noteworthy phenomena concern us here.

The first is the 'narrative identity' of the characters of the story. At the same time that the recounted actions receive the temporal unity of a story from the plot, the characters of the story can also be said to be plotted out (*mise en intrigue*). They are recounted at the same time as the story itself. This first remark has many consequences of which the following is the most important: narrative identity is not that of an immutable substance or of a fixed structure, but rather the mobile identity issuing from the combination of the concordance of the story, taken as a structured totality, and the discordance imposed by the encountered events. Alternatively put, narrative identity takes part in the mobility of the story, in its dialectic of order and disorder. An important corollary is suggested here: it is possible to revise a recounted story which takes account of other events, or even which organizes the recounted events differently. Up to a point, it is possible to tell several stories based on the same events (however we may then give meaning to the expression: the same events). This is what happens when we endeavour to take account of other people's stories.

This last remark leads to the second phenomenon which needs to be emphasized here. If each of us receives a certain narrative identity from the stories which are told to him or her, or from those that we tell about ourselves, this identity is mingled with that of others in such a way as to engender second order stories which are themselves intersections between numerous stories. Thus, the story of my life is a segment of the story of your life; of the story of my parents, of my friends, of my enemies, and of countless strangers. We are literally 'entangled in stories', according to W. Schapp's beautiful title, *In Geschichten Verstrickt*.

From these two phenomena taken together – 1) narrative constitution of each personal identity, and 2) the entanglement of personal incidents in stories conveyed by some and heard by others and above all told by some about others – a model of memory-exchange emerges whose ethical import is easy to grasp. To communicate at the level where we have already conducted the work of translation, with its art of transference and its ethics of linguistic hospitality, calls for this further step: that of taking responsibility, in imagination and in sympathy, for the story of the other, through the life narratives which concern that other. This is what we learn to do in our dealings with fictional characters with whom we provisionally identify through reading. These mobile identifications contribute to the reconfiguration of our own past and that of the past of others, by an incessant restructuring of stories that we tell, some of them about others. But a more profound engagement is required by the transition from the level of fiction to that of historical reality. It is not of course a matter of actually reliving the events that happened to others; the inalienable character of life experiences renders this chimerical 'intropathy' impossible. More modestly, but also more energetically, it is a matter of exchanging memories at the narrative level where they are presented for comprehension. A new ethos is born of the understanding applied to the complex intertwining of new stories which structure and configure the crossroads between memories. It is a matter there of a genuine task, of a genuine labour, in which we could identify the *Anerkennung* of German Idealism, that is, 'recognition' considered in its narrative dimension.

The transposition to the level of the European problematic is evident. But the second lesson, that drawn from the entanglement of stories at the interpersonal level, reaches its objective only if the first – the narrative constitution of specific identity – has been well under-stood and completely accepted. The identity of a group, culture, people, or nation, is not that of an immutable substance, nor that of a fixed structure, but that, rather, of a recounted story. Now the contemporary implications of this principle of narrative identity have not yet been perceived. A rigid and arrogant conception of cultural identity prevents us from perceiving the corollaries of this principle mentioned above: the possibilities of revising every story which has been handed down and of carving out a place for several stories directed towards the same past. What really prevents cultures from allowing themselves to be recounted differently is the influence exercised over the collective memory by what we term the 'founding events', the repeated commemoration and celebration of which tend to freeze the history of each cultural group into an identity which is not only immutable but also deliberately and systematically incommunic-able. The European ethos which is sought does not of course require the abandonment of these important historical landmarks, but rather an effort of *plural reading*: one first example of which is the dispute among French historians about the meaning of the French Revolution; another is the dispute among German historians regarding the significance of the criminal episodes of the Second World War. *Recounting differently* is not inimical to a certain historical reverence to the extent that the inexhaustible richness of the event is honoured by the diversity of stories which are made out of it, and by the competition to which that diversity gives rise.

This ability to recount the founding events of our national history in different ways is reinforced by the exchange of cultural memories. This ability to exchange has as a touchstone the will to share symbolically and respectfully in the commemoration of the founding events of other national cultures as well as those of their ethnic minorities and their minority religious denominations.

In this exchange of memories it is a matter not only of subjecting the founding events of both cultures to a crossed reading, but of helping one another to set free that part of life and of renewal which is found captive in rigid, embalmed and dead traditions. In this regard, I deferred up to now any mention of 'tradition'. Indeed, it is only at the end of the twofold linguistic and narrative course just proposed that we can go beyond clichés and anathemas concerning tradition. It is necessary for us to have gone through the ethical requirements of translation – what I call linguistic hospitality – and through the requirements of the exchange of memories – narrative hospitality – in order to approach the phenomenon of tradition in its specifically dialectical dimension. Tradition means transmission, transmission of things said, of beliefs professed, of norms accepted, etc. Now such a transmission is a living one only if tradition continues to form a partnership with innovation. Tradition represents the aspect of debt which concerns the past and reminds us that nothing comes from nothing. A tradition remains living, however, only if it continues to be held in an unbroken process of reinterpretation. It is at this point that the reappraisal of narratives of the past and the plural reading of founding events come into effect.

What remains to be considered now is the second pole of the partnership of tradition and innovation. With regard to innovation, an important aspect of the rereading and the reappraisal of transmitted traditions consists in discerning past promises which have not been kept. Indeed, the past is not only what is bygone – that which has taken place and can no longer be changed – it also lives in the memory thanks to arrows of futurity which have not been fired or whose trajectory has been interrupted. The unfulfilled future of the past forms perhaps the richest part of a tradition. The liberation of this unfulfilled future of the past is the major benefit that we can expect from the crossing of memories and the exchange of narratives. It is principally the founding events of a historical community which should be submitted to this critical reading in order to release the burden of expectation that the subsequent course of its history carried and then betrayed. The past is a cemetery of promises which have not been kept. It is a matter of bringing them back to life like the dry bones in the valley described in the prophecy of Ezekiel (Ch. 37).

III The model of forgiveness

What has just been said about the revival of promises of the past which have not been kept leads to a third opening: that of forgiveness. The considerations which follow are linked in a double sense to the preceding discussion. On the one hand, the role of the story in the constitution of narrative identity has indicated what we have called the revision of the past, a revision which is effected by recounting in a different way. Forgiveness is a specific form of the revision of the past and, through it, of the specific narrative identities. On the other hand, the entanglement of life stories gives occasion for a revision which is neither solitary nor introspective of its own past, but rather a mutual revision in which we are able to see the most valuable yield of the exchange of memories. Forgiveness is also a specific form of that mutual revision, the most precious result of which is the liberation of promises of the past which have not been kept.

The novelty of this third model is connected to a phenomenon – a complement of the founding events which a historical community glories in – namely, the wounds inflicted by what Mercea Eliade called the 'terror of history'. What has been said above under the heading of the exchange of memories must no longer be investigated through the perspective of glorious deeds but rather through this new perspective of suffering. Suffering appears twice, then, in the tableau of our meditation: it appears in the first instance as endured suffering which transforms the agents of the story into victims; it appears a second time as suffering inflicted on others. This point is so important that it is necessary to reverse the order followed above when we passed from narrative identity to the entanglement of life stories. It is necessary this time to proceed from the suffering of others; imagining the suffering of others *before* re-examining one's own.

A major feature of the history of Europe is the extraordinary weight of suffering which the majority of states, great or small, taken in pairs or in interposed alliances, have inflicted in the past. The history of Europe is cruel: wars of religion, wars of conquest, wars of extermination, subjugation of ethnic minorities, expulsion or reduction to slavery of religious minorities; the litany is without end. Europe is barely emerging from this nightmare. We know only too well what tendencies lead back to these horrors: the perverse recourse to a narrative identity which is devoid of the important correctives already noted, namely the examination of one's own stories and the entanglement of our stories with the stories of others. To these important correctives we now add the following complement: that of understanding the suffering of others in the past and in the present. According to this new model, then, the exchange of memories required by our second model calls for the exchange of the memory of sufferings inflicted and sustained. This exchange demands more than the imagination and sympathy which were called for above. This 'extra' has something to do with forgiveness insofar as forgiveness consists in 'shattering the debt', according to the beautiful subtitle of the volume dedicated to the theme of forgiveness by Editions Autrement.

Forgiveness, in its full sense, certainly far exceeds political categories. It belongs to an order – the order of charity – which goes even beyond the order of morality. Forgiveness falls within the scope of an economy of the gift whose logic of superabundance exceeds the logic of reciprocity; we have already seen an application of this above (namely the exercise of recognition presupposed by the model of translation and by that of crossed narration). Insofar as it exceeds the order of morality, the economy of the gift belongs to what we would be able to term the 'poetics' of the moral life if we were to retain the twofold sense of the term 'poetics', that is, the sense of creativity at the level of the dynamics of acting and the sense of song and hymn at the level of verbal expression. It is thus to this spiritual economy, to this poetics of the moral life, that forgiveness essentially belongs. Its 'poetic' power consists in shattering the law of the irreversibility of time by changing the past, not as a record of all that has happened but in terms of its meaning for us today. It does this by lifting the burden of guilt which paralyses the relations between individuals who are acting out and suffering their own history. It does not abolish the debt insofar as we are and remain the inheritors of the past, but it lifts the pain of the debt.

We have said that these considerations do not have their primary employment in the political sphere whose principle is justice and reciprocity, and not charity and the gift. Could we not suggest, nevertheless, that the order of justice and reciprocity can be touched by that of charity and the gift – touched, that is to say, affected, and, if I may say, moved to pity? Have we not some examples of this in the sphere of penal justice, with the royal pardon, prescription and sentence reductions? And are there not further examples found in the social sphere in certain affective expressions of solidarity? But what would it be at the level of peoples and nations? I spoke above of an 'extra' called for by the exchange of memories of injury, and I suggested that this 'extra' has something to do with forgiveness. It is necessary in reality that the peoples of Europe show compassion for each other, imagining – I repeat – the suffering of others just as they are about to call for vengeance for those injuries which have been inflicted upon them in the past. What is demanded here strongly resembles forgiveness.

However, we must enter on to this path with the greatest caution guided by sober circumspection. Two pitfalls must be avoided. The first would be that of confusing forgiveness and forgetting. On the contrary, we can forgive only where there is no forgetting, where the humble have been released from a promise. 'Shattering the debt and forgetting' is the subtitle of the book mentioned earlier. Nothing would be more loathsome than that which Jankélévich called the forgetful forgiveness, a product of shallowness and indifference. This is really why the work of forgiveness must be grafted on to the work of memory in the language of narration. The second pitfall would be to take forgiveness under its worst aspect. The first relation that we have to forgiving is not the exercise of an easily granted forgiveness – that which once again is reduced to forgetfulness – but the difficult practice of responding to a request for forgiveness. As to the victims of imprescriptible crimes – crimes that they consider to be unforgivable – there is no other advice than to wait for better times. These times will see the first cathartic effect of the drawing-up of wrongs suffered by the injured, who will see the offender attain full understanding of the crimes that he or she has committed. There is a time for the unforgivable and a time for forgiveness. Forgiveness requires enduring patience.

In this respect, the recourse to the model of forgiveness does not take us as far from the political sphere as we might think. The history of recent years offers us some wonderful examples of a kind of short circuit between the poetical and the political. We have all retained the image of Willy Brandt kneeling at Warsaw; we think also of Vàclav Havel writing to the President of the Federal Republic of Germany in order to seek forgiveness for the sufferings inflicted upon the Sudeten Germans after the Second World War; we remember too the for-giveness sought by the German authorities from the Jewish people and their scrupulous care in atoning to the survivors of the final solution in numerous ways. Finally, we think of Sadat's stunning visit to Jerusalem. But to the same degree that charity exceeds justice we must guard against substituting it for justice. Charity remains a surplus; this surplus of compassion and tenderness is capable of giving the exchange of memories its profound motivation, its daring and its momentum.

We proposed three models for the mediation of identity and

alterity. We stated that translation is the best way of demonstrating the universality of language (*le langage*) in the dispersal of languages (*les langues*). We added that crossed narration is the best way of sharing in the memory of others. We then concluded with the claim that forgiveness is the best way of shattering the debt, and thus of lifting impediments to the practice of justice and recognition. From beginning to end we have held to the blueprint of 'mediations'. In this sense, the proposed models may be seen as contributing to the crucial ongoing debate between the right to universality and the demand of historical difference.[1]

[Translated by Eileen Brennan, Trinity College Dublin]

Notes

This essay is translated from the French, 'Quel éthos nouveau pour l'Europe', in *Imaginer l'Europe*, sous la direction de Peter Koslowski (Paris: Editions du Cerf, 1992), pp. 107–19. We would like to thank Paul Ricoeur, the editors and the publishers for permission to publish this translation.

1   Christian denominations also have a role to play in this threefold work of translation, crossed narration and mutual compassion insofar as they have received a legacy of evangelical words about forgiveness and loving one's enemies. In this sense, their manner of approaching the problems discussed here would begin with forgiveness as the dominant theme which is thereby placed above the two other themes (of the crossing of memories and of the translation from one cultural language to another). But the Christian communities also pay a price for being heard. This price is twofold: they must, on the one hand, thoroughly pursue the course of relinquishing power, power which is sometimes exercised directly, sometimes indirectly by the intervention of the secular arm, and sometimes, more subtly, by increasing their authority through the vertical dimension of domination – characteristic of the phenomenon of sovereignty found principally in the context of nation-states – at the expense of the horizontal relation of wishing to live together. To the extent that the Christian communities will, at some future point, clearly break with a certain 'theological politics' – where theology primarily justifies the dimension of domination in political relations – and to the extent that they will be

capable, in contrast, of giving a free rein to another 'theological politics' – where the ecclesia, asserting itself as a place of mutual aid with a view to salvation, would truly become a model of fraternity for all the other institutions – to that extent will the message of the gospel be likely to be heard by politics on the grand scale of Europe. This leads us to say – and it is the second price to pay by the Christian communities – that the primary context in which the model of forgiveness is designed to be put to the test is that of interdenominational exchanges. It is primarily with regard to each other that the Christian communities must exercise mutual forgiveness in order to 'shatter the debt' inherited from a long history of persecution, inquisition, repression, acts of violence which were perpetrated by some communities against others or by all of the communities against non-Christians and non-believers. The new evangelization of Europe is a project which carries this twofold price.

Paul Ricoeur

Fragility and responsibility

This article will discuss the *fragility*, rather than the *tragedy*, related to the public exercise of human action, despite an important relationship between the two phenomena. This relationship consists in the fact that both the fragile and the tragic arise from a conflict among human beings of quality who must confront each other's grandeur. Moreover, both the fragile and the tragic reveal a sort of obstination in finitude, an imperviousness to the other on the part of the grandeur which action confronts. Nevertheless, the major difference between the fragile and the tragic resides in their different relation to responsibility. The tragic evokes a situation where a human awakens painfully to the conscious-ness of a destiny or fatality which weighs on his or her life, nature, or very condition. The conflict's dimension of 'fatality' or 'destiny' consists in its irremediability and in the fact that the 'collision,' to use Hegel's term in his *Lectures on Aesthetics*, results in the mutual destruction of the protagonists. On the contrary, the fragile does not compromise the fatality by virtue of which the protagonists head for ruin through their very efforts to ward off disaster. Fragility calls for action by virtue of an intrinsic relation, which I shall now demonstrate, with the idea of responsibility. Yet, perhaps one should not forget this unsettling relationship with the tragic whenever the best-intentioned human interventions tend to aggravate the evils they claim to cure.

The intrinsic relationship between fragility and responsibility can be demonstrated from the idea of responsibility itself. I shall say with Hans Jonas in *Principe Responsabilité* that responsibility has the fragile as its specific vis-a-vis, that is to say, both what is perishable through natural weakness and what is threatened under the blows of historical violence.[1] The philosopher calls it a 'principle' because it is expressed from the very first instance as an imperative which nothing precedes. Yet we discover this principle enshrouded in a feeling by which we are affected at the level of a fundamental mood. We feel – under the multiple figures which will be evoked below – required or enjoined by the fragile to do something, to help, but, even better, to foster growth, to allow for accomplishment and flourishing.

The strength of this sentiment initially consists in making us experience a situation which is, but should not be. The imperative is embodied in what we perceive as deplorable, unbearable, inadmissible, unjustifiable. Consider the birth of a child – its mere existence obliges. We are rendered responsible by the fragile. Yet what does 'rendered responsible' mean? When the fragile is not something but someone – an individual, groups, communities, even humanity – this someone appears to us as entrusted to our care, placed in our custody. Let us be careful, however. The image of custody, or the burden which one takes upon oneself, should not render us inattentive to the other component emphasized by the expression 'entrusted to our care' – the fragile as 'someone' who relies on us, expects our assistance and care, and trusts that we shall fulfil our obligations. This bond of trust is fundamental. As intimately related to the request, the injunction, or the imperative, it is important that we encounter trust before suspicion. The result, accordingly, is that in the feeling of responsibility we *feel* that we are *rendered* responsible for, and by, someone.

Let us pause here to measure the gap between an analysis of responsibility introduced by its relation to fragility and a more traditional analysis according to which responsibility consists in the ability to designate oneself as the author of one's own acts. This definition certainly is not abolished. If, after the event, we could not recapitulate the course of our acts in a brief recollection and gather them around the pole which we say is *us* – authors of these acts – neither could anyone rely on us, nor expect that we keep our promises. But notice the incompleteness of this notion of responsibility occurring in the aftermath of action: it is turned towards the past rather than the future. This incompleteness remains even when we are *willing to repair the damages caused by our actions* (definition of responsibility according to civil law), or when we *assume the penal consequences of punishable actions* (definition of responsibility according to the penal code). The assumed consequences certainly constitute a slice of future with regard to the acts themselves. Yet the consequences have already happened when the judgment is passed. Thus it is always towards *retrospection* that we are drawn. The appeal coming from fragility differs greatly in this respect. The question becomes: what shall we do with this fragile being, what shall we do for her or him? We are directed towards the future of a being in need of help to survive and to grow. This future can be very remote from our present, as in the cases observed by Hans Jonas which essentially concern the threats inflicted upon the environment in which the human adventure unfolds. The imperative which requires us to act in such a way that there may still be human life after us, orients us towards a future as vast and as distant as the effects of our technological interventions. Here I shall not address the examples chosen by Jonas. I merely note this reversal from past to future.

Yet this is not the most important reversal. The ability to designate oneself as author of one's acts is affirmed, or, better, attested, in the relation of self to self: I . . . myself, you . . . yourself, he . . . himself, she . . . herself. The appeal, the injunction, and also the trust which proceed from the fragile, result in its being always *another* who declares us responsible, or, as Lévinas says, calls us to responsibility. Another, by relying on me, renders me accountable for my acts.

I shall not address the sterile debate concerning the priority between the ability to designate oneself as author of one's acts and the appeal of the fragile. Suffice it to say that a capability must be awakened in order to become real and actual; and that it is in the midst of others that we become effectively responsible. Inversely, as soon as the other relies on or trusts in me, what he or she expects is precisely that I shall keep my word and behave as an agent, the author of my own acts. Ultimately, the question at stake concerns mutual recognition – a recognition through which the other ceases to be alien and is treated as my peer according to a fundamental human fellowship?

Having reached this point, we must pass from generalities and seek to outline something like a typology of fragility – essentially of human fragility – in the field of public praxis.

Rival cities

Let us first consider the viewpoint of civil society as distinct from political society (which essentially is defined by the state-controlled institution and by the exercise of power related). Today, sociologists, economists and political scientists recognize the permanent character of the conflict affecting the organizational and institutional structures of civil society. Yet to describe the conflict as permanent is hardly enough; rather, it seems to grow in proportion with the increasing complexity of social structures.

I shall mention here two important contemporary analyses which attribute a strategic position to conflict. The first analysis, developed by Michael Walzer in *The Spheres of Justice*, sets conflict in direct relation to both the idea of justice and the discussion of justice in the abstract, formal, or procedural sense expounded by John Rawls in *A Theory of Justice*. Rawls distinguishes two notions of justice – equality before the law, and equality of opportunities – considering the status of privileged classes in unequal distributions. Yet each can be considered unitary in the sense that it presides over distribution according to an identical rule – arithmetical in the first case, geometrical or proportional in the second – regardless of what is being distributed (remuneration, patrimony, authority, etc.). The deconstruction of the unitary notion of justice performed by Walzer rests on the consideration that the distributed goods are heterogeneous. This fact is emphasized by the concept of distribution itself, and this qualitative heterogeneity is obvious when marketable and non-marketable goods are compared. However, our firm belief is that everything cannot be sold or bought. Consider indeed citizenship, which is the first good, the right to belong to a political community according to certain rules of admission and exclusion. Consider health, education, security, access to public functions and in general to positions of authority or command. Nonetheless, our societies are permeated with compulsions which foster the infringement of one sphere on to another. Besides the inequalities internal to each sphere (with respect to citizenship, consider the difficulties related to the right to asylum, the fate of immigrants, the vote of foreigners, etc.), there arise the most grievous conflicts between spheres. For example, education or health appear at once as marketable and non-marketable goods – both cost, but their value exceeds the monetary. The compromises called for by the conflicts between spheres are at the heart of a European politics which seeks a social market economy, arbitrating between efficiency, competitiveness and the solidarity required to compensate for the inequalities created by the market itself.

The second analysis is developed by L. Boltanski and L. Thevenot in their work *De la justification: les économies de la grandeur*.[2] Combining the respective abilities of sociologist and economist, the authors explore the conflicts generated by the strategies of justification. These strategies are used by social actors to determine a course of action in the situation created by their respective belonging to spheres of activity which are coherent, but multiple and irreducible to one another. The authors thus arrive at a limited plurality of models capable of fostering agreement in litigious situations. These models regulate systems of justified actions, which deserve to be called 'cities' insofar as they give a sufficient coherence to an order of human transactions, and 'worlds' insofar as things, objects, or devices serve as stable references in ordeals experienced by a 'given city', after the manner of a 'common world'. Thus, in the 'inspired city' greatness is granted grace unrelated to money, glory, or usefulness; it is the city of artists and contemplatives. In the 'city of opinion', greatness depends on fame, the opinion of others; it is the dwelling of sportsmen, artists, professionals of mediatic appearance and performance. In the 'commercial city', unity among people is fostered by the rarity of certain goods desired by all and the competition of desires. The 'domestic city', which approximates to what Hannah Arendt called the 'household', is ruled by values of loyalty, faithfulness and reverence. The 'civil city' is grounded on the subordination of private interest to common will as expressed through positive law. The 'industrial city' is dominated by functional rules subjected to the superior principles of usefulness.

On the whole, the significance of the work resides chiefly in its contribution to a theory of conflict and compromise. The collective models outlined above are the scene of two types of conflict. In each 'city', or-deals related to the establishment of greatness result from conflicts. The objects which establish the 'city' as a 'world' are then called to witness. To the internal contestations and legitimations are added the border-conflicts among distinct orders. The authors write: 'everything that allows us to constitute the grandeur of a city can thus be used to deconstruct the grandeur established in reference to other superior common principles. The same means therefore serve alternatively topical composition and critical disclosure.' A typology of disagreement situations is thus added to the presentation of 'worlds' and their foundation of agreement. It appears then that the internal constraint of justification results from the confrontation of a 'world' to the critique imposed by the existence of other differently ordered 'cities'. The corollary of this theory of conflicts is a theory of compromises, which gives the book its point and bite: 'in a compromise, one agrees to compose, that is to say to suspend the contention, without resolving it by appealing to an ordeal in a single world.' In other words, compromises are fragile and ill-founded.

One can see where the conflict borders on tragedy: Max Weber and Raymond Aron have both meditated on the unsettling fact that all values called for by civil society cannot be satisfied at once. Yet the conflict, insofar as it calls for an accomplished art of negotiation and compromise, eludes the law of tragedy, that is to say the collision leading to destruction. Furthermore, the individuals have the capacity to identify the proper rules, the objects pertinent to a particular 'city', and the appropriate ordeals. They can borrow from the neighbouring 'city' critical arguments needed. Finally, in the course of time, they have the power to shift from one 'city' to another. This ability to inhabit several 'worlds' through the agency of judgement is finally constitutive of the individual. The authors speak therefore of justification, rather than justice. In this respect, the key concept in a pragmatics of judgement is the concept of ordeal. It is through ordeal, in my opinion, that the ideas of fragility and responsibility beget one another, or, as Hegel would say, enter into one another.

The paradoxes of political society

Inasmuch as political society is irreducible to civil society, it involves its own sources of fragility and responsibility which are related to the central phenomenon of power. I would like to insist on two fundamental sources of conflict characteristic of political society.

First, power as such proceeds from the encounter of two major forces in the course of history. On one hand, there is the violence of masters, who gathered lands, seized inheritances, and oppressed ethnic, cultural, or religious minorities. On the other hand, there is the institutionalization of the initial violence under the pressure of legal rationality. At this point of equilibrium which characterizes the legal state, political power is defined both as force, inasmuch as it holds the legitimate violence, and as form, inasmuch as it is submitted to the constitutional rule by which the initial violence was humanized and institutionalized. The legal state thus stands between two extremes, namely the initial violence and the residual violence. Residual violence can be recognized in the police force which has progressively stripped citizens of their right to retaliate, of their private relations of violence. Such is the first fragility of political power, as it were an institutional and constitutional fragility.

A second source of fragility proceeds from the intersection at the level of power between a vertical relation of domination/ subordination and a horizontal relation constituted by the will to live together of a historical community. The intersection of these two axes constitutes a second source of fragility inasmuch as the authority resulting from the hierarchical relations tends to hide, or even inhibit, the will to live together. Yet the will to live together is the true origin of power. Thus it is the ultimate fragility, as it ignores its own significance as foundation of power and recognizes itself only in situations of danger – the fatherland is in danger! This recognition is even more painful in defeat. Defeat dissolves the bond of cooperation, which is so hidden behind the relation of domination that it is almost forgotten. Yet this relation of domination functions only through what Boethius called 'voluntary submission'.

Another source of fragility results from the nature of the modern democratic state. Indeed, the state's sovereignty proceeds only from a virtual social pact – which was theorized by Rousseau and thus elevated to the rank of fictitious founding act. Furthermore, its most widely spread variant is representative democracy. Yet the latter appears increasingly fragile, since my elected representative (who is considered in principle my alter ego) turns out, once elected, to belong to another world – the political world which obeys its own laws of gravity. This symptom of fragility, which affects the Western form of democracy, is doubtless related in depth to the paradox of democracy itself, namely that it proceeds from a self-authorized auto-foundation. The bond of trust underlying the fictitious pact which constitutes the political contract carries therefore all the burden of the vertical and horizontal power relations.

Enumerating the weaknesses of politics would be endless. Elsewhere I have discussed the fragility of political language, whose relation to rhetoric forces it to oscillate between rational argumentation and sophism which proceeds by seduction, or, worse, by intimidation.

I have said enough about the internal tensions which bring the fragility of political action close to the Greek sense of tragedy. Moreover, the fact that it unfolds in the midst of confronted greatnesses of power is not fortuitous. Nevertheless, it seems that I have thereby designated the field of responsibility inasmuch as it is the field of fragility itself. Let us recapitulate the facts in an inverse order. I start with responsibility at the level of language. The task is to clarify and conceptualize the notions obscured by political rhetoric, to shed light on the interests at stake. The facts must also show the relations between properly political choices and choices required at the level of civil society by the conflict between different spheres of justice and by the competition of the 'cities' and 'worlds' which we inhabit through our multiple roles. Yet responsibility does not belong only to the intellectuals. It is even more important that each citizen is aware of his or her own responsibility. He or she must know that the great city is fragile, that it rests on a fiduciary bond. He or she must feel particularly responsible for the constitutive horizontal bond of the will to live together. In short, he or she must ascribe public safety to the vitality of the associate life which regenerates the will to live together.

[Translated by Elisabeth Iwanowski]

Fragility and responsibility

Notes

This paper is an edited version of a lecture given by Ricoeur at the Department of Philosophy of the University of Naples, 26 May 1992, published in Italian in *Il Tetto* 171 (Naples): 325–36.

1   Hans Jonas, *Principe Responsabilité*, trans. J. Greisch (Paris: CERF, 1990).
2   L. Boltanski and L. Thevenot, *De la justification: les économies de la grandeur* (Paris: Gallimard, 1991).

Paul Ricoeur

Love and justice

Talking about love may be too easy, or rather too difficult. How can we avoid simply praising it or falling into sentimental platitudes? One way of finding a way between these two extremes may be to take as our guide an attempt to think about the dialectic between love and justice. Here by dialectic I mean, on the one hand, the acknowledgment of the initial disproportionality between our two terms and, on the other hand, the search for practical mediations between them – mediations, let us quickly say, that are always fragile and provisory.

The insight promised by such a dialectical approach seems to me to have been overlooked by the method of conceptual analysis that seeks to extract from some selection of texts by ethicists or theologians who talk about love the most systematic recurrent themes. This, of course, is the approach used by many of our colleagues in philosophy and theology influenced by the discipline of analytical philosophy. To cite just one example of such a work, and it is a noteworthy one, in Gene Outka's *Agape* the subtitle *An Ethical Analysis* is indicative of the general orientation.[1] For this author it is a matter of isolating the 'basic normative content' that Christian love or agape 'has been said to possess irrespective of circumstances'.[2] By using what method? His answer is what my own approach would like to call into question: 'Such an inquiry is formally similar to the one philosophers have pursued in discussing, e.g. utilitarianism as an ultimate normative standard, criterion, or principle for judgments of value and obligation'[3] The whole issue for me is contained in this response: Does love in our ethical discourse have a normative status comparable to that of utilitarianism or even of the Kantian categorical imperative?

I shall provisionally set aside the three fundamental features of agape that Outka sees as being the most systematic and the most recurrent ones in the literature he considers. Far from neglecting them completely, however, we shall return to them below in some closing remarks devoted to the practical mediations between love and justice linked to the exercise of moral judgment in a particular situation. For the moment, though, I will limit myself to listing these features without commenting on them, in order to give some idea of the ultimate end of our own investigation: first, an equal 'regard for the neighbor which in crucial respects is independent and unalterable'; then, self-sacrifice, 'the inevitable historical manifestation of agape insofar as agape was not accommodated to self-interest'; and, finally, the mutuality characteristic of those actions 'which establish or enhance some sort of exchange between the parties, developing a sense of community and perhaps friendship'.[4]

We cannot reproach Outka for not having caught sight of the conceptual incoherencies that such a typology seeks to lay bare. In fact, each of his basic features is constructed at the expense of setting aside variations, disagreements and confusions which he deplores more than once throughout his study. What is more, it is obvious that his third feature, the one that in fact seems most decisive to him, is highly discordant with the second one. Yet these deceptions encountered in the process of an ethical analysis devoted to isolating a 'basic normative content' are, to me, an indication that such a direct method is, in fact, inappropriate to our making sense of the relationship between love and justice, and that we should instead start from what in the topos of love resists such treatment of love as 'an ultimate normative standard, criterion, or principle for judgments of value and obligation'.

I would like to put this first part of my own remarks on our topic, dedicated to the disproportionality between justice and love, under the emblem of a quotation from Pascal:

> All bodies together and all minds together and all their products are not worth the least impulse of charity. This is of an infinitely superior order. Out of all bodies together we could not succeed in creating one little thought. It is impossible, and of a different order. Out of all bodies and minds we could not extract one impulse of true charity. It is impossible, and of a different, supernatural order.[5]

I will not conceal the fact that this harsh judgment of Pascal's will make it more difficult subsequently to find the mediations required by moral judgment in a particular situation, provoked by the question, What ought I to do here and now? For the moment, however, my question is the following. If we begin by acknowledging disproportionality, how can we avoid falling into one or other of the dangers mentioned above, exaltation or emotional platitudes? In other words, unthinking sentimentality?

It seems to me that one possible way presents itself which would consist in looking for those forms of discourse – which are sometimes quite complicated – that resist the kind of leveling down brought about by the kind of conceptual analysis carried out by analytic philosophy. For love does speak, but it does so in a kind of language other than that of justice, as I shall phrase it at the end of my remarks.

I

I would like to focus on three aspects of such language as it is shaped by the biblical tradition, aspects that are indicative of what I shall call the strangeness or oddness of the discourse of love.

The first of these aspects has to do with the link between love and praise. Indeed, we may say that the discourse of love is initially a discourse of praise, where, in praising, one rejoices over the view of one object set above all the other objects of one's concern. In this abbreviated formula, the three elements – rejoicing, seeing and setting above all else – are equally important. By saying this, do we fall once again into a kind of conceptual analysis or into sentimentality? Neither, I suggest, if we are attentive to those original features of praise for which such verbal forms as the hymn are particularly appropriate. For example, the glorification of love by Paul in I Corinthians 13 is akin to those 'songs of praise' indicated by the Hebrew title of the book of Psalms: *mizmôrê tĕhillîm*. Beyond this, we should also bring together the hymn and the discourse of benediction: 'Blessed is the man who walks not in the counsel of the wicked. . . . He is like a tree planted by streams of water' (Psalm 1.1, 3). 'O Lord of hosts, blessed is the man who trusts in thee!' (Psalm 84.12). In this way we are brought to the literary form of the macarism, familiar to readers of the Beatitudes: 'Blessed are the poor in spirit, for theirs is the kingdom of heaven' (Matthew 5.3). Hymn, benediction, macarism – in these forms of discourse we find a complex interweaving of literary expressions which we can link together in terms of the central aspect of 'praise'.

In turn, such praise refers us back to the more general, broader domain of biblical poetry, which Robert Alter has shown functions discordantly in relation to the rules of a discourse that would seek univocity at the level of principles.[6] In such poetry the key words undergo amplifications of meaning, unexpected assimilations, hitherto unseen interconnections, which cannot be reduced to a single meaning.

As an example, we may consider the rhetorical strategies at work in

I Corinthians 13. The initial strophe exalts the greatness of love by a kind of negative hyperbole, announcing the annihilation of everything that is not love: 'If I speak in the tongues of men and of angels, but have not love, I am a noisy gong or a clanging cymbal'. The same formula recurs a number of times: 'And if I have . . . but have not love . . . I am nothing'. The second strophe then develops the vision of the eminence of love in the indicative mode, as though everything were already consummated: 'Love is patient and kind; love is not jealous or boastful; it is not arrogant or rude. Love does not insist on its own way; it is not irritable or resentful; it does not rejoice at wrong, but rejoices in the right. Love bears all things, believes all things, hopes all things, endures all things.' The reader will have noted the interplay of assertion and denial, as well as the playful use of synonyms that makes akin quite distinct virtues, all of which run counter to our legitimate concern to isolate individual meanings. Finally, in the third strophe, a movement of transcendence beyond all limits carries the day: 'Love never ends; as for prophecy, it will pass away; as for tongues, they will cease; as for knowledge, it will pass away. . . .' And, as a final passing to the limit: 'So faith, hope, love abide, these three; but the greatest of these is love'.

This is the first kind of resistance that love opposes to 'ethical analysis', in the strong sense of the term 'analysis', that is, as conceptual clarification.

The second oddity of the discourse of love has to do with the disturbing imperative form in such well-known expressions as 'You shall love the Lord your God . . . and you shall love your neighbor as yourself.' If we take the imperative in the usual sense of obligation, whose case is so powerfully stated by Kantian ethics, there seems to be something scandalous about commanding love, that is, about ordering a feeling. Kant diminishes this difficulty by distinguishing 'practical' love, which is nothing but respect for persons as ends in themselves, from 'pathological' love, which has no place in the sphere of ethics. Freud is more obviously indignant over what is at stake here. If so-called spiritual love is just a sublimated erotic love, the commandment to love can only be the expression of the tyranny of the superego over the affective sphere. At this point in our reflections, the difficulty, however, does not have to do with the status of love within the realm of feelings (to which I shall return), but rather with the status of the commandment, particularly as a commandment to love. Does this commandment, on the plane of acts of discourse, have the same illocutionary force as, let us say, those ordinary commands that call for obedience, such as closing a door or opening a window? And, on the ethical plane, is this commandment comparable with moral principles, that is, with those first propositions that govern subordinate maxims, as do the utilitarian principle or the Kantian categorical imperative?

I found an unanticipated source of help in responding to this question in Franz Rosenzweig's *Star of Redemption*.[7] It may be recalled that this work, which itself is far from the commonplace, is divided into three sections, corresponding respectively to the idea of creation (or the eternal before), revelation (or the eternal present of encounter), and redemption (or the eternal not yet of messianic expectation). Coming to the second section, revelation, the reader may expect to be instructed concerning the Torah, and in a sense this is what happens, but the Torah, at this stage of Rosenzweig's meditation, is not yet a set of rules. Rather, it becomes so, because it is preceded by the solemn act that situates all human experience in terms of the paradigmatic language of scripture. And what is the most apt symbol for this imposing of a primordial language on the human sphere of communication? It is the commandment to love. Yet, contrary to our expectation, the formula for this commandment for Rosenzweig is not that of Exodus, nor that of Leviticus, nor that of Deuteronomy, but rather that of the Song of Solomon, which is read at every Passover celebration. Love, says the Song of Songs, 'is as strong as death'.[8] Why does Rosenzweig refer to the Song of Solomon at this place? And with what imperative connotation? At the beginning of this section on revelation, he considers just the intimate colloquy between God and an individual soul, before any 'third' person comes on the scene, which is taken up in the section on redemption.[9] His insight is to show in this way how the commandment to love springs from the bond of love between God and the individual soul. The commandment that precedes every law is the word that the lover addresses to the beloved: Love me! This unexpected distinction between commandment and law makes sense only if we admit that the commandment to love is love itself, commending itself, as though the genitive in the 'commandment of love' were subjective and objective at the same time. Or, to put it another way, this is a commandment that contains the conditions for its being obeyed in the very tenderness of its objurgation: Love me!

If anyone should doubt the validity of this ever-so-subtle distinction Rosenzweig makes between commandment and law, I would reply by adding that we need to relate this deviant use of the imperative to the forms of discourse referred to earlier – praise, hymn, benediction, macarism – and thereby dare to speak of a poetic use of the imperative. This poetic use of the imperative has its own connotations within the broad range of expressions extending from the amorous invitation, through pressing supplication, through the summons, to the sharp command accompanied by the threat of punishment.[10] Thanks to this kinship between the command 'Love me!' and the song of praise, the commandment of love is revealed as being irreducible, in its ethical overtones, to the moral imperative, so legitimately equated by Kant to obligation, or duty, with reference to the recalcitrance of human inclinations.

It is from this gap between what I have called the poetic use of the commandment and the commandment in the properly ethical sense of the term that I shall undertake my attempt below at a dialectic centered on the economy of the gift.

But before attempting this dialectic, I should like to add a third feature to our canvassing of the strange and odd expressions of love. This time, I should like to consider those expressions that have to do with love as a feeling. I have held off until this point any consideration of such expressions so as not to give in to the sirens of sentimentality. But now it is under the sign of the poetics of the hymn and the commandment that we can place this third feature, which I will sum up in terms of the power of metaphorization linked to the expressions of love. We may take up this theme beginning where we left off the preceding one: the pressing appeal – Love me! – which the lover addresses to the beloved, confers on love the dynamism thanks to which it becomes capable of mobilizing a wide variety of affects which we designate by their end states: pleasure versus pain, satisfaction versus discontent, rejoicing versus distress, beatitude versus melancholy, and so on. What is more, love is not limited just to deploying this wide variety of affects around itself like some vast field of gravitation. It also creates a kind of ascending and descending spiral out of them, which it traverses in both directions.

And what I have just described in the psychological terms of affects and end states has its linguistic counterpart in the production of a vast field of analogies among all of the affective modes of love, thanks to which they mutually signify one another. Thus it is thanks to what I have called the process of metaphorization on this linguistic plane that erotic love is capable of signifying more than itself and of indirectly intending other qualities of love. But it is the underlying analogy between an affect and the linguistic process of metaphorization that we must emphasize. This is what Anders Nygren and all those who have followed him in setting up a dichotomy between eros and agape have underestimated.[11] Analogy on the level of feelings and metaphorization on the linguistic plane refer to a single phenomenon, which implies that here metaphor is more than just a trope, or rhetorical ornament. To put it another way, in this instance the trope expresses what we might call the substantive tropology of love: that is, both the real analogy between feelings, and the power of eros to signify agape and to put it into words.

II

I want to end these initial remarks by considering those features of the discourse of justice that most obviously are opposed to these aspects of the discourse of love. I shall consider justice first on the level of social practice (where it is identified with the judicial structure of a society and characterizes a state based on law), then on the level of those principles of justice that govern our use of the predicate 'just' as applied to such institutions.

Beginning with justice as a kind of social practice, I would like rapidly to recall the circumstances or occasions where justice arises, how it is applied, and what arguments it makes use of. As regards the circumstances of justice, taken as judicial practices, they form one part of the activities of communication in a society. More specifically, justice is at issue when a higher court is asked to decide between the claims of parties with opposed interests or rights. How this is carried out depends on a judicial structure which itself includes a number of aspects: for example, a body of written laws; courts of justice, invested with the function of passing judgment; judges – that is, individuals like us, held to be independent, and charged with passing a just sentence for a particular situation. To this we must add that these structures are held to have the monopoly of power, that is, the power to impose their decision regarding what is just by using the public means of force.

As we can see, neither the circumstances nor the means of justice are those of love. Still less are the arguments of justice those of love. In fact, love does not argue, if we take the hymn from I Corinthians 13 as our model. Justice does argue. And it does so in a quite specific way, by confronting reasons for and against some position, which are taken as plausible, capable of being communicated, and worth discussing by all parties involved. Thus to say, as I suggested earlier, that justice is one part of the communicational activity of a society takes on its full meaning here. A confrontation between arguments before a tribunal is a noteworthy example of the dialogical use of language, and this kind of communication even has its own ethics: *Audi alteram partem* (Listen to the other side).[12]

There is one aspect of this argumentative structure of justice that we must not overlook in our comparison between justice and love. The clash of arguments is in a sense infinite, inasmuch as there is always the possibility of a 'but . . .'; for example, through recourse to a higher court of appeal. Yet it is also finite inasmuch as the conflict ends with the rendering of a decision. So the exercising of justice is not just a case of arguments, it also involves a decision, and this is the responsibility of the judge, as the last link in the chain of procedures, wherever this may occur. And when the judge's words are those of condemnation, we recall that statutes of justice carry a sword as well as a balance scale. Taken together, all these characteristics of judicial practice allow us for the first time to define the formalism of justice – not as a fault, but as a sign of force.

However, I do not want to take up the too-easy task of reducing justice to that judicial apparatus that makes it a part of social practice. We have also to take into consideration the idea or ideal of justice, whose borderline with love is less easy to trace. Nevertheless, taken even at the quasi-reflective level of social practice, justice can be opposed to love in terms of some well-marked features that will bring us to the threshold of our reflections devoted to the dialectic between love and justice.

These distinctive features result from the almost complete identification of justice with distributive justice. This has been the case from Aristotle's *Nicomachean Ethics* right up to John Rawls's *A Theory of Justice*, and it is the significance of this identification that we now have to consider.[13] It presupposes that we give the idea of distribution an amplitude that surpasses the realm of economics. It is society as a whole, seen from the angle of justice, that appears as an assigning of roles, tasks, rights and duties, of advantages or disadvantages, of goods and costs. The strength of this representation of society as a system of distribution is that it avoids the double trap of wholism (which makes society an entity distinct from the members who compose it) and individualism (which makes society an additive sum of individuals and their interactions). In a distributive conception of society, society does not exist apart from the individuals among whom the 'parts' are distributed and who thus 'take part' in the whole. These individuals have no social existence apart from the distribution rule that confers on them a place within the whole. This is where justice comes in as the undergirding virtue of the institutions presiding over this division. To render each his or her due – *suum cuique tribuere* – is, in some particular situation of distribution, the most general formula of justice.

But in what way is there a virtue involved here? With this question, we raise the question of the status of the predicate 'just' in our moral discourse. Since Aristotle, ethicists have sought an answer in the tie that binds justice and equality. On the judicial plane, this equation is easy to justify: treat similar cases in similar ways is the very principle of equality before the law. But how does this apply to those notoriously unequal distributions of wealth and property, of authority and responsibility, of honor and status, that have characterized human society? Aristotle was the first who, when he found himself confronted with this difficulty, distinguished between proportional equality and mathematical equality. A division is just if it is proportional to the social importance of the parties involved. At the other end of history, we rediscover the same attempt to preserve the equation between justice and equality in the aforementioned work of John Rawls, when he argues that the increase in the advantages of the most favored is compensated for by a decrease in the disadvantages of the least favored. This is his second principle of justice, which completes the first principle of equality before the law. To maximize the smallest portion, this is the modern version of the concept of proportional justice stemming from Aristotle. With it, we have in a second manner characterized the legitimate formalism of justice, this time not just as judicial practice but as the ideal of an equitable division of rights and goods to the benefit of everyone.

What are the consequences for our reflections? Let us consider further the two concepts of distribution and equality which are the pillars of the idea of justice. The concept of distribution, taken in its broadest extension, confers a moral basis on the social practice of justice, in the sense we have given it, as the regulation of conflicts. Here society is seen, in effect, as the space of a confrontation between rivals. The idea of distributive justice covers all the operations of the judicial apparatus by giving them the end of upholding the claims of each person within the limit that the freedom of the one does not infringe on that of the other. As for equality, as the mathematical equality of rights and the proportional equality of advantages and responsibilities within an unequal division, this idea indicates both the strength and the limits of the very idea of the highest form of justice. The equality of rights, completed by that of chances, is certainly a source of social cohesion. Rawls even expects his principles of justice to reinforce social cooperation. But what kind of bond is thereby instituted between social partners? My own suggestion would be that the highest point the ideal of justice can envision is that of a society in which the feeling of mutual dependence – even of mutual indebtedness – remains subordinate to the idea of mutual disinterest.

We may in this regard recall Rawls's striking formula of a 'disinterested interest', by means of which he characterizes the basic attitude of the parties in the hypothetical situation of the original social contract. The idea of mutuality is by no means absent from this formula, but the juxtaposition of interests prevents the idea of justice from attaining the level of a true recognition and a solidarity such that each person feels indebted to every other person. I shall attempt to show below that these ideas of recognition, of solidarity, of mutual indebtedness, can be seen as the unstable equilibrium point on the horizon of the dialectic of love and justice.

III

In the next part of my essay I would like to build a bridge between the poetics of love and what we might now call the prose of justice, between the hymn and the formal rule. We cannot avoid this confrontation once one or other of these terms makes some claim concerning individual or social practice. In our reflections on the hymn, this relation to praxis was not considered. As we saw, love was simply praised for itself, for its elevation and its moral beauty. And in the rule of justice, no explicit reference was made to love, this latter if anything being left to the realm of possible motives. Yet both love and justice are addressed to action, each in its own fashion, for each makes a claim on action. Our dialectic must therefore move beyond our separate examination of love and justice to consider their interaction.

Rather than just confusing them or setting up a pure and simple dichotomy between love and justice, I think a third, difficult way has to be explored, one in which the tension between two distinct and sometimes opposed claims may be maintained and may even be the occasion for the invention of responsible forms of behavior. Where might we find the paradigm of such a living tension? Perhaps we can find it in the fragment of the Sermon on the Mount in Matthew and the Sermon on the Plain in Luke or, in what is a single context, in the new commandment, where love of one's enemies and the golden rule are brought into juxtaposition. These two commandments are stated in the greatest proximity in Luke 6: 'But I say to you that hear, Love your enemies, do good to those who hate you, bless those who curse you, pray for those who abuse you' (6.27–8). And just a bit further on: 'And as you wish that men would do to you, do so to them' (6.31). Before trying to make sense of this strange contiguity, let us ask two preliminary questions. How, on the one hand, is the commandment to love one's enemies linked to the hymn of love? In what way, on the other hand, does the golden rule announce the rule of justice?

Our first question is equivalent to asking how the poetic quality of the hymn gets converted into an obligation. What was said above regarding Rosenzweig's discussion of the commandment 'Love me!' points us in the direction of an answer. To put it briefly, the commandment to love one's enemies is not sufficient by itself; rather, it is the hyperethical expression of a broader economy of the gift, which has many other modes of expression besides this claim on us to act. This economy of the gift touches every part of ethics, and a whole range of significations confers a specific articulation of it. At one extreme, we find the symbolism, which itself is quite complex, of creation, in the most basic sense of an originary giving of existence. The first use of the predicate 'good' applied to all created things in Genesis 1 belongs to this symbolism: 'And God saw everything that he had made, and behold it was very good' (1.31). The hyperethical dimension of this predicate extended to all creatures is what we must emphasize, for the result is that it is as a creature that we find ourselves summoned. The sense of radical dependence that is at stake here, insofar as it is attached to the symbolism of creation, does not leave us face to face with God; rather it situates us within nature considered not as something to exploit but as an object of solicitude, of respect and admiration, as we hear in St Francis's *Canto de Sole*. The love of neighbor, in its extreme form of love for one's enemies, thus finds its first link to the economy of the gift in this hyperethical feeling of the dependence of the human creature, and our relation to the law and to justification stems from this same economy. These two relations even constitute the core of the recital of this economy, for, on the one hand, the law is a gift inasmuch as it is bound to the history of liberation, as told, for example, in Exodus 20.2 – 'I am the Lord, your God, who brought you out of the land of Egypt, out of the house of bondage.' Justification, on the other hand, is also a gift inasmuch as it is a free pardon.

At the other end of the range of significations that articulate the economy of the gift we find the symbolism, symmetrical to creation and no less complex, of the final end, where God appears as the source of *unknown* possibilities. In this way, the God of hope and the God of creation are one and the same God at both extremes of the economy of the gift. At the same time, our relation both to the law and to salvation is shown to belong to this economy by being placed 'between' creation and the eschaton.

Now it is from its reference to this economy of the gift that the 'new' commandment draws the signification we have termed hyper-ethical. Why 'hyperethical'? It is ethical owing to its imperative form, akin to what we considered above in discussing the commandment 'Love me!' However, the commandment here is more determinate inasmuch as it is linked to a structure of praxis, the distinction between friends and enemies, which this new commandment abolishes. It is ethical, therefore, but also hyperethical in that this new commandment constitutes in a way the most adequate ethical projection of what transcends ethics, the economy of the gift. In this sense, an ethical approximation of this economy is set forth which may be summed up in the expression '*since* it has been given you, give . . .'. According to this formula, and through the force of the 'since', the gift turns out to be a source of obligation.

Yet this approximation is not without its paradoxes. By entering into the practical field, the economy of the gift develops a logic of superabundance that, at first glance at least, opposes itself to the logic of equivalence that governs everyday ethics.[14] If we consider the other pole of the opposition, it appears as though it is from the logic of equivalence, which we have just opposed to the logic of super-abundance of the 'new' commandment, that the golden rule stems, the rule that the Sermon on the Mount and, even more so, the Sermon on the Plain, juxtapose in great contextual proximity with the command-ment to love one's enemies. That the golden rule does stem from a logic of equivalence of some kind is indicated by the reciprocity, or the reversibility, that this rule establishes between what one person does and what is done to another, between acting and being acted upon – hence by implication between the agent and the patient, which, although irreplaceable, are proclaimed as being able to substitute for each other.

A reconciliation between this logic of equivalence, illustrated by the golden rule, and the logic of superabundance, incarnated in the new commandment, is made almost impossible if, following certain exegetes such as Albrecht Dihle in *Die Goldene Regel*, we link the golden rule to the law of retribution, the *jus talionis*, which is the most rudimentary expression of the logic of equivalence and its corollary, the rule of reciprocity.[15] Yet this incompatibility between our two logics even seems to be sanctioned by the declaration of Jesus that, in Luke 6.32–4, somehow leads to the statement of the golden rule:

> If you love those who love you, what credit is that to you? For even sinners love those who love them. And if you do good to those who do good to you, what credit is that to you? For even sinners do the same. And if you lend to those from whom you hope to receive, what credit is that to you? Even sinners lend to sinners, to receive as much again. But love your enemies, and do good, and lend, expecting nothing in return.

Is not the golden rule retracted by these harsh words?

This apparent condemnation of the golden rule has to disturb us inasmuch as the rule of justice can be taken as a reformulation of the golden rule in formal terms.[16] This formalization is already visible in justice considered as a social practice, as the precept *Audi alteram partem* bears witness, and as does the rule, Treat similar cases in similar ways. It is given a more complete statement in the principles of justice referred to earlier with reference to the work of John Rawls. This does not, however, prevent our recognizing the spirit of the golden rule in even the quasi-algebraic form of Rawls's second principle: maximize the smallest portion. This formula is equivalent in effect to equalizing portions as much as permitted by the inequalities imposed by economic and social efficiency. Therefore it is legitimate for us to extend to the social practice of justice and to the principles of justice themselves the suspicion that strikes the golden rule through the logic of superabundance underlying the hyperethical commandment to love one's enemies. The rule of justice, the expression *par excellence* of the logic of equivalence and reciprocity, thus seems to suffer the same fate as the golden rule when put under the judgment of the new commandment.

But must we remain with this assertion of incompatibility? Let us return to our paradigm, the Sermon on the Mount (or the Plain). If the difference between our two logics were merely as we have stated it, how are we to explain the presence in one and the same context of the commandment to love one's enemies and the golden rule? Another interpretation is possible, wherein the commandment of love does not abolish the golden rule but instead reinterprets it in terms of generosity, and thereby makes not just possible but necessary an application of the commandment whereby, owing to its hyperethical status, it does not accede to the ethical sphere except at the price of paradoxical and extreme forms of behavior, those forms which are in fact recommended in the wake of the new commandment:

> Love your enemies, do good to those who hate you, bless those who curse you, pray for those who abuse you. To him who strikes you on the cheek, offer the other also; and from him who takes away your cloak do not withhold your coat as well. Give to every one who begs from you; and of him who takes away your goods, do not ask them again. (Luke 6.27–30).

These are those unique and extreme forms of commitment taken up by St Francis, Gandhi and Martin Luther King, Jr. Yet from what penal law and, in general, from what rule of justice can we deduce a maxim of action that would set up non-equivalence as a general rule? What distribution of tasks, of roles, or of advantages and obligations could be established, in the spirit of distributive justice, if the maxim of lending while expecting nothing in return were set up as a universal rule? If the hypermoral is not to turn into the non-moral – not to say the immoral; for example, cowardice – it has to pass through the principle of morality, summed up in the golden rule and formalized by the rule of justice.

Yet the opposite is no less true. In this relation of living tension between the logic of superabundance and the logic of equivalence, the latter receives from its confrontation with the former the capacity of raising itself above its perverse interpretations. Without the corrective of the commandment to love, the golden rule would be constantly drawn in the direction of a utilitarian maxim whose formula is *Do ut des*: I give *so that* you will give. The rule 'Give *because* it has been given you' corrects the 'in order that' of the utilitarian maxim and saves the golden rule from an always possible perverse interpretation. It is in this sense that we may interpret the harsh words of Luke 6.32–4), just after the reaffirmation of the golden rule in 6.31 and just before the reaffirmation of the new commandment in 6.35. In these intermediary verses the critical point of the logic of superabundance is directed not so much at the logic of equivalence of the golden rule as against its perverse interpretation. The same rule is capable of two readings, of two interpretations, one of which is based on interest, the other of which is disinterested. Only the commandment can decide the case in favor of the second against the first.

Having said this, can we not extend to the rule of justice the same test and the same critical interpretation? We have already referred to the dissimulated ambiguity of the rule of justice. We saw the rule of justice oscillate between the disinterested interest of parties concerned to increase their own advantage as far as the accepted rule will allow, and a true feeling of cooperation going as far as the confession of being mutual debtors to one another. In the same way that the golden rule, given over to itself, sinks to the rank of a utilitarian maxim, the rule of justice, given over to itself, tends to subordinate cooperation to competition, or rather to expect from the equilibrium of rival interests the simulacrum of cooperation.

If such is the spontaneous tendency of our sense of justice, must we not admit that if it were not touched and secretly guarded by the poetics of love, even up to its most abstract formulation, it would become merely a subtly sublimated variety of utilitarianism? After all, does not even the Rawlsian calculation of the maximum run the risk in the final analysis of appearing as the dissimulated form of a utilitarian calculation?[17] What saves Rawls's second principle of justice from falling into this subtle form of utilitarianism is finally its secret kinship with the commandment to love, inasmuch as this latter is directed against the process of victimization that utilitarianism sanctions when it proposes as its ideal the maximization of the average advantage of the greatest number at the price of the sacrifice of a small number, a sinister implication which utilitarianism tries to conceal. This kinship between Rawls's second principle of justice and the commandment to love is finally one of the unspoken presuppositions of the well-known reflective equilibrium which this theory warrants in the last resort between its abstract theory and our well-considered convictions.

The tension we have discerned in place of our initial antinomy is not equivalent to the suppression of the contrast between our two logics. Nevertheless, it does make justice the necessary medium of love;

precisely because love is hypermoral, it enters the practical and ethical sphere only under the aegis of justice. As I have said elsewhere about the parables of Jesus, which reorient by disorienting, this effect is obtained on the ethical plane only through the conjugation of the new commandment with the golden rule and, in a more general way, through the synergistic action of love and justice. To disorient without reorienting is, in Kierkegaardian terms, to suspend the ethical. In one sense, the commandment to love, as hyperethical, is a way of suspending the ethical, which is reoriented only at the price of a reprise and a rectification of the rule of justice that runs counter to its utilitarian tendency.

Allow me to say in conclusion that the formulas we find in reading analytical philosophers concerned, as is Outka, with disengaging the normative content of love, are formulas that describe those figures of love that have already been mediated by justice, in a culture marked by our Jewish, Greek and Christian heritages. In this sense, we come back once again to Outka's three definitions: equal regard, self-sacrifice and mutuality.

It is the task of both philosophy and theology to discern, beneath the reflective equilibrium expressed in these compromise formulas, the secret discordance between the logic of superabundance and the logic of equivalence. It is also their task to say that it is only in the moral judgment made within some particular situation that this unstable equilibrium can be assured and protected. Thus we may affirm in good faith and with a good conscience that the enterprise of expressing this equilibrium in everyday life, on the individual, judicial, social and political planes, is perfectly practicable. I would even say that the tenacious incorporation, step by step, of a supplementary degree of compassion and generosity in all of our codes – including our penal codes and our codes of social justice – constitutes a perfectly reasonable task, however difficult and interminable it may be.

[Translated by David Pellauer]

Notes

From *Radical Pluralism and Truth: David Tracy and the Hermeneutics of Religion*, ed. Werner G. Jeanrond and Jennifer L. Rike (New York: Crossroad). Copyright © 1991 by Werner G. Jeanrond and Jennifer L. Rike. Reprinted by permission of the editors and Crossroad Publishing Co., New York.

1 Gene Outka, *Agape: An Ethical Analysis* (New Haven, CT and London: Yale University Press, 1972).

2 ibid., p. 7.

3 ibid.

4 ibid., pp. 9, 24, 36.

5 Blaise Pascal, *Pensées*, trans. A. J. Krailsheimer (Harmondsworth, Middlesex: Penguin, 1966), p. 125.

6 Robert Alter, *The Art of Biblical Poetry* (New York: Basic Books, 1985).

7 Franz Rosenzweig, *The Star of Redemption*, trans. William W. Hallo (New York: Holt, Rinehart & Winston, 1971).

8 ibid., p. 202.

9 If anyone is surprised to see all reference to the neighbor put off until the third category, redemption, it should be recalled that Rosenzweig's three categories are contemporaneous with one another even though the third also develops the second one. Thus the historical dimension unfolds beyond the solitary I–thou conversation. From here on there are laws and not just the commandment: Love me, at the same time as there are others. In other words, the second great commandment proceeds from the first, insofar as the always imminent future of a history of redemption, with all its historical and communal implications, proceeds from the Today of the commandment to love. In this sense, there is not just a lover and a beloved, but a self and an other than oneself – a neighbor.

10 There is here a broad semantic field whose exploration calls for the insightfulness and subtleness of a second J. L. Austin!

11 Cf. Anders Nygren, *Agape and Eros*, trans. Philip S. Watson (Philadelphia, PA: Westminster, 1953).

12 In the case of a crime and the pronouncing of a guilty verdict that the accused does not accept, the passing of sentence is still a form of communication. As J. R. Lucas puts it, 'Punishment is a language. It translates the disesteem of society into the value system of the recalcitrant individual' (*On Justice* [Oxford: Clarendon, 1980], p. 134).

13 John Rawls, *A Theory of Justice* (Cambridge, MA: Harvard University Press, 1971).

14 This logic of superabundance finds a great variety of expression in the New Testament. It governs the extravagant twist of many of Jesus's parables, as is evident in those called parables of growth: one seed that produces 30, 60, 100 grains; a tiny mustard seed that becomes a tree where birds may nest, etc. In a different context, Paul interprets the whole history of salvation following the same law of superabundance: 'If because of one man's trespass, death reigned through that one man,

much more will those who receive the abundance of grace and the free gift of righteousness reign in life through the one man Jesus Christ' (Romans 5.17). The extravagance of the parables, the hyperbole of the eschatological sayings, the logic of superabundance in ethics, are all different expressions of what I am calling the logic of super-abundance.

15 Albrecht Dihle, *Die Goldene Regel* (Heidelberg: C. Winter, 1989).

16 In truth, a certain formalism already appears in the golden rule. We are not told what it is that we are to love or hate if it is done to us; however, this formalism is imperfect inasmuch as it still appeals to emotions, to love and hate, which Kant will put on the side of 'pathological' desires.

17 This calculation would run as follows. If, once the veil of ignorance were lifted, the worst portion were to fall to me, would it not be better to choose behind the veil of ignorance the rule of distribution that, undoubtedly, would deprive me of the highest gains I might attain under a less equitable division, but that would also protect me from the greater possible disadvantages of another form of division?

Peter Kemp

Ricoeur between Heidegger and Lévinas: original affirmation between ontological attestation and ethical injunction

This article takes a stand on the opposition between Martin Heidegger and Emmanuel Lévinas in order to show Paul Ricoeur's method of taking other philosophers into account and going with them as long as possible. It is Ricoeur who, more than anyone else, has taught me that to do philosophy is to follow the thought of the other to its end in order to surpass that thought and push one's own reflection a little further. A good example of this is Ricoeur's way of reading, interpreting and criticizing Heidegger – how he appropriates Heidegger's thinking by remaining faithful to the texts while nevertheless indicating the points with which he cannot agree.

I Legacy

1 From Jaspers to Lévinas

Lévinas appears very late in the work of Ricoeur as not only an important translator of Husserl, but also a first-rate interlocutor. Heidegger, on the other hand, appears very early in Ricoeur's work as a philosopher in relation to whom Ricoeur wants to situate himself. This is not to say that Lévinas's philosophical standpoint, at least in broad outline, was not an earlier consideration of Ricoeur's; but, before Lévinas, Ricoeur attributed this position to another name, Karl Jaspers. Thus, in Ricoeur's first book in collaboration with Mikel Dufrenne, *Karl Jaspers et la philosophie existentielle*, Jaspers is presented as the philosopher who at the same time thought Being as the Other, truth as veracity, and human existence as living before Transcendence.

However, Jaspers's idea of the Other as Transcendence, to which human existence must reply by interpreting the symbolic figures, is different from Lévinas's Other, which comes from the outside without mediation as a command inscribed in the epiphany, or the face of the other. Still, in *Karl Jaspers et la philosophie existentielle*, Ricoeur already shows a strong interest in ontology which, following Jaspers, considers the human situation *in front of* Transcendence. Accordingly, just as Ricoeur's interest in Jaspers shows an early concern with the Other whom he later recognizes in the ethics of Lévinas, Ricoeur also, from the beginning of his authorship – which is quite remarkable for our purposes here – saw the idea of Transcendence challenged by the *other* existential philosophy developed by Heidegger in *Being and Time*.

In fact, in one of the last paragraphs of *Karl Jaspers et la philosophie existentielle*, where Jaspers is contrasted to Heidegger, Ricoeur claims that the opposition is between a philosophy having two focal points and a philosophy having one. The two focal points in Jaspers are those of freedom and Transcendence; whereas Heidegger's single focal point is that of freedom in the world which denies any Transcendence in the sense of Being as Other beyond the world.[1] It follows that the concept of world claimed by Heidegger is other than that claimed by Jaspers and that their conceptions of the relationship to death are very different. To Jaspers, death belongs to the sensual life from which one must be liberated by hope; whereas, to Heidegger, death gives humankind its highest possibility of recovering lucidity and understanding itself as a finite totality, as a coherence of human time from the beginning of existence to its end.

Today's reader who knows the later works of Ricoeur will certainly wonder why, in this paragraph on the opposition between Heidegger and Jaspers, the author makes (or the authors make) no effort to employ this opposition dialectically in order to create a third way of thinking. Heidegger appears only in order to put Jaspers in relief; and the discussion at the end of the book on the split in Jaspers's philosophy between the criticism of religion and its reconciliation by belief makes no appeal to Heidegger in the search for a solution. However, it is true enough that it could not do so because this distinction brings up the question of religious philosophy excluded by Heidegger.

However, after that book, and after an attempt to utilize the philosophy of Jaspers in developing a philosophy of existence and communication by approaching it via the thought of Gabriel Marcel's 'twofold sympathy' in his 1947 work, *Gabriel Marcel et Karl Jaspers*, Ricoeur abandoned Jaspers as a sparring partner and replaced him with Heidegger. Why? Ricoeur himself answered this question[2] on the occasion of Jeanne Hersch's translation of Jaspers's great work, *Philosophy*, by declaring that despite Jaspers's intention to take the consequences of the double shock of Kierkegaard and Nietzsche by performing a 'destruction' of the world-views belonging to traditional ontology, Jaspers's efforts nevertheless remain classic in his attempt to unify the ideas of freedom and rational clarity. Whereas Heidegger, in addition to his original way of thinking existence in the world, was showing himself to Ricoeur and all others seeking a radical existential philosophy, as the most radical renovator in the rupture with classical metaphysics.

However, for Ricoeur, the idea of Transcendence in the sense of the Other who breaks with self-sufficient existence – an idea which Ricoeur also found in Gabriel Marcel and Karl Barth – is never abandoned. And it was his late discovery of Lévinas which allowed Ricoeur to oppose Heidegger through yet another philosophy of transcendence and communication[3] – now in a dialectical way which allows him to state: 'in the debate between Heidegger and Lévinas, I find myself at the same time a little on both sides'.[4] How is it that Ricoeur has succeeded in situating himself between Heidegger and Lévinas? This is the question which will guide us in the following.

2 Jean Nabert

The philosopher who made possible Ricoeur's approach to Heidegger is certainly Jean Nabert, who published the book *Eléments pour une Ethique* in 1943. Thus, it is not surprising that recently, in an article on testimony, Ricoeur presented Nabert as a mediator between Heidegger and Lévinas.[5]

Like Jaspers, Nabert reflects on defeat, fault and solitude, but he does not oppose these negative phenomena to a Transcendence which overcomes them. On the contrary, he shows that by thinking an existential negation to its end, one is brought to an affirmation of existence which he calls 'original affirmation'. For example: 'from the moment that the feeling of solitude has acquired an intensity strong enough to produce the disarray and the unhappiness . . . [it] gives the self the presentiment that, alone with itself, it is perhaps not more separated from itself than it is from the other consciousnesses in the communication.'[6] By deepening solitude, the self discovers that it receives from others all that it appreciates in its own being, and consequently that it is not alone. The self's negation of others is itself negated by the original affirmation of the desire to exist with the other and of the experience of a present community.

According to this reflective philosophy, the world is no longer primarily an obstacle or a border to existence as it was to Jaspers; rather, as Ricoeur described it in his remarkable 1956 analysis of Sartrean negativity, 'Negativity and Original Affirmation',[7] the world is the correlate to existence. Thus, although the fundamental feeling in Nabert is not anxiety for 'my own existence', as it is in Heidegger's *Being and Time*, he nevertheless takes negative feelings as starting-points in order to show that they limit themselves and are rooted in the original affirmation which does not sink into Nothingness, but which makes existence, in immanence, open for Transcendence.

3 Heidegger

Thus, Nabert played an essential role in allowing Ricoeur to dissociate himself from Jaspers and to approach Heidegger without being captivated by the analysis in *Being and Time* of the lonely and heroic existence of *Dasein* which finally owes nothing to the other. How then has Ricoeur managed this approach?

First, he recognized Heidegger's concept of world, or rather the concept of being-in-the-world, as more true than classic concepts which grasp the world as perceived and material nature, as objective to the knowing subject, and as that which blocks the spiritual aspirations of the human mind.

Rémi Brague showed that Heidegger rightly claimed that his concept of world is original and that it does not come from Greek philosophy which identifies world with nature.[8] One may ask if Heidegger's concept of world is a transformation of the later Husserl's concept of life-world; or, as suggested by Tomonobu Imamichi, if it comes from Japanese thought, in particular from Kakuzo Okakura's *The Book of Tea*, written in English in 1906 and translated into German 12 years later.[9] In this book Okakura speaks of Taoism as 'the art of being in the world' (translated in the German edition as *Kunst des In-der-Welt-Seins*). He also claims that the world is no mere objectivity or border, but familiarity and atmosphere which open around life. 'It deals with the present-ourselves', he claims.[10] In any case, the concept of world which Ricoeur integrated is that of the surroundings of and correlate to existence, not that of objectivity opposed to subjectivity. Thus the influence of Maurice Merleau-Ponty on his application of the Heideggerian concept of world is undeniable.

This new concept of world is not yet recognized in *Le volontaire et l'involontaire* (Freedom and Nature)[11] which he finished in 1948 and which still identifies world with nature; but it appears in the introduction to Ricoeur's translation of the first volume of Husserl's *Ideas* when he discusses Eugene Fink's interpretation of the concept of *Lebenswelt* in the late Husserl.[12] In addition, in a note at the end, he refers to the Heideggerian conviction in Merleau-Ponty's *Phenomenology of Perception* that the world is always 'already there' and constitutes the facticity of our 'being-in-the-world'.[13] Ricoeur's interest in this concept reaches its climax in his programmatic essay 'Existence and Hermeneutics' from 1965 (in the same year appeared his great work *Freud and Philosophy: Essay on Interpretation*, where he presents his thinking as hermeneutical). In 'Existence and Hermeneutics' he unambiguously acknowledges that he follows a Heideggerian understanding of the Husserlian concept of *Lebenswelt*[14] and that he also aims for a fundamental ontology which presupposes that 'before objectivity there is the horizon of world'. It is against this background of agreement with Heidegger that Ricoeur claims the disagreement to which I will return.

Ricoeur also followed Heidegger's criticism of the pretensions of the theories of knowledge. Instead of asking for the transcendental conditions for the knowing subject to know objectively, he asks what Being is, *since* there is comprehension and knowledge. Moreover, like Heidegger, Ricoeur recognizes with Aristotle that Being 'has several meanings' (*Metaphysics*, E.2) and he focuses on two principal distinctions: (1) between true-Being and false-Being, and (2) between Being as substance and Being as power and act. It was Franz Brentano's 1862 dissertation, 'Von der mannigfaltigen Bedeutung des Seienden nach Aristoteles', which gave Heidegger the idea of questioning Being as *true* and as *act* and of dissociating the *Vorhandensein* (being present-at-hand) from these two modes of *Dasein*. We see these same concerns in Ricoeur's latest work *Soi-même comme un autre* (*Oneself as Another*) when he considers the question of ontology by a 'reappropriation of Aristotle through Heidegger', going so far as to reconstruct an unsaid Aristotelian distinction in order to elaborate his own fundamental distinction between *ipse* and *idem* (selfhood and sameness) as two modes of identical Being.[15]

Finally, we must note the importance Ricoeur affords to the Heideggerian notion of 'conscience' (*Gewissen*) in *Oneself as Another*. Conscience expresses the attestation by which existence is called to recognize its own potentiality-for-Being. Following the author of

Oneself as Another, the idea of conscience, which bears witness to a potentiality of existence in a pre-moral manner (i.e. before designating the capacity to distinguish good and evil), confirms his 'working hypothesis that the distinction between selfhood and sameness does not simply concern two constellations of meaning but involves two modes of being'.[16] However, Heidegger's notion of conscience is perhaps not so far from Jaspers's, as Ricoeur already noted in his work on Jaspers.[17]

Recently,[18] Ricoeur has shown a certain regret for having abandoned Jaspers, for whom 'in a broad sense the whole of philosophy . . . is ethics',[19] in favor of Heidegger, whose analytic of *Dasein* 'did not permit him to have moral and political criteria' to judge his own time. This weakness undoubtedly has been fatal for Heidegger and for all who took him as the only *maître à penser*; but, even if today we should perhaps return to Jaspers in our reflections on ethics, we do not need to regret Ricoeur's approach to Heidegger's thought. Thanks to Ricoeur's appropriation, his opposition to Heidegger is more fruitful, especially insofar as he has taken care not to use Heidegger's philosophy as a basis for ethics.

4 Lévinas

On the other hand, even though in Ricoeur's eyes Lévinas has replaced Jaspers as the thinker of the Other, Ricoeur does not intend to base the comprehension of ethics on Lévinas's thought. He refers much more to Aristotle — following the interpretation by Alasdair MacIntyre and others — in order to outline the foundation of ethics as 'the aim of true life'.[20] For Ricoeur, it is important 'to give solicitude a more fundamental status than obedience to duty'.[21] Solicitude also constitutes a dimension of selfhood's own being by which it always surpasses itself as '*solus ipse*'.

However, Ricoeur recognizes that Lévinas, through his famous phenomenology of the face, has dared reverse the statement, ' "no other-than-self without a self", substituting for it the inverse statement, "no self without another who summons it to responsibility" '.[22] Moreover, it is Lévinas to whom Ricoeur refers when he looks for expression of the selfhood's pure personal identity as self-constancy (*maintien de soi*). Ricoeur considers this concept of self-constancy essentially ethical: 'Self-constancy is for each person that manner of conducting himself or herself so that others can *count on* that person.'[23] This accountability of one's own actions is what Lévinas expresses when he explains the way I am responsible before another by the testimony, 'Here I am!' which constitutes an answer to the question

'Where are you?'[24] For Ricoeur, this answer is a statement of self-constancy.

The summons to responsibility through the injunction from the other constitutes Lévinas's strength for Ricoeur. But, in his description of the ethical relationship of responsibility between selfhood and otherness, Lévinas refuses reciprocity to such an extent that his philosophical position reaches its climax in opposition to Heidegger, whose selfhood cannot receive the other. Let us consider more closely how Ricoeur distances himself from these two philosophers.

II Criticism

1 Heidegger or the ontology of properness

(a) Ricoeur's reproach. As already mentioned in reference to 'Existence and Hermeneutics', Ricoeur agrees with the Heideggerian desire for ontology; but, he refuses the short cut of breaking with all debates on method in order immediately to establish a fundamental ontology, i.e. through a direct description of *Dasein* who exists by the mode of understanding. On the contrary, he follows the long way, a 'more winding and harder way', in order progressively to reach ontology 'by deepening the methodological claims of exegesis, of history and of psychoanalysis'.[25] While he calls this longer way a grafting of the hermeneutical problem on the phenomenological method,[26] it is, rather, the grafting of reflection on methodological problems on to phenomenological ontology – since finally it is a question of an ontological debate with Heidegger.

For Ricoeur, the long way through the problem of method is necessary for the very understanding of existence because of the aporia which the author of *Being and Time* cannot escape. Indeed, Heidegger argues for the necessity of grounding every understanding of real historical time, which the historian speaks of when he or she tells a story (*die Historie*), on the comprehension of historicality (*Geschicht-lichkeit*) in such a way that the written history of historical sciences is considered to be derived from the understanding of history. Yet, Ricoeur claims that Heidegger does not give us 'any means to show in what sense the real historical understanding is derived from this original understanding'.[27] It follows that Heidegger's ontology does not help us to understand how historical sciences are dissociated from natural sciences and, more profoundly, how one can arbitrate conflicts between competing interpretations, often inside even the same science.

Heidegger's fundamental ontology, which in *Being and Time* he still calls a hermeneutics, is qualified not to *resolve* conflicts of interpretation, but rather to *dissolve* them.[28]

The price Heidegger must pay for refusing to consider methodological problems of the sciences is the fact that the history of historians acquires a kind of intermediary position which is finally unthinkable and impossible between the intimate time of *Dasein* and the vulgar time of everyday which the natural sciences formalize and employ for calculations. But, did humans from the past not also exist and did they not also have an understanding of their temporal existence which historians today can tell us about?

In his essay 'Existence and Hermeneutics', Ricoeur lets us only suspect the dilemma of understanding, whereas later on, in *Time and Narrative*, he presents the dilemma in its full extent. The solution he proposes in the earlier essay is 'that one takes the starting point on the level itself where [historical] understanding is performed, i.e. on the level of language'.[29] Thus, he emphasizes that an understanding of one's own existence already presupposes a reflection on the language of understanding. However, in *Time and Narrative*, the language by which we understand our existence itself appears to be the story, i.e. the narrative language by which the application of three 'connectors' – the *calendar*, the *sequence of generations*, and the *trace* – constitutes historical time, through which we join not only our predecessors, contemporaries and successors, but also the universe and cosmological time. Thus, Ricoeur's criticism, which begins by reproaching Heidegger for wanting to derive an understanding of history from an understanding of *Dasein*'s existence, ends in reproaching Heidegger for an incapacity to think historical time itself.

In addition, do we not find Heidegger's incapacity to relate his own existence to what has been but is no longer in his denouncement of the whole of western thinking that precedes him as substantializing metaphysics? Accordingly, in *La métaphore vive* (*The Rule of Metaphor*), Ricoeur turns against the manner in which Heidegger opposes all other ontologies by confining them inside the bounds of 'the' metaphysical.[30] This 'destruction of metaphysics' signifies in Ricoeur's eyes an 'unacceptable claim . . . [to put] an end to the history of being',[31] a claim which is no more legitimate than the Hegelian attempt to demonstrate the closing of history. In particular, Ricoeur cannot follow Heidegger's refusal to acknowledge that metaphor can serve thought when Heidegger claims that 'the metaphorical exists only within the metaphysical'.[32] As Ricoeur reminds us, Heidegger himself frequently uses metaphors. Therefore, his polemics must be seen as a pretense of rupturing the very history that he himself is a part of in order to master it from inside his own world, rather than as an attempt at real rupture which would mean an end to all use of metaphor in philosophy.

Instead of performing the 'destruction of metaphysics', Ricoeur asks: 'Which resources of ontology are capable of being reawakened, liberated and regenerated by coming in touch with a phenomenology of Self?'[33] and finally by aiming at an ontology of being? Thus, in Ricoeur's criticism of Heidegger as the 'deconstructor' of the history of metaphysics, one can see a demonstration, in a very precise sense, of his more fundamental criticism of the absence in Heidegger of a non-vulgar understanding of historical time.

There is yet another absence in Heidegger's *Being and Time* which is undoubtedly connected to his incapacity to think historical time – the lack in his main work of a focus on corporeal existence. Thus, when Ricoeur in *Oneself as Another* uses the concept of *flesh*, by which Merleau-Ponty in his posthumous work *The Visible and the Invisible* indicates a human being's own body, he notes that 'Heidegger [in *Being and Time*] has not developed the notion of flesh as a distinct existentiale'.[34] At first this absence is astonishing – that an author who considers things in the world to be 'ready-to-hand' (*zuhanden*) or 'present-at-hand' (*vorhanden*) should not also consider things to be at the disposal of one's body; and it is even more surprising when we take into account that his teacher Husserl focused much on the body (*Leib*). Thus, Ricoeur wonders why the author of *Being and Time* did not apply this Husserlian notion to his analysis of the facticity in which *Dasein* discovers itself to be 'thrown' (*geworfen*). What we find is only an analysis of the spatiality in which *Dasein* has at its disposal things and persons in everydayness. According to Ricoeur, the reason is that Heidegger avoided any analysis which might favor an interpretation of ourselves according to the things we care about. Thus, Heidegger sticks to an analysis of the spatiality and temporality of existence which, to his mind, do not involve the same risks.

(b) A more severe criticism? What is coherent in the criticism Ricoeur turns against Heidegger and has he carried it fully to its end?

In order to answer these questions we must first notice that all of Ricoeur's reservations about Heidegger can be summarized as a criticism of his analytic of the human world, for giving no room for *the other* at the border of or outside the world which is mine. There is no place for the other – whether it is my body as the other I am in an ambiguous way (to be body is indeed to take care of oneself as another), or the other here and now, absent in the past or in the future to which I must ascribe his or her own world – if it is true that this other being is more than the image I have of him or her. It is not by accident that Heidegger, on the level of fundamental ontology, does not consider the question of ethics and in particular the question of ethical relationships both to the other and to oneself (as Kant spoke of duties both to the other and to oneself). According to Heidegger, neither the other nor the self which is also another are known outside fallen existence and, consequently, these others cannot exist on a fundamental level. *Mitsein* (Being-with) is 'proximally and for the most part' the other in everydayness (*das Man*, the they). Although Heidegger cannot avoid speaking of the 'resolute' relationship to others completely, he claims only that *Dasein* must let them 'be' (*'sein' zu lassen*): 'Dasein's resoluteness towards itself is what first makes it possible to let the Others who are with it "be" in their ownmost potentiality-for-Being'.[35] Fundamentally, care for the other consists in letting him or her be in peace, liberating the other to his or her own solitude or 'mineness'.

However, with the ontology at which Ricoeur aims – which implies recognition and respect for the other as its own body, as the other being, and as conscience which judges itself – we have the grounds for a more severe criticism of Heidegger.

The reason why French philosophers in general and Ricoeur in particular have often been too lenient in their criticism of Heidegger is related perhaps to the traditional French translation (the same can be said of the traditional English translation) of the German terms *Eigentlichkeit* and *Uneigentlichkeit*. Since 1930 these words have been translated into French as *authenticité* (in English, 'authenticity') and *inauthenticité* (in English, 'inauthenticity'). These translations do not take into account what is essential for the author of *Being and Time*. Lévinas, in his 1991 lectures on *La mort et le temps* (*Death and Time*), mentions this fact when he claims that for Heidegger the being who wants to be *eigentlich* is the being of an entity 'which has to make it its own, to *sich zu ereignen*'.[36] This appropriation succeeds in 'the aspect where it is in possession of itself, where it is, properly, *eigentlich*'.[37] Moreover, Lévinas considers that *das Ereignis*, the event analyzed in Heidegger's later works, presupposes this *Eigentlichkeit*. Thus, we must translate *eigentlich* by *propre* (in English, 'own' or 'proper') rather than by *authentique* (in English, 'authentic'). However, this translation goes against nearly all of the French philosophers, from Sartre to Ricoeur,[38] who have employed Heideggerian terminology, and also against Emmanuel Martineau, who for very good reasons is generally recognized as the best French translator of *Being and Time*. As an exception, at this point in translating one must follow François Vezin; his translation is for the most part heavy and loaded with awful and useless neologisms, but, as a Danish proverb says, 'a blind chicken can also find the grain'. Vezin translates *eigentlich* and *uneigentlich* by *propre* (in English, 'own' or 'proper') and *impropre* (in English, 'improper') and *Eigentlichkeit* and *Uneigentlichkeit* by the more artificial terms *propriété* (in English, 'properness' or 'ownness') and *impropriété* (in English, 'improperness').

Why is this question of translation so important? Because Heidegger gives the terms *Eigentlichkeit* and *Uneigentlichkeit* meanings which are quite his own and very unusual even in German. Heidegger's *Eigentlichkeit* has a sense of solitude, even of cloistering and confinement. Let us take some examples of the employment of *Eigentlichkeit* and *Uneigentlichkeit* in *Being and Time*. Both notions are introduced in section 9 of the analytic of *Dasein* regarding the Being of an entity which is 'in each case mine'.[39] Take the following statement:

> That entity which in its Being has this very Being as an issue, comports itself towards its being as its ownmost possibility (*als seiner eigensten Möglichkeit*). . . . And because Dasein *is* in each case essentially its possibility, it *can*, in its very Being, 'choose' itself and win itself; it can also lose itself and never win itself; or only 'seem' to do so. But only in so far as it is essentially something which is *mögliches eigentliches, das heißt sich zueigen ist.*

Martineau translates: 'est un *Dasein authentique* possible, c'est-à-dire peut être à lui-méme en propre'; whereas Vezin translates: 'à la possibilité d'être *proprement*, c'est-à-dire d'être à soi.'[40] The English translation by John Macquarrie and Edward Robinson uses the same term as Martineau: 'in so far as it is essentially something which can be *authentic* – that is something of its own – can it have lost itself and not yet won itself.'[41] However, in a note the English translators frankly acknowledge that in their translation 'the connection between "*eigenlich*" ("authentic", "real") and "*eigen*" ("own") is lost'.[42] Therefore, the last part of the statement should have been translated into English as 'insofar as it is essentially something which can be *proper* – that is, something of its own – can it have lost itself and not yet won itself'. Consequently, Heidegger's words should be translated as follows: 'As modes of Being, *properness* and *improperness* (these expressions have been chosen terminologically in a strict sense [*im strengem Worsinne*]) are both grounded in the fact that any *Dasein* whatsoever is characterized by mineness.'

While it is true that *Eigentlichkeit* in ordinary German can often be translated as 'authenticity' or 'literalness' (in the latter case, for example, Hegel, in his *Aesthetics*, talks about the 'literal sense' of a word, and Husserl, in the sixth of his *Logical Investigations*, considers 'literal thought'), the Heideggerian use of the term is so peculiar, not only because it concerns *die eigene Existenz* (my own or proper existence), but also because he emphasizes the distinction between *Eigentlichkeit* and *Echtheit*. In English one often renders *Echtheit* by either 'genuineness' or 'authenticity'. While Macquarrie and Robinson translate it by 'genuineness' in a statement on p. 142 of *Being and Time*, they, on the same occasion, blur the difference between *Eigentlichkeit* and *Echtheit* by rendering *eigentlich* by 'really' – 'Fearing-about does not lose its specific genuineness even if it is not "really" afraid.'[43]

The difference between *Eigentlichkeit* and *Echtheit* is clearly stated by Heidegger in section 31, 'Being-there as Understanding' (here my revisions to the English translation are in italics):

> Understanding is either *proper*, arising out of one's own Self as such (*aus dem eigenen Selbst als solchem entspringendes*), or *improper*. The '*im*' of '*improper*' does not mean that Dasein cuts itself off from its Self and understands 'only' the world. The world belongs to Being-one's-Self as Being-in-the-world. On the other hand, *proper* understanding, no less than that which is *improper*, *can* be either genuine or not genuine (*Das eigentliche ebensowohl als das uneigentliche Verstehen können wiederum echt oder unecht sein*).[44]

Heidegger gives several examples: one can 'fear about' without 'being-afraid', so that fear is an 'improper' feeling nevertheless having its genuineness;[45] interpretation (*Auslegung*), according to the pre-paratory analyses of everyday *Dasein*, is developed 'in *improper* understanding, and indeed in the mode of its genuineness' (*uneigent-liche Verstehen und zwar im Modus seiner Echtheit*);[46] and,

> Inasmuch as Dasein understands itself in a way which, proximally and for the most part, is *improper*, we may suppose that 'time' as ordinarily understood does indeed represent a genuine [*echtes*] phenomenon, but one which is derivative [*ein abkünftiges*]. It arises from *improper* temporality, which has a source of its own [*Es entspringt der uneigentlichen Zeitlichkeit, die selbst ihren eigenen Ursprung hat*].[47]

It follows that when we want to emphasize the proper understanding of proper existence, it is not enough to say that according to Heidegger this understanding must be authentic in the sense of veracious, i.e. a reliable philosophical discourse. What is essential is that this understanding concerns my proper existence, the mineness, *die Jemeinigkeit*. As Heidegger claimed on several occasions: 'Dasein exists for the sake of a potentiality-for-Being itself.'[48] This message is exactly what we see in his analysis of Being-towards-death, which is not only anticipation of itself but 'anticipation of a potentiality-for-Being'. This anticipation 'turns out to be the possibility of understanding one's *ownmost* and uttermost potentiality-for-Being (*des eigensten äusßersten Seinkönnens*) – that is to say, the possibility of *proper existence (das heißt als Möglichkeit eigentlicher Existenz)*'.[49]

However, if the analytic of *Dasein* is not, as one may assume, an analysis intended to describe human existence with as much veracity as possible, but rather is an analysis in which properness (*Eigentlichkeit*) must be understood in the strict sense, then the *care of oneself (die Sorge)* is fundamentally *care of Myself*. This Self is certainly not a psychological ego, but rather an ontological Self who in its mineness or ownness implies that the other is totally excluded as a partner. Finally, *Dasein* is unable to understand that the other is in its existence another mineness, an irreplaceable other in the world. According to Heidegger, ultimately the other can give me nothing of real importance. Likewise, in my ownness, I am fundamentally unable to give something to others except – if this can be more than a *flatus vocis* in the Heideggerian universe – to 'let them be'.

Thus, it is not surprising that Heidegger's thought cannot really make room for ethics. One may even say that it is properly (*eigentlich*) anti-ethical. Paradoxically however, Heidegger, as the author of *Being and Time*, addresses himself to a reader; and this is why the reader of that work is able to read the work against the saying (*die Rede*) of the author. Thus, when I read this work, it bears witness to the proper existence of *another*. This testimony indicates that the existence of the other selfhood is 'proximally and for the most part' fallen (*verfallen*); it discovers itself as guilty (*schuldig*) of this fall; and its conscience (*Gewissen*) allows it to become lucid and resolute (*entschlossen*) in its understanding of itself, so that it does not understand itself as being-present-at-hand (*Vorhandensein*) but as a potentiality-for-Being (*Sein-können*). Thus, the reader who listens to this testimony can receive it, at least to a certain extent, as an interpretation of the meaning of existence which applies to every human being and which opposes any conception of human existence which reduces it to being present-at-hand without potentiality-for-Being and without responsibility for its acts. That reader thus appropriates the Heideggerian analyses of proper existence as elements for an ethic (according to the title of the work already quoted by Nabert).

It follows that the reason why we need not reject *Being and Time* as egocentric to the highest degree, is that we understand Heidegger despite himself. But, precisely from an ethical point of view, we cannot accept his work totally – as in the case of his incapacity and refusal to think the other in his or her proper existence, the corporeality of *Dasein*, and the history of historians.[50] Against these errors in thought one must be even more severe than Ricoeur. The very fact that the reader, despite the defeat of Heidegger's entire project, can interpret his work as offering elements for ethics is a marvelous demonstration of how ontology ends in a cul-de-sac if it claims to be valuable for everybody and to present the truth of all human beings and of the world as such and yet avoid ethics.

2 Lévinas and the ethics of the face

(a) Ricoeur's reproach. We find Ricoeur's criticism of Lévinas in the essay on testimony[51] already mentioned and in the final chapter of *Oneself as Another*. These two texts point to the dialectics between the two radical positions which, for Ricoeur, are represented by Heidegger and Lévinas – the former analyzing the attestation of self, conscience (*Gewissen*) without the other's injunction, and the latter claiming the injunction by the other without attestation of the self-affection of conscience. To Heidegger he objects 'that attestation is primordially injunction, or attestation risks losing all ethical and moral significance'; and to Lévinas he objects 'that the injunction is primordially attestation, or the injunction risks not being heard and the self not being affected in the mode of being-enjoined'.[52] Ricoeur proposes a third position that claims 'being enjoined as the structure of self-hood'.[53] This third position also opposes Husserl's attempt to derive from his own ego the other as *another ego*. According to Ricoeur, this derivation is a contradiction by the fact that it presupposes the other who should be derived.

The reason why Ricoeur can oppose Lévinas to Husserl and Heidegger is that he considers the ethics of Lévinas to be a radical rupture with the self that relates to itself by identifying itself. To Ricoeur, the author of *Totality and Infinity* (1961) presents the self before the encounter with the other as 'a stubbornly closed, locked up, separate ego'.[54] The phenomenology of separation is that 'of egotism',[55] which implies, as Lévinas himself says, that the 'I is ignorant of the Other'.[56] Thus, the Other is an ab-solute exteriority which can present itself to the separate ego by the *epiphany* of the face. The face accomplishes the rupture with the closed Ego and with its world of representation where I find only myself or the Same.

However, according to Ricoeur, this representation of *separation* is characterized by hyperbole, i.e. by a practice of *excess* in philosophical argumentation which serves to provoke the reader to make the rupture Lévinas speaks about. This manner of communication is brought to its extreme in the other great work of Lévinas, *Otherwise than Being or Beyond Essence* (1974), which, particularly in the last chapter on 'the substitution', 'employs even greater hyperbole, to the point of paroxysm'.[57] Thus Ricoeur finds hyperbole when Lévinas carries the assignment of responsibility 'back to a past more ancient than any past of memory',[58] or when he declares that injunction comes from that which is prior to any beginning and speaks of 'a responsibility that is justified by no prior commitment'.[59] The point of paroxysm in this work is reached when Lévinas speaks about responsibility which 'under accusation by everyone'[60] goes to the point of *substitution of the I for the Other*. Here the Other is no longer, as in *Totality and Infinity*, the master of justice who says, 'You shall not commit murder', he is 'the offender, who, as offender, no less requires the gesture of pardon and expiation'.[61] In this ethics 'a subject is a hostage'.[62]

Ricoeur does not like these hyperboles because they make reception of the other and the distinction between oneself and myself inconceivable. Self-esteem is identified with egoism because interiority is 'determined solely by the desire for retreat and closure'.[63] The Other has become my executioner and my persecutor who is there not to convince me, but to oppress me into total passivity.

However, Ricoeur recognizes that even in *Otherwise than Being* there are positive statements about selfhood as 'unique and irreplaceable'.[64] In addition, Lévinas says selfhood is not-thematizable, preferring to speak of it in the accusative ('It is me here'), aiming to refuse every 'idealistic priority of the I',[65] and testifying about the height called 'glory of the Infinite'.[66] Thus, there is in Lévinas a self who bears testimony. For these reasons, Ricoeur asks the question: 'Is this testimony so far from what we constantly have named attestation?'[67]

(b) A less severe criticism? Ricoeur's criticism of Lévinas is based primarily on *Otherwise than Being*. He only refers to *Totality and Infinity* to the extent that he wants to show what anticipated the theses in *Otherwise than Being* and which theses were strengthened by the latter. From *Otherwise than Being* it is not difficult to get an impression of a philosopher who, in order to emphasize the ethical demand, pushes his strategy of hyperbole to paroxysm and scandal. In addition, if one agrees with Ricoeur that grounding ethics requires one to ascribe to solicitude a more fundamental status than obedience to duty, then one may consider Lévinas's description of the assignation of responsibility excessive by its demonstration, by way of the absurd, of the weakness of an ethics founded on the idea of obedience.

From this standpoint, Ricoeur's criticism is not too severe, though Lévinas's analysis of substitution is without doubt marked by the terrible experiences and extreme situations of the Nazi Holocaust. However, if one chooses to consider *Totality and Infinity* as the key work in Lévinas's thinking, then the interpretation of his philosophy can certainly be seen differently from the view taken by Ricoeur. In particular, one should not read the analysis of separation as Ricoeur does. In fact, in *Totality and Infinity* there is an equilibrium between the levels of analysis which Ricoeur has not identified and, consequently, a separation without contradiction between ethical existence and pre-ethical life. It is only when seen from *Otherwise than Being*, totally forgetting *Totality and Infinity*, that Ricoeur can write that the 'I' before the encounter with the 'other' is 'a stubbornly closed, locked up, separate ego'.[68] However, even from this point of view, I doubt that this interpretation is fair to Lévinas.

In *Totality and Infinity* there are three levels of description of existence: that of enjoyment and habitation (called 'Interiority and Economy'); that of the face (called 'Exteriority and the Face'); and that of love and fecundity (called 'Beyond the Face'). None of these levels excludes the others. In interiority we live by all the elementary things – we love life and find ourselves happy as in Paradise. This analysis is clearly part of Lévinas's 'showdown with Heidegger', since he opposes interiority to Heidegger's analysis of being-thrown (*Geworfensein*). Moreover, the world of separation in *Totality and Infinity* is not the world of 'the they' (*das Man*) in *Being and Time*. Human existence in Lévinas is not first fallen (*verfallen*), but is first received as a gift. In its self-satisfaction existence is certainly egoist and 'ignorant of the other',[69] but is 'innocently egoist and alone'.[70] Thus, the term 'other' which Lévinas uses when he speaks of the ignorance of the other should be understood in a strictly ethical manner as face, command. Enjoyment indeed is experienced in a habitation where the other, although not yet being 'face', nevertheless is not absent, but, on the contrary, present in intimacy and sweetness, in familiarity and femininity.

It seems to me that it is impossible to understand this analysis otherwise than as praise of the goodness of life in the sense in which this goodness is given by the creation of human existence. The same should be said of Lévinas's analysis of the economy of labor – in the home – by the hand which first gropes and then progressively learns to take and comprehend (*prendre et comprendre*). In addition, habitation is not total passivity in relation to the foreigner – it is in principle a home of hospitality. But, the hand is fallible, it *may* be a manipulator, and one *may* close one's house instead of opening it to the poor and the stranger. In these cases, the Same at all levels of praxis, including philosophical or metaphysical praxis, closes in on itself, so that interiority and the economy of the home cannot constitute an ethics. Indeed, it is only the face entering from the exteriority which assigns us to responsibility.

Thus, Lévinas's description of separation does not have the negative and even masochistic accent which Ricoeur ascribes to it, although there are certain passages of *Otherwise than Being* concerning substitution which could indicate such an accent. Neither does the part of *Totality and Infinity* where existence 'beyond the face' is described have such an accent. On the contrary, it is a marvelous description of sensual love and paternity. This part of the work, courageously elaborated from the point of view of the lover and the father, begins with the following revealing statement: 'The relation with the Other does not nullify separation.'[71] Thus, relation with the other does not refuse innocent loneliness and the right to existence of love and fecundity in their authenticity (*Ectheit*).

All of the above disappears when Ricoeur interprets Lévinas; and for this reason I consider his criticism too severe. One cannot blame Lévinas for the absence of attestation of self-affection. While it is true that attestation, as it is explained in *Totality and Infinity*, is implicit in love of life and happiness, this is less apparent in *Otherwise than Being*. However, even in that work, attestation is indirectly indicated by the analysis of the self as 'denuded and destitute', a self who, according to Lévinas, is 'vulnerable, that is to say, sensible'.[72]

III Farewell praise

I have tried to show that in our criticisms we should be more severe in relation to Heidegger and less severe in relation to Lévinas than Ricoeur has been. More fundamentally, my intention was to praise the philosopher and master who, by applying the idea of original affirmation taken in an independent and renovating manner from Spinoza, Maine de Biran and particularly Nabert, has taught us about the royal way to philosophical reflection which is neither pure self-attestation nor pure injunction that makes me guilty, but concerns both a self who lives by the other and another who invites the self to community.

If that is true, one has to go even further, I think, and claim that ethics, as the guardian of veracity, is the foundation and the justification of ontology regarding the multiple senses of Being.

University of Copenhagen, Denmark

Notes

This paper was originally given in honor of Paul Ricoeur in Naples, 7–8 May 1993.

1 Mikel Dufrenne and Paul Ricoeur, *Karl Jaspers et la philosophie existentielle* (Paris: Editions du Seuil, 1947), p. 371.

2 Paul Ricoeur, *Lectures I* (Paris: Editions du Seuil, 1991), p. 156.

3 Bengt Kristensson Uggla's Swedish dissertation on Ricoeur, 'Kommunikation på bristningsgränsen. En studie i Paul Ricoeurs projekt' (Communication at the bursting point: the philosophical project of Paul Ricoeur), prepared for a doctorate degree at the University of Lund, Sweden and defended on 1 October 1994, addresses the role that the idea of communication developed by Jaspers plays in Ricoeur's entire work.

4 *Le Monde*, 27 June 1987.

5 Paul Ricoeur, 'Emmanuel Lévinas, penseur du témoignage', in *Répondre d'autrui, Emmanuel Lévinas*, comp. Jean-Christophe Aeschlimann (Neuchâtel: De la Baconnière, 1989), pp. 17–40.

6 Jean Nabert, *Eléments pour une Ethique* (1943), preface by Paul Ricoeur (Paris: Aubier, 1962), p. 50; English translation (ET) published as *Elements for an Ethic* (Evanston, IL: Northwestern University Press, 1969).

7 Paul Ricoeur, *Histoire et vérité* (1955), 2nd edn (Paris: Editions du Seuil, 1964), p. 310; English translation: *History and Truth: Essays* (Evanston, IL: Northwestern University Press, 1965).

8 Rémi Brague, *Aristotle et la question du monde* (Paris: PUF, 1988), Ch. 1.

9 Tomonobu Imamichi, *Betrachtungen über das Eine* (Tokyo: University of Tokyo, 1968), pp. 89 and 154.

10 Kakuzo Okakura, *Das Buch vom Tee*, trans. Horst Hammitzsch (Frankfurt: Insel Verlag, 1918), p. 29; English translation (ET) published as *The Book of Tea* (Tokyo and New York: Kodansha International, 1991 [1906], p. 64.

11 Paul Ricoeur, *Le volontaire et l'involontaire* (Philosophie de l'esprit) (Paris: Aubier, 1950), pp. 397 et seq.; English translation: *Freedom and Nature. The Voluntary and Involuntary* (Evanston, IL: Northwestern Univesity Press, 1966).

12 Edmund Husserl, *Idées directrices pour une phénoménologie*, trans. and intro. Paul Ricoeur (Paris: Gallimard, 1950), p. xxvii et seq.

13 ibid., p. xxxviii.

14 Paul Ricoeur, *Le conflit des interprétations* (Paris: Editions du Seuil, 1969), p. 12.

15 Paul Ricoeur, *Soi-même comme un autre* (Paris: Editions du Seuil, 1990), p. 361; English translation (ET) published as *Oneself as Another*, trans. Kathleen Blamey (Chicago, IL and London: University of Chicago Press, 1992), p. 311.

16 ibid., p. 358; ET: p. 309.

17 Dufrenne and Ricoeur, *Karl Jaspers et la philosophie existentielle*, p. 216.

18 *Le Monde*, 27 June 1987.

19 Dufrenne and Ricoeur, *Karl Jaspers et la philosophie existentielle*, p. 210

20 Ricoeur, *Soi-même comme un autre*, p. 194 note, et seq.; ET: p. 164, note 31, et seq.

21 ibid., p. 222; ET: p. 190.

22 ibid., p. 219; ET: p. 187.

23 ibid., p. 195; ET: p. 165.

24 Cf. Emmanuel Lévinas, *Autrement qu'être ou au-delà de l'essence* (The Hague: Martinus Nijhoff, 1974), pp. 184 and 186; English translation (ET) published as *Otherwise than Being or Beyond Essence*, trans. A. Lingis (The Hague: Martinus Nijhoff, 1981), p. 180.

25 Ricoeur, *Le conflit des interprétations*, p. 10.

26 ibid., p. 7.

27 ibid., p. 14.

28 ibid.

29 ibid.

30 Paul Ricoeur, *La métaphore vive* (Paris: Editions du Seuil, 1975), p. 395 et seq.; English translation (ET) published as *The Rule of Metaphor*, trans. by Robert Czerny with Kathlin McLaughlin and John Costello (Toronto and Buffalo, NY: University of Toronto Press, 1977), p. 311.

31 ibid., p. 397; ET: p. 312.

32 Cited by Ricoeur in *La métaphore vive*, p. 357; ET: p. 280.

33 Paul Ricoeur, 'L'attestation: entre phénoménologie et herméneutique', in Jean Greisch and Richard Kearney (eds) *Les métamorphoses de la raison* (Paris: Cerf, 1991), p. 398.

34 Ricoeur, *Soi-même comme un autre*, p. 378; ET: p. 327.

35 Martin Heidegger, *Sein und Zeit* (1927) (Tübingen: Niemeyer, 1960), § 60, p. 298; English translation (ET) published as *Being and Time*, trans. John Macquarrie and Edward Robinson (Oxford: Blackwell, 1962), p. 344; cf. *Sein un Zeit*, § 26, p. 122; ET: pp. 158–9.

36 Emmanuel Lévinas, *La mort et le temps* (Paris: Herne, 1991), p. 29; republished as Part One of *Dieu, la mort et le temps* (Paris: Grasset, 1993).

37 ibid., p. 48.
38 As concerns Ricoeur, see especially *Temps et Récit*, Vol. III, p. 97 et seq.; he is well aware of the fact that Heidegger claimed a 'personal conception' of *Eigentlichkeit* (p. 100); but his criticism of this conception might have been stronger had he considered a translation of *Eigentlichkeit* other than as 'authenticity'.
39 Heidegger, *Sein und Zeit*, p. 41; ET: p. 67.
40 ibid., p. 41; ET: p. 68, fn; cf. translation by Emmanuel Martineau, *Etre et Temps* (Paris: Authentica [édition privée], 1985), p. 54; translation by François Vezin, *Etre et Temps* (Paris: Gallimard, 1986), p. 74.
41 Heidegger, *Being and Time*, p. 68.
42 ibid.
43 ibid., p. 181.
44 ibid., (revised) p. 186.
45 Heidegger, *Sein und Zeit*, § 30, p. 142; ET: p. 181.
46 ibid., § 32, p. 148; cf. ET (revised): p. 189.
47 ibid., § 65, p. 326; cf. ET (revised): p. 374.
48 ibid., § 69c, p. 364; ET: p. 416.
49 ibid., § 53, pp. 262–3; ET (revised): p. 307.
50 Heidegger, *Being and Time*, § 77, 'The Connexion of the Foregoing Exposition of Historicality with the Researches of Wilhelm Dilthey and the Ideas of Count York', is very revealing of the defeat of Heidegger's entire project by the fact that – very unusual for the author – it consists almost entirely of a series of quotations.
51 Ricoeur, 'Emmanuel Lévinas, penseur du témoignage', *Répondre d'autrui, Emmanuel Lévinas*, pp. 17–40.
52 Ricoeur, *Soi-même comme un autre*, p. 409; ET: p. 355.
53 ibid.; ET: p. 354.
54 ibid., p. 389: ET: p. 337.
55 ibid.
56 Emmanuel Lévinas, *Totalité et Infini* (The Hague: Martinus Nijhoff, 1961), p. 34, English translation (ET) published as *Totality and Infinity*, trans. A. Lingis (The Hague: Martinus Nijhoff and Duquesne University Press, 1969/1979), p. 62; quoted in Ricoeur, *Soi-même comme un autre*, p. 389; ET: p. 337.
57 Ricoeur, *Soi-même comme un autre*, p. 390; ET: p. 338.
58 ibid., cf. Lévinas, *Autrement qu'être*, p. 133; ET: p. 104.
59 Lévinas, *Autrement qu'être*, p. 129; ET: p. 102.
60 Ricoeur, *Soi-même comme un autre*, p. 390; ET: p. 338. Cf. Lévinas, *Autrement qu'être*, p. 142; ET: p. 112.
61 Ricoeur, *Soi-même comme un autre*, p. 390; ET: p. 338.
62 Lévinas, *Autrement qu'être*, p. 142; ET: p. 112.

63 Ricoeur, *Soi-même comme un autre*, p. 391; ET: p. 339.

64 Ricoeur, *Répondre d'autrui*, p. 38.

65 ibid.

66 ibid., p. 35; cf. Lévinas, *Autrement qu'être*, p. 183 et seq.; ET: p. 144 et seq.

67 Ricoeur, *Soi-même comme un autre*, p. 392; ET: p. 340.

68 ibid., p. 389; ET: p. 337.

69 Lévinas, *Totalité et Infini*, p. 34; ET: p. 34.

70 ibid., p. 107; ET: p. 134.

71 ibid., p. 229; ET: p. 251.

72 Lévinas, *Autrement qu'être*, p. 69; ET: p. 54.

Domenico Jervolino

Gadamer and Ricoeur on the hermeneutics of praxis

The following remarks deal with the relation between interpretation and praxis or, more specifically, between the hermeneutics of praxis (in its different varieties) and Marxism, understood in a Gramscian fashion as a philosophy of praxis.

On the one hand, a number of theories inspired by or linked to hermeneutics have sprung up in contemporary philosophy, all of which center on the problem of action, as related to the essentially linguistic character of human experience and behavior. Put succinctly, they all focus on humans speaking and acting (and suffering) and seek a new, more productive and dynamic equilibrium between word and deed.

On the other hand, these theories, which come to conceive of themselves as practical philosophy or hermeneutics of praxis, do not actually succeed in intruding on the domain of that systematic body of thought on history and humanity that was once known and defined as the 'philosophy of praxis'. Thus, between contemporary hermeneutics and Marxism a peculiar relationship of proximity and distance is established, and that relationship itself requires interpretation. It is not only the name of Marx that is absent from, or seldom present in, the works of the fathers of contemporary hermeneutics, but also human labor itself, which is dealt with only marginally, and whose absence weighs even more heavily.

For our part, we share the evaluations of Marek J. Siemek, according to whom 'there is no doubt that in contemporary theory, i.e. in the thought of the second half of the present century, the phenomenon of hermeneutics, or hermeneutic philosophy, holds a prime position. The philosophers of 'sense' are today among those who bear the greatest responsibility for the deep transformations undergone by the form and structure of problematic philosophy over the last twelve years and more'. Siemek was writing in 1975:

> Any system of thought that wants to keep abreast of this process of transformation and intends to take part actively in it, cannot fail to consider hermeneutic philosophy a major participant in the debate. This is especially true of Marxism, which clearly has more shared interests with hermeneutics than with any other philosophy, and finds more possibilities for deep dialogue there than anywhere else.[1]

If we reflect on how much time has passed since these words were written, we have to conclude that the dialogue, which for the Polish philosopher required a 'many-sided meeting of minds', carried out in depth, has not taken place. Instead, one of the two possible interlocutors, Marxist philosophy, has been stricken by a rapid withering, or rather a defeat due to political oppression, of its liveliest formulations (we are thinking of the phenomenological or ontologico-phenomenological Marxism that seemed so promising in the central and eastern European countries in the 1960s, and still in the early 1970s; but has 'western' Marxism fared much better?). If Marxism seems to have vanished from the face of the earth, the other interlocutor, hermeneutics, has enjoyed considerable success, to the point of presenting itself as a sort of common tongue, a *koinè*, for European and North American thought. Perhaps, however, in these worldly triumphs (especially in the 'big time' of mass communications and cultural showbusiness) hermeneutics runs no little risk of losing its critical force, presenting itself in designedly 'weak' versions, not only on account of its declared abandonment of old-fashioned metaphysical research on basics, but also on account of a more or less resigned, more or less convinced reconciliation with the concealed metaphysics of present world reality (that technological era the Marxist interlocutor cannot fail to interpret as the era of capital triumphant). The very dialogue that to Siemek seemed an 'urgent task', however 'unfashionable' it may seem today, actually is the only route open.

In the present article I have chosen, as the main partners in this dialogue, Gadamer and Ricoeur, allowing forebears such as Heidegger and interlocutors such as Habermas to remain somewhat in the background, although their importance in the history of hermeneutics is, of course, beyond doubt.[2]

Theoria and praxis in Gadamer

With his 1960 opus magnum, *Wahrheit und Methode*, Hans-Georg Gadamer, more than any other thinker, placed the hermeneutic problem at the core of contemporary philosophy. In Habermas's memorable phrase, he 'urbanized the Heideggerian province'. Explicitly, and with the clarity that is a constant in his crystalline, masterly philosophical style, he dealt with the relationship between theory and practice.[3]

Gadamer strives to move beyond the opposition between the two terms as it exists in our consciousness as persons who live and operate in the age of science ('im Zeitalter der Wissenschaft'). This going beyond presumes a reappropriation of the authentic meaning of *theoria* and *praxis*, for which Gadamer goes back to their source in the language and civilization of ancient Greece. It is not mere chance that, even in his modern usage, he prefers the Greek terms that preserve the memory of their origins. What have we to do, then, with a return to the past which neglects the different context, consolidated and endurable, of the modern world with its sciences and technologies – where 'instrumental reason' reigns supreme along with the will to power that is closely linked to it?

In spite of the impassioned plea Gadamer makes to his contemporaries – 'Be Greek!' – he hardly seems to favor some sort of impossible flight into the bygone; rather, he urges a reappropriation of the roots of our present. A reappropriation that is possible thanks to the mediation offered by language, which is the finite, historical heir to the objective spirit and which conserves and quickens our bonds with tradition. In the spirit of language there lives again – if we may be allowed some verbal juggling – the language of the Hegelian Spirit, albeit free of its final apotheosis in the absolute of a definitive, omnipotent knowledge. For Gadamer, Hegel is the philosopher who brings to fullness the modern concept of subjectivity while, at the same time, proposing to reconcile the modern conception of reason with the one that has its roots in the thought of ancient Greece.

According to Greek philosophy, what is worthiest of being honored is the divine order of the cosmos, which human reason contemplates in the privileged moment of theoretical activity. *Theoria*, then, is not something that can be assembled as modern scientific theories are, but is rather a belonging to and an approaching of the rationality of being. In ancient times *theoria* meant a procession or delegation sent to the feast in honor of a god: 'To contemplate the epiphany of a god does not mean merely to consider a state of affairs in an aloof fashion, nor even to be an interested onlooker at a marvelous spectacle. This contemplation means participating authentically in what goes on, a true, genuine presence.'[4] Gadamer adds that the rationality of being, which is to say the great hypothesis of Greek philosophy, is not a distinctive feature of the self-awareness of the subject, but a determination of being – which is that *All* of which human reason must be thought a part. Hegel's accomplishment is to have taken this idea of rationality seriously and to have sought for a dialectical synthesis between it and Christian interiority: 'The grandiose result of his logic was to have acknowledged in logic a foundation capable of supporting and reuniting all that which is opposed to it. Whether Hegel calls it *nous* or God, this basis is in any case both the most complete exteriority and, as the mystical vortex into which the Christian plummets, the deepest interiority.'[5]

Although it is impossible simply to go back to the Greeks, the Greek *theorein* is introduced somewhat as an ideal corrective, a different possibility which, once it has been taken up in its historical dimension, prevents the subject from being turned into an absolute, with a pseudo-scientific, overweening knowledge of the world. Likewise, the appeal to Hegel does not imply a 'return' to Hegel in the sense of a retrieval of his system, but rather, we feel, a reappropriation of the spirit of dialectics beyond any possibility of a system. Of the rational visions our philosophical tradition is heir to, Gadamer says explicitly, at the conclusion of the cited essay, that we can adhere to none of them as a whole cloth but must pay heed to all. What does hold valid is the need for a unity of reason that continually forces us to conceptualize, preventing us from being shut up within the confines of a pseudo-scientific, positivistic type of philosophy, or yielding to the enticements of overly aesthetic conceptions of reality. The striving for conceptualization is enacted in what Hölderlin called, in a famous phrase, the 'dialogue which we are' – the one in which we are involved and which never ceases to involve us. This dialogue, in the spirit of Gadamerian hermeneutics, is the true locus of dialectics.

These, then, are the premises for Gadamer's 'praise of theory', which paradoxically becomes a 'praise of praxis',[6] as long as praxis is no longer the opposite of theory (as it is for modern scientific positivism) but rather the other side of that fundamental relationship with being, which, since it can be understood, is language. Language is the basic relation that unites us with binding ties not only to being itself but also to the other speaking and conversing beings that coexist and co-participate in this essential colloquy.

How, then, are we to understand 'praxis' in such a context? It is certainly not the applied science of the moderns, if only because the 'science' of the modern sciences, as we have just seen, is far from identifying itself with the theoretical attitude in its deepest acceptance. Again we must look back to our Greek roots. These, however, bring us to a still broader scenario – a vast articulation of human phenomena quite familiar to anthropologists and present from the most remote expressions of primitive mankind – from burial rites to work, from the birth of language to the administration of justice and the terrible phenomenon of war. Everything converges to show that humans are beings who go beyond the instinct of conservation. Human practice is not limited to adapting to the living conditions imposed by nature, as with certain animal species organized in social forms of life. Specifically human action is such precisely because it goes beyond mere survival needs. If the term praxis designates the behavior of a living being in a general sense,[7] genuinely human praxis is a behavior that conforms wittingly to the common goals desired by all, exceeding mere utility and involving a dimension the Greeks called *kalon*. The term does not refer simply to what is beautiful in the aesthetic sense but also to something that all humans, without exception as rational beings, would find desirable – where 'rational' means *logon echon*, equipped with reason and speech (*logos*), capable of the theoretical life (*bios theoretikos*), in the sense of *theoria* defined above.

From this standpoint, if praxis is not exclusive to human beings – since animals, too, have a certain modus vivendi of their own, a certain *praxis* and *bios* – human practice is human because, moving beyond the dimension of pure neutrality, it reaches the area of *theoria*, which is, in a certain sense, the loftiest form of practice.

Aristotle's distinction between theoretical, practical and 'poietic' disciplines must not be read in terms of opposition. Rather than an opposition between *theoria* and *praxis*, one would stress another opposition within the realm of action between the acting of *praxis* and the producing by *poesis*. It can be said that the three disciplinary levels correspond to three moments of realization of human rationality, which ascends to the summits of *theoria*, the speculative activity (in any case, a *praxis tis*, a kind of practice), but also requires the many kinds of knowledge that support productive activities (the arts, *technai*). Praxis (and the knowledge specific to it, viz. practical philosophy, which is both ethical and political) exerts a mediating and unifying function among the many branches of human activity proper to the rational, free man, who lives and partakes in a community of free, rational people (the *polis*).

Evidently, a yawning gap opens at this point between the sensitivity of modern people (Christian or post-Christian) and that of the ancient Greeks; the latter limited their ideal of human rationality to male, free Greeks, excluding outsiders ('barbarians'), women and slaves from the commonwealth of citizens. But this fact cannot be used against Gadamer who, in effect, is far from proposing any sort of revival of the Greek *polis*. His intent is simply to draw lessons from our past, while being fully aware of the historical distance between us and the Greeks. The task, then, is to understand how we can be served by a concept of *praxis* that we could not fail to extend to all human beings, to every citizen of man- and womankind. 'What is praxis? Praxis is to dwell and act in solidarity. Solidarity is hence the determining condition and basis of all social reason. There is a saying of Heraclitus, the "weeping" philosopher: "the *logos* is common to all, but men behave as if each had his own private reason. Must this continue?"'[8]

Posing this question, the master of Heidelberg shows he is far from basking in an attitude of tranquil optimism – being well aware of the obstacles and resistance to a human solidarity based on the acknowledgement of a common rationality. Hegel's saying, 'All that is rational is real, all that is real is rational', is to be understood not as a justification of our sloth, but as a pointer to a task. To interpret history in a Hegelian fashion as a history of freedom (in the Oriental world only one is free, in the Greek world few are free, in the Christian-Germanic world all are free) does not mean to overlook the obstacles to the recognition and, above all, realization of the principle of freedom; it only means that by now the principle that all men and women are free, having emerged historically, can never be rescinded or called into doubt and that it becomes the task of universal history to carry it out.[9]

> 'Praxis' means . . . that everyone belongs to society, the nation, and mankind in the whole and is responsible to them all. As citizen, or world citizen, not even a scientist enjoys any longer that proud autonomy that once made him a scientist; the sphere of praxis imposes upon him, like anyone else, to make choices and decisions without any guarantee as to the results of his action.[10] . . . The Greeks ended their letters with the formula *eu prattein*, which we might translate as 'be well.' Praxis is the way one *is*. However things go, whether well or ill, praxis indicates the fact that we are not the masters of our existential situation but depend on external circumstances: obstacles, disappointments or – as we hope – happy outcomes beyond our wildest dreams. Praxis, understood in these terms, is clearly much closer to the concrete position of mankind in the world, with its dimensions of temporality and finitude, of programming and expecting, of remembering and forgetting. In other words, we are dealing with a set of meanings that goes under the name of 'historicity' and in our century has become one of the main themes of philosophical inquiry.[11]

Praxis takes its bearings from practical knowledge, the Aristotelian virtue of *phronesis* (*prudentia* in Latin) which signifies a capacity for discernment in a concrete situation and determines a specific level of philosophical reflection – practical philosophy. This philosophy is, *par excellence*, an historical and finite knowledge without any a priori guarantees; but it is also the only form of knowledge that can come across as 'concrete logic'. Furthermore, 'practical philosophy' is philosophical hermeneutics: 'To understand, just as to act, is always a risk and does not allow the application of general rules for understanding statements or given texts. . . . Understanding is an adventure and, as such, contains risks.'[12] The relationship between hermeneutics and praxis is not confined to the moment of *applicatio*, nor does it challenge only the *subtilitas applicandi* that ancient hermeneutic theory required of the interpreter;[13] rather, it runs through the whole hermeneutic field.

Probably Gadamer's effort to re-propose the ethico-practical dimension of wisdom can be sufficiently appreciated only if it is seen against the background of the great tragedies of our century – a history of ruins and rubble with a part of its theoretical roots in the presumption to know and enthrall the world – in accord with the canons of scientific objectivism that have been modernized into a perilous ideology of social techniques and technologies (the Promethean paradigm of human self-production). Behind the irenical serenity of the wise Heidelberg humanist one finds, drawn as ever from our Hellenic ancestors, the tragic wisdom of one who has learned through suffering (*pathei mathos*)[14] and lived through the great tragedies of our century.[15]

Perhaps a suitable comparison can be made with another great humanist from the beginning of the modern era. Just as Gadamer stands as a presence, nourished with ancient wisdom, at the turning-point of this half millennium; so stood Erasmus of Rotterdam, with his irenical message and his faith in reason, ironically dissimulated under the form of a praise of folly in an era during which the mind of Europe was rent and torn. Let us listen once more to the voice of Gadamer the sage, the Erasmus of our times:

> It is clear that the modern state has little in common with the Greek *polis* and its forms of civil communion. Still, both rest on one immutable premise that I would call the assumption of solidarity. I mean an unstudied, spontaneous accord on the basis of which common decisions, valid for all, can be made on moral, social and political issues. For the Greeks this idea was self-evident and unquestionable, and was reflected even in language. In fact, life in Greek society revolved around the concept of 'friend' (*philos*). According to a still more ancient Pythagorean inheritance that permeates Greek thought, friends are those who share everything. . . . Not that anybody should yield to the romantic illusion that friendship and universal love were the effective cornerstones of the ancient *polis*

any more than of the modern technological state. It seems to me, however, that if one wants to come to grips with the vital problems of the modern world, the decisive assumptions are not at all different from those formulated by the ancient Greeks. In any case, the progress of science and its instrumental applications to society will never create a situation so original that one can do without 'friendship', i.e. a basic solidarity that permits people to live side by side with each other. It would be quite misleading to think that past ideological systems can be resuscitated *in toto*. The task is rather to use past lessons as a corrective, acknowledging at the same time that subjectivism and 'voluntarism' are modern blind alleys. These errors must not be attributed to human kind or to science but to the scientific superstition that has ultimately overwhelmed our society.[16]

To come back to our initial premiss – a productive encounter between the Marxian and Gramscian theory of practice and contemporary hermeneutics – the question must be raised, quite seriously, as to how much of 'scientific superstition' has penetrated even the ranks of the working class and its ideological patrimony (in the era of positivism and, more subtly, in the American 'neo-positivistic' era that Gramsci himself so lucidly defined and criticized), and whether a rereading of the most genuine meaning of praxis – such as that proposed by Gadamer – might not be precious in order to free the praxis that claims to transform the world from its Promethean features[17] in order to understand it as a project of liberation on the part of finite, historically situated subjects, bound together in a bond of *philia* (the prospective that André Tosel quite appropriately called a 'communism of finitude'[18]). 'Friends are those who have something in common', the Heidelberg master tells us, quoting from ancient Pythagorean wisdom that goes back to the most distant origins of the tradition of thought we call 'philosophy'. What does the idea of 'communism' become once it has been rethought in its pacific, non-violent essence of universal friendship – as compared with the conceptions, infected by scientific superstition, that have been at the bottom of most of the tragic experiences of our century, inspired by the paradigm of the 'self-production of man'?

Action as text in Ricoeur

If we pass from Gadamer to the other great contemporary hermeneutics scholar, Paul Ricoeur, we note a certain change in the air. The hermeneutic and linguistic turn finds Ricoeur already giving thought to a major, phenomenologically founded philosophy of the will. A pupil of Husserl and Marcel more than of Heidegger, he develops the hermeneutic project in an original fashion. He takes his position in the camp of methodic hermeneutics rather than in the opposing Gadamerian camp of 'truth' and 'method', and systematically seeks a dialogue and a mediation with human sciences. In Ricoeur's intention, the role of hermeneutics, the obligatory passage through the world of language and signs, is to free phenomenological reflexion from the idealistic temptations to which it is prone. Ricoeur polemicizes openly with the trend that treats language as if it were a universe closed in itself, forgetting that the meaning of language is the uttering of what is the other of self.

Furthermore, whereas Gadamer, as we have seen above, takes a position on the hither side of the modern opposition between theory and practice by seeking in and through language the Greek roots, still alive and usable, of philosophy, Ricoeur, while having never ceased to ponder the lessons of the ancient philosophers, would seem to have chosen a different strategy with respect to philosophical modernity. In Christian terms, his strategy could be described as taking up the cross of the contradictions of the present in hopes of being able to gather the rose of a future reconciliation. But such a reconciliation – and here emerges the emphasis on human finitude which the two masters of hermeneutics share – is not viable in the Hegelian form of a total knowledge, but rather as a unity among opposing tensions producing mediations that are always finite and 'imperfect'.

A distinctive feature of Ricoeur's hermeneutics is his attention to the 'conflictual' nature of human experience. The 'conflit des interprétations' gives the title to the first collection of his essays on hermeneutics, published in 1969. Furthermore, his hermeneutics is characterized by the search for mediations between different positions. Ricoeur never forgets that behind the texts and the works of literature there are human beings who act and suffer and that the texts themselves, as discourse, are actions. 'Du texte à l'action' is the hermeneutic arc according to Ricoeur (as is suggested, almost 20 years later, by the title of his second volume of essays on hermeneutics, published in 1986).[19]

We do not intend to yield to the temptation to set up a 'Greek' Gadamer against a 'Christian' Ricoeur. Ricoeur is no less aware of the lessons of classic philosophy than Gadamer, who, in his own fashion, is aware of the lessons of the Christian fathers. However, there is no doubt that a post-Reformation Christian sensitivity permeates all Ricoeur's works without compromising their philosophical validity. He is especially concerned with the theme of guilt – and, hence, human fallibility and frailty – in addition to connected themes such as responsible action, reconciliation and Grace.

To sum his hermeneutics up in a theological nutshell, we can say that, whereas Gadamer turns to ancient Greek philosophy for his key words, Ricoeur's philosophy could be seen in the light of a New Testament expression from St Paul, the 'veritatem facientes in charitate' (Ephesians. 4.15). Make truth, a truth to be made: this is Ricoeur's way of overcoming, or rather rejecting, the opposition between theory and practice.

On this question, let us take a look at a text of Ricoeur's that goes back to a phase of his work that was not explicitly hermeneutic, the 1955 preface to the first edition of *Histoire et vérité*:

> I believe in the efficacity of reflexion because I believe that man's greatness lies in the dialectic of work and the spoken word. Saying and doing, signifying and making are intermingled to such an extent that it is impossible to set up a lasting and deep opposition between 'theoria' and 'praxis.' The word is my kingdom and I am not ashamed of it. To be more precise, I am ashamed of it to the extent that my speaking shares in the guilt of an unjust society which exploits work. I am not ashamed of it primordially, that is with respect to its destination.[20]

In effect, the essay 'Travail et parole' in *Histoire et vérité*, alluded to in the passage quoted, stands as a happy exception to the scarce attention to the problems of human labor we have lamented in hermeneutic theories of action; it is unfortunate that the subject has not been further developed in Ricoeur's works. Still, the space dedicated to a given theme is not always directly proportional to its real importance among an author's deep motivations. We can say with some confidence that this essay lies close to the heart of the most genuine and profound reasons for Ricoeur's intellectual involvement. He has never cut away from the roots of his youthful socialism, which carried over into the *Esprit* movement. Furthermore, having been published for the first time in *Esprit* (January 1953), the essay reveals an early presence in Ricoeur – even before there was talk of hermeneutics – of the motif (clearly an anticipation of the hermeneutics to come) of a dialectical relationship between saying and doing. Doing is identified here with labor, human activity in general. We are nearer to the Marxian idea than to the more ancient concept of praxis. Work is here opposed universally to the 'parole', living language.

We can do no more here than touch briefly on the various passages within the dialectic of word versus deed – from the word as an imperative cry, a mere appendix to action, to the dubitative, optative, indicative, or poetic word. If the whole edifice of culture can be seen as one long itinerary starting from action and returning to action, then even the form of the word that is closest to the pragmatic dimension of action contains in itself *in nuce* a critique of labor; it suspends the mere question of survival and opens out on reflection and the discerning of oneself and one's neighbor (one's other) through signs. The dubitative word 'effects the decisive revolution within the order of signification: it introduces the dimension of the *possible*'.[21] Here, on this level, the world of dialogue is introduced into the world of work, penetrating it and going beyond it at the same time. This phenomenology of the word continues with the word of desire and of prayer, of self-consciousness and poetic meditation. In this connection we find mention of the same passage in Aeschylus's *Agamemnon* of which Gadamer was fond, containing a reference to '*pathei mathos*' – learning wisdom through the experience of pain: 'The imperative word by which I come to a decision, bringing judgement upon my affective confusion; the dubitative word by which I question myself and bring myself into question; the indicative word by which I consider, deem, and declare myself to be such; but also the lyrical word by which I chant the fundamental feelings of mankind and of solitude.'[22] Such are the manifold forms of the *puissance de la parole* – that word which is closely linked with the historically determined forms of labor, only to transcend them and, in some fashion, complete them in a project for mankind.

At this point Ricoeur distinguishes between the alienation of labor and its objectifying. The former is linked to the wage-earning condition typical of capitalism; the latter depends on the technological form of labor in the various forms of the industrial revolution which lives on into socialist society, where, however, it can better be dealt with. Alienation implies that the finitude of human action is closed in upon itself, with problems such as work's being limited to a single, apparently senseless task, with a consequent loss of overall perspective.

The struggle against alienation due to labor requires a *civilisation du travail*, which coincides, in Ricoeur's description, with a markedly democratic socialism in which the centralized planning of the economy is accompanied by multiple forms of control and participation from below – with room for a division and broad sharing of power and a new culture built on labor, untrammeled by ideological or bureaucratic management. Ricoeur states explicitly that such a civilization of labor does not yet exist anywhere on earth; there exist only certain economies of labor 'in a part of the world' (in the countries that we today would call 'state socialist'). And he adds, such economies are 'even present in some degree everywhere in the world', given that during the early 1950s he correctly saw some elements of 'labor economy' even in certain capitalistic countries (in a phase in which Keynes and the social or welfare state had not yet been challenged).[23]

On the other hand, the matter of the objectifying of work is a still more complicated problem, the solution of which requires a deeper, more radical cultural transformation. Here, more than ever, the labor question involves the question of the word. Ricoeur concludes with remarks on the service that the word can offer to labor – as a corrective to the division of labor, as a compensatory factor thanks to leisure time, as a foundation for theory, and finally as poetry.

We have chosen deliberately, one might say provocatively (in a positive sense of the term), to pay some attention to this early, explicitly 'socialist' text of Ricoeur's, which today runs the risk of being forgotten. At the same time, it is incumbent upon us to point out those places in his main works that contain many useful teachings relative to our premiss that the theme of action needs to be taken up again in view of a productive dialogue with Marxism.

In the mature phase of Ricoeur's hermeneutics, the terms '*discours*' and '*texte*' are preferred to '*parole*'. Whereas a hermeneutics like Gadamer's has its paradigmatic moment in dialogue (the dialogue that we are), in Ricoeur it is the text, understood as objectified discourse fixed in writing, that has that role.

The relationship between text and action is absolutely central; the text, as discourse, presumes action (utterance itself is a form of action), and action, polymorphous and multiple like human speech, can be treated as a text. What follows from this is that the methodology of the human sciences having meaningful action as their object can garner precious teachings from a textual hermeneutics that does not oppose but tends to integrate explication and comprehension. *Expliquer* presumes the consideration of the text (and, by analogy, of any social phenomenon) as a closed system, an analogue of the *langue*, understood as a system of signs. This is the logic behind the structuralist explanation, which has value but is limited as well. According to Ricoeur the structuralist explanation needs to be dialecticized by incorporating the moment of *comprendre*, which presumes a 'semantic' consideration of the text (and hence of action). The text says something about the world; it is a world project. The meaning of the text (in its fullness as sense plus reference) is not something lying behind it (a hidden intention) but something situated before it that interrogates or engages us. This holds as well for meaningful action and social phenomena in general.

De la même manière que les jeux de langage sont des formes de vie, selon l'aphorisme fameux de Wittgenstein, les structures sociale son également des tentatives pour se mesurer avec les perplexités de l'existence et les conflits profondément enfouis dans la vie humaine. En ce sens, ces structures elles aussi ont une dimension référentielle. . . . La référence du texte, à savoir son pouvoir de déployer un monde.[24]

We cannot help being involved with this 'world of the text', but this takes place at the end of a cognitive process requiring an ascetic submission to the rigors of explicative discipline. Ricoeur does not oppose the stereotype of a neutral social science with the opposite stereotype of partisan science, but rather with an original hermeneutic theory of personal engagement; for this is what any genuine knowledge, as well as any reading of a text, implies. Such is the hermeneutic, practical appropriation of meaning; it is the transforming, refiguring effect that texts (hence, also the text of social action, the text of the history in which we are immersed) have on our practice. In other words, an answer to the question of the 'meaning of history' – no longer framable in terms of Hegel's absolute knowledge – can be found in the force of the present, that moment of intersection between memory and expectation, between *l'espace d'expérience* and *horizon d'attente*. This is to say, it can be found in the historically situated and ethically responsible initiative of subjects, finite and plural, through mediations that are themselves historical, finite and imperfect. Here we note the convergence with Gadamer, to be found also in the importance assigned to 'practical reason' and the assertion that the goal is not an unattainable science of praxis[25] but a practical knowledge, one that cannot be spliced on to the reductive concepts of modern science.

The dialectical relations between text and action are developed more broadly in Ricoeur's grand trilogy, *Temps et récit*. Narration, *mimesis praxeos* or the creative imitation of action, has the power to prefigure, configure and refigure praxis. In this threefold dialectic it responds poetically to the aporias of the intimate awareness of time, experiencing and preserving a human sense of temporality and history. The identity of historical subjects (acting, suffering human beings), won in the course of a reflexive journey through the whole field of human action, taken as an analogical unity of plural, polysemic forms – this is the theme of Ricoeur's recent major work, *Soi-même comme un autre*.[26]

Throughout these studies, deserving fuller discussion than the present context permits, a concept of action emerges that is subtly and dialectically entwined with human utterance, whence it draws force and vigor. At the same time, action partakes, together with utterance, in the finite, fallible condition of mankind. Thus one of the possible conclusions of a hermeneutic reappropriation of praxis may be a reflection on the fragility of language and ethico-political action. We mean the fragility of a subject who has no absolute yardstick for what is good and just but must strive mightily to win meaningfulness for his or her utterance and action. Yet just this fragility calls up an unavoidable 'element of responsibility that quickens and bolsters our perseverance in action, in search of meaning, in the face of the dramas and conflicts of history.[27]

We leave it to the reader's intelligence to grasp what a similar view of action, and of the suffering that always comes with it, implies for a praxis that takes on the immense challenge of transforming the world and freeing humanity.

Rome, Italy
[Translated by Gordon Poole]

Notes

1 M. J. Siemek, 'Marxismus und hermeneutische Tradition', in B. Waldenfels, J. M. Broekman and A. Pazanin (eds) *Phänomenologie und Marxismus*, Vol. I (Frankfurt am Main: Suhrkamp, 1977), p. 45 (the text was written in 1975).

2 On Habermas's hermeneutics as an example of 'hermeneutics without an ontological foundation' see B. Ineichen, *Philosophische Hermeneutik* (Munich: Alber, 1991), pp. 211–20. The main texts of the famous debate between Gadamer and Habermas, which we will only touch upon here, are contained in the collective volume by K. O. Apel et al., *Hermeneutik und Ideologiekritik* (Frankfurt am Main: Suhrkamp, 1971). The debate, in which numerous scholars have taken part, deals with the relationship between tradition and rationality, authority and prejudice, language and being. Habermas practices a 'hermeneutics of suspicion' with regard to Gadamer's rehabilitation of tradition, authority and prejudice. On the other hand, Gadamer accuses the social therapy developed by the critique of ideology, along the lines of the psychoanalytical model, of re-proposing a sort of Hegelian 'absolute knowledge'. Instead he privileges a form of practical knowledge patterned on ancient rhetoric. The reciprocal acknowledgement of opposed reasons and the overcoming of the alternative between hermeneutic awareness and

critical awareness are proposed by Ricoeur in a 1973 essay, 'Herméneutique et critique des idéologies', now in *Du texte à l'action* (Paris: Editions du Seuil, 1986), pp. 333–7, in which he favors a 'critical hermeneutics'. At the conclusion of a recent re-examination of this debate, twenty years later, Graeme Nicholson stresses that Gadamer's last word in the debate is found in the postface to the third edition (1972) of *Wahrheit und Methode*. The German philosopher reasserts the value of practical rationality (*phronesis*) and the exemplary character of rhetoric as a form of knowledge that does not pretend to an absolute determination of good; at the same time, he expresses his agreement with Habermas on the importance of the emancipatory project and 'seeks to make it clear to his readers that he too shares the hope that hermeneutics will prove to be an emancipatory discipline' (G. Nicholson, 'Answers to Critical Theory', in H. J. Silverman (ed.) *Gadamer and Hermeneutics* [New York and London: Routledge, 1991], p. 161).

3 J. Habermas, 'Urbanisierung der Heideggerschen Provinz. Laudatio auf Hans-Georg Gadamer', in H. G. Gadamer and J. Habermas, *Das Erbe Hegels. Zwei Reden aus Anlass des Hegels-Preises* (Frankfurt am Main: Suhrkamp, 1979), pp. 11–31.
4 H. G. Gadamer, *Vernunft im Zeitalter der Wissenschaft* (Frankfurt am Main: Suhrkamp, 1976), p. 28
5 ibid., p. 34.
6 H. G. Gadamer, *Lob der Theorie. Reden und Aufsätze* (Frankfurt am Main: Suhrkamp, 1983), p. 49: 'Is theory, when you come right down to it, a praxis, as Aristotle insisted, or is praxis, if it is truly human praxis, theory as well? Is it not, if it is human praxis, a looking away from oneself, turning one's gaze on others, standing aside from oneself and listening to others? Thus life is that unity of theory and practice that is everybody's opportunity and duty.'
7 Gadamer, *Vernunft*, p. 81. Where pertinent studies by Ritter are cited.
8 ibid., p. 77.
9 ibid., pp. 24–5.
10 H. G. Gadamer, *Das Erbe Europas* (Frankfurt am Main: Suhrkamp, 1989), p. 26.
11 ibid., pp. 24–5.
12 Gadamer, *Vernunft*, p. 106.
13 H. G. Gadamer, *Wahrheit und Methode* (Tübingen: J. C. B. Mohr, 6th edn, 1990 [1960]), pp. 358 et seq.
14 ibid., p. 362.
15 Especially enlightening, in this connection, is Gadamer's fascinating intellectual autobiography, *Philosophische Lehrjahre. Eine Rückschau* (Frankfurt am Main: V. Klostermann, 1977).

16 Gadamer, *Das Erbe Europas*, pp. 123–4.

17 Worth coming to grips with is Rüdiger Bubner's critique of the Marxian concept of praxis from the viewpoint of a neo-Aristotelian 'philosophy of praxis', where he also takes analytical philosophy and sociological theories of action into account: R. Bubner, *Handlung, Sprache und Vernunft. Grundbegriffe praktischer Philosophie* (Frankfurt am Main: Suhrkamp, 1976).

18 A. Tosel, 'Autoproduction de l'homme ou communisme de la finitude?', *M* (juin–juillet 1990): 14–20. The Italian translation by M. N. Pierini in *A sinistra* 1 (1991): 47–58, is followed by an article by G. Prestipino, 'Comunismo della finitudine e comunità etico-politica', ibid.: 59–63.

19 Paul Ricoeur, *Le conflit des interprétations. Essais d'herméneutique* (Paris: Editions du Seuil, 1969) and *Du texte à l'action. Essais d'herméneutique II* (Paris: Editions du Seuil, 1986).

20 Paul Ricoeur, *Histoire et vérité* (Paris: Editions du Seuil, 3rd edn, 1967 [1955]), p. 9; English translation published as *History and Truth*, trans. Charles A. Kelbley (Evanston, IL: Northwestern University Press, 1965), p. 5.

21 ibid., p. 220; Eng. trans., p. 207.

22 ibid., p. 223; Eng. trans., p. 209.

23 ibid., p. 228; Eng. trans., p. 215. Nowadays most scholars would probably be less sanguine about 'labor economy', both in the East and in the West. Ricoeur's essay, expressing the hopes of so many socialist-leaning or 'personalist' intellectuals after the Second World War, to some might seem rather out-of-step when read today. But just for this reason, because it is against the mainstream, it seems to me to be extraordinarily up-to-date.

24 Ricoeur, *Du texte à l'action*, pp. 210–11.

25 ibid., p. 250. On the general question see Ricoeur's essays 'La raison pratique', ibid., pp. 237–59 and 'L'initiative', ibid., pp. 261–77. In his treatment of the theme of 'practical philosophy', one characteristic element is the attention he gives to a 'theory of action' drawn from analytical philosophy and applied in hermeneutics. Another is his search for a mediation between the Aristotelian principle of a teleological conception of ethical life and the Kantian moral imperative. On this, see the 'petite éthique', as developed in *Soi-même comme un autre* (Paris: Editions du Seuil, 1990), pp. 199–344.

26 Paul Ricoeur, *Temps et récit*, 3 vols (Paris: Editions du Seuil, 1983–5) and Ricoeur, *Soi-même comme un autre*. As I have scarcely dwelt on these two Ricoeurian masterpieces in the present essay, the reader may wish to see my other works on Ricoeur: *Il cogito e l'ermeneutica. La questione del soggetto in Ricoeur* (Naples: Procaccini, 1984); see also

the postface to the second Italian edition (Genova: Marietti, 1993); English translation published as *The Cogito and Hermeneutics. The Question of the Subject in Ricoeur*, trans. Gordon Poole (Dordrecht/ Boston, MA/London: Kluwer, 1990); 'Herméneutique de la praxis et éthique de la libération', in J. Greisch and R. Kearny (eds) *Paul Ricoeur. Le métamorphose de la raison herméneutique* (Paris: Cerf, 1991), pp. 223–30; 'Du bon usage de la pensée de Ricoeur', in *Agone*, 2–3 (Marseilles, 1991): 81–91.

27 'Fragilité et responsabilité' is the title of a lecture given by Ricoeur at the Department of Philosophy of the University of Naples, 26 May 1992, published in Italian in *Il Tetto* 171 (Naples, 1992): 325–36; published in English in this volume, pp. 15–21. On the fragility of political language, see 'Langage politique et rhétorique', in P. Ricoeur, *Lectures I: Autour du politique* (Paris: Editions du Seuil, 1990), pp. 161–75.

Jean Greisch

Testimony and attestation

No one testifies for the witness. (Paul Celan, *Atemwende*)

The title of this discussion suggests that two close yet distinct notions, which define a twofold source of reflection in Paul Ricoeur's hermeneutical philosophy, can be reconciled. They are on the one hand the *hermeneutics of testimony*, and on the other the *hermeneutics of the self*, whose hidden core is, in my opinion, attestation. It is important not to confuse the notions of testimony and attestation, even if the one invokes the other. Their closeness and their difference outline a sort of ellipse with two foci. I will examine in turn each focus of this ellipse by asking in what sense these two notions arise out of a common hermeneutical problematic.

I The hermeneutics of testimony

1

Testimony has been an important theme in Paul Ricoeur's hermeneutical thought since at least 1972. It was Enrico Castelli, the tireless *spiritus rector* of the hermeneutical scene at that time, who drew him into this area. Ricoeur presented his first contribution on this theme[1] as part of the Castelli symposium on testimony which took place between 5 and 11 January 1972 at Rome and several aspects of this contribution have been taken up in his later works, up to recent times. In fact, the 1972 work determines in an almost authoritative fashion the philosophical problematic of testimony that hermeneutics is supposed to resolve. It opens up the following threefold thesis: testimony only becomes a problem for a philosophy in which the *question of the absolute* is a *sensible question*; for a philosophy that requires an *experience of the absolute to be combined with the idea* of the absolute; and for a philosophy that does not find the depth of this experience in either the example or the symbol (*HT*: 119/35). The study concludes with an equally important declaration: 'We must choose between the philosophy of absolute knowledge and the hermeneutics of testimony' (*HT*: 153/61; translation slightly altered). The formulation of these three preliminary theses involves the admission of a very clear debt – which will never be subsequently repudiated – to Jean Nabert, in particular to his posthumous work *Le désir de Dieu*, which taught Ricoeur to link together originary affirmation and hermeneutical testimonies of the absolute. His own hermeneutics of testimony seeks to resolve the paradox that a reader of *Le désir de Dieu* cannot fail to come up against: 'how . . . are we to understand the interiority of the originary affirmation and the exteriority of actions and beings that are supposed to testify to the absolute?' (*HT*: 122/37; translation altered).

Despite the considerable debt to Jean Nabert, the elaboration of the problem of testimony follows a double detour that traditional reflexive philosophy would no doubt have great difficulty approving. Before there can be any question of establishing that a philosophy can only be a hermeneutics, that is to say a philosophy of *interpretation*, (*HT*: 143/59), we have to master not only the prophetic and kerygmatic dimension of testimony revealed by biblical exegesis (*HT*: 130–42/38–49), but also the *semantic* one, by submitting the ordinary notion of testimony to a semantic analysis (*HT*: 123–30/44–53). The philosophy of interpretation which takes care of this double dimension itself exhibits the behavior of an 'ellipse with two foci' (*HT*: 143/53) for the interpretation of testimony is a twofold act: 'an act of consciousness of itself and an act of historical understanding based on the signs that the absolute gives of itself' (*HT*: 143/53). The hermeneutics of testimony is located at the very junction of these two operations. It must spend its time reducing the distance between the two foci of the ellipse – without ever being able to completely neutralize it, which would risk pushing the hermeneutics of testimony (or rather testimonies) over into absolute knowledge.

So the hermeneutical possibility of a philosophy of testimony is tied to two conditions. First, the exegesis of historical testimonies must be able to approach self-exegesis, which can take place only if the testimony *gives* something to be interpreted, namely the immediacy of the absolute which challenges us – and if at the same time the testimony itself becomes the *object* of interpretation, by virtue of the threefold dialectic which inhabits it (meaning and event, testimony and prosecution, witness and testimony). Second, the originary affirmation and the criteriology of the divine, which convey the most detailed analysis that a human consciousness is capable of, must 'make a detour through an interpretation of the contingent signs that the absolute gives of itself in history' (*HT*: 149/57).

2

That is, in a nutshell, the initial determination which allowed Paul Ricoeur to lay out the program of a hermeneutics of testimony. In a number of later works he takes up the active elements of this problematic, in particular in the study devoted to the hermeneutics of the idea of revelation.[2] An even more recent study devoted to 'Emmanuel Lévinas, thinker of testimony'[3] suggests that the initial program is still valid, even if the author introduces a new working hypothesis: the characteristic of a philosophy of testimony is the simultaneous conjunction of the dimension of Height and Exteriority (*EL*: 17). Ricoeur examines the soundness of this link through a 'biased' reading of three philosophers who in his opinion truly deserve the title of 'thinkers of testimony': Martin Heidegger, Jean Nabert and Emmanuel Lévinas. The arrangement of the reading of these three names is intended to show the growing emergence of the two themes in question. Along the axis of Height, Ricoeur tries to compare the Heideggerian theme of *Gewissen*, the originary affirmation of Jean Nabert, and the 'glory of the infinite' in Lévinas. Similarly, along the axis of Exteriority, we can begin a dialogue between Heideggerian strangeness (*Unheimlichkeit*), the mediation of other consciences which testify completely to the absolute in Nabert, and the 'state of being hostage' in Lévinas.

The course he follows consists of simultaneously increasing the gradient of Height and Exteriority. Of the three thinkers of testimony, Ricoeur distances himself most from Heidegger, because he is the one who grants the least to Height and Exteriority, even if these two dimensions are present in the framework of his existential analytics. Since in Heidegger 'an exteriority without alterity corresponds to a height without transcendence' (*EL*: 19), it is necessary to let oneself be guided by 'the ethical cut' in Nabert, which allows us to strongly articulate the criteriology of the divine and the hermeneutics of absolute testimonies before turning to Lévinas, in whom Height and Exteriority receive their most extreme expression, an excess in accord with the very exaggeration of ethical responsibility. One could then think that upon the completion of his course of reading, Ricoeur would have lined up completely with Lévinas's position, which is as far removed from the horizon of ontology as it is from the philosophy of consciousness. However, Ricoeur shows that the Lévinasian pathos of 'denial', if it turns its back completely on identity-*sameness*, will only paradoxically bring to light the identity-*ipseity* of the self in its state of being hostage. 'Here I stand, in the name of God', says the prophet-witness. This paradoxical affirmation of an ipseity at the heart of passivity, which is more passive than any other passive thing, 'marks the site of a path which would go from Lévinas to Nabert and from Nabert to Lévinas' (*EL*: 38). The hermeneutics of testimony, for which Ricoeur could be considered the spokesperson, consists of nothing less than this very path. The way in which Ricoeur himself carries out this journey tempts us to apply to him the title of his own study on Lévinas: 'Paul Ricoeur, philosopher of testimony!' His own thinking about testimony – his hermeneutics of testimony – seeks to 'uncover the traces of a philosophy where the attestation of the self and the glory of the absolute would be co-originary' (*EL*: 39). And it is precisely in this continuous coming and going between Nabert and Lévinas that this hermeneutics of testimony (which appears to fulfill at least in part the project of a 'poetics of will') opens on to the problematics of attestation that is found at the heart of the hermeneutics of self.

II Attestation at the heart of the hermeneutics of self

Let us now move on to an examination of the second focus of our ellipse: the essential role that attestation plays in the formulation of a hermeneutics of the self, a program that Ricoeur defines in *Oneself as Another* at the same time that he puts it to work in a rudimentary form in the ten studies that make up this work.[4] A note, relating to the semantic proximity of the German terms *Überzeugung* (conviction) and *Bezeugung* (attestation), underlines the fundamental role of this notion of 'attestation', 'the password for this entire book' (*OA*: 289/335). Indeed, the author defines the role he intends to create for this notion in the preface; however, it is only really thematized in the tenth study. This role is directly linked to the position that the hermeneutics of the self assumes in the face of the philosophies of the subject: aware of the strange oscillations that these philosophies offer, torn between the Cartesian cogito with its foundational claim ('the exalted subject') and the Nietzschean anti-cogito (the humiliated subject), it 'is placed at an equal distance from the apology of the cogito and from its overthrow' (*OA*: 4/15). But this 'equal distance' is not an exact midpoint between two extremes. The hermeneutics of the self is found to be 'at an equal distance' because it has left behind these two antagonistic positions and occupies an *epistemic* and *ontological* place 'situated beyond this alternative' (*OA*: 16/27; translation altered).

So attestation plays a decisive role both in the epistemic desig-nation and in the ontological characterization of this site. With regard to the epistemic aspect, it is useful to underline two remarks relating to the style and the method adopted. The fundamental stylistic character-istic of the work is a rather special 'rivalry' between analytical philosophy and hermeneutics which exhibits a different face in each of the ten studies. What seems at the beginning to be rivalry is progressively transformed into complementarity. In this transform-ation, the borrowings from phenomenology play a special role, which is rather difficult to analyze. While the encounter between hermeneu-tics and analytical philosophy clearly occupies the foreground of the scene, the reader slowly discovers that a certain phenomenology, which has been working behind the author from the start, eventually erupts – sometimes in a rather untimely and surprising way. This aspect is by no means irrelevant to our concerns. Indeed, we should ask ourselves what in the notion of attestation is derived from a phenom-enological description, and what on the other hand is in the region of conceptual analysis, namely the semantic field of acting.

The second aspect of the analysis is presented as a *fragmentary* series of studies, each having its own autonomy and the ensemble constituting the open examination of the *purely analogical* unity of the field of human acting (*OA*: 20/32). Such diversity can only thwart the aspiration of an ultimate foundation which characterizes the philo-sophies of the cogito, even if this aspiration does not find its expression in the production of a system of knowledge conceived in the manner of speculative idealism. Now it is precisely the total renunciation of the claim to foundation and of the type of certitude which characterizes it, which defines the epistemic originality of the hermeneutics of the self. It is a matter of defining a new type of *certitude*. It is at this point that the notion of attestation comes in and, before even becoming a theme of special investigation, defines in Ricoeur's eyes the *alethic* (or veritative) mode which characterizes his entire investigation. From this point of view, attestation represents precisely the 'sort of certainty that hermeneutics claims' between (or rather *beyond*) the epistemic exal-tation of the cogito beginning with Descartes and its humiliation beginning with Nietzsche.

In the first, or phenomenological, aspect of the analysis, attestation implies a moment of *belief* which 'is less demanding than the certainty belonging to the ultimate foundation' (*OA*: 21/33). But the type of belief it implies avoids the classical opposition of *doxa/episteme*. 'Belief' here means credence rather than opinion. We can then understand the relationship that exists between attestation and testimony (*Bezeugung* and *Zeugnis*), *even* if they are not identical (*OA*: 22/34). Weakness in regard to the claim to the final foundation, fragmentation and historical contingency of questioning, 'vulnerability of a discourse aware of its own lack of foundation' (*OA*: 22/34) – these are so many aspects which suggest that attestation could well be a description of the 'wounded cogito' on the level of a hermeneutics of the self. But this wounded cogito is not a cogito *crushed* by the weight of a relentless suspicion. For the credence which characterizes attestation is also the 'trust' which copes with suspicion, thus making an 'attestation of the self' out of attestation.

'As credence without any guarantee, but also as trust greater than any suspicion, the hermeneutics of the self can claim to hold itself at an equal distance from the cogito exalted by Descartes and from the cogito that Nietzsche proclaimed forfeit' (*OA*: 23/35). Ricoeur's reader can confirm the assurance, the confidence of the author which is expressed in his lines and which incites the reader to trust him, while adding that if this happens it is due to attestation!

We can then try to test this presence of attestation on each of the four levels where the analysis takes place: (1) the power of speaking; (2) the power of doing; (3) the power to recognize oneself as a character in a narrative; and (4) the power to assume ethical responsibility. First we must add a final remark: at the end of the preface, the author points out that he has excluded from his inquiry the part of the Gifford Lectures concerning the religious status of the self. The additional question that can be raised in connection with our problematic would be this: does not the relationship already pointed out between attestation and testimony become strongest at the level of a hermeneutics of the religious self?

1 The power to speak and the aporias of ascription

Let us then try to confirm, at each stage of the inquiry, the presence of the phenomenon of attestation which is very discreet at the beginning of *Oneself as Another* but becomes more explicit as the analysis develops. We must begin with an admission: at first sight, the first two studies, whose stated aim is to establish an 'integrated theory of the self (at least on the linguistic level)' (*OA*: 40/55) using the united resources of semantics and pragmatics, do not refer to attestation at all. This is easily understood. For we are here at the lowest level of identification, in the double disguise of the identifying reference of the 'basic characteristic' (in Peter Strawson's terminology) that forms the person or of the self-description of the speaker in the act of utterance. It is above all the problems of location, identification and reidentification which occupy the foreground of the scene; while the question of the self, and therefore the phenomenon of attestation as well, remains hidden.

However, from the first study, as a note points out (the first of several notes in the work which draw our attention to the 'broader problematics of attestation' [OA: 45/60]), the place of the phenomenon of attestation is etched in. Without being named, the problem of attestation 'emerges for the first time on the occasion of the relation of ascription of psychic predicates to a personal entity' (OA: 45/60). One could say it is hidden in what the author calls in his first study 'the strange structure of mental events' (OA: 35/48; translation altered), which, a little further on, overlaps that of the body proper; which compels us to wonder if the mineness of the body proper is really of the same nature as the possession of a predicate by a logical subject (OA: 37/51). Here we can glimpse for the first time the distance *between* ascription and (logical) attribution, a distance which reveals all its importance only in a later stage of the analysis. But from the first study onwards ascription definitely seems to be the phenomenon which a more explicit theory of attestation would come to be grafted on.

Would the 'reflexivity' characteristic of the phenomenon of the utterance provide better possibilities for this apprehension? First, let us dispel a terminological misunderstanding. Far from supporting the notion of the subject presupposed in the philosophies of reflection, 'the reflection of the act of utterance in the sense of the statement' (OA: 42/57) brings in an additional element of opacity: the subject (the speaker) presupposed in the act of utterance, far from being presented as transparent to itself, is a subject basically more questionable than that which makes the object of an identifying reference. Without doubt, the illocutionary or perlocutionary force of any discursive act whatever can be explained by a prefix which 'attests' the presence of the speaker in the heart of the act. So instead of saying 'Open the window' I can say 'I *order* you to open the window', etc.; but we must be careful not to confuse this type of reflexivity with a self-awareness (OA: 47/63). We are dealing with a 'reflexivity without ipseity', with 'a "self" without "oneself"' (OA: 47/64; translation altered). This is why pragmatics, in its analysis of the concept of *self*-reference, puts the main stress on the *factualness* of the utterance, which in its turn creates new aporias that Ricoeur analyzes at length; in particular, the aporia of anchoring which represents 'the ultimate aporia of the speaking subject' (OA: 51/68), the equivalent of the aporia of ascription on the pragmatic level. Ludwig Wittgenstein has given this its authoritative formulation: how are we to bring together the *I* as limit of the factual world and the *proper name* which indicates a real person recorded in the register of the civil state? This inscription itself presupposes a special act of utterance, *appellation*, which brings about the connection between the two. As a hypothesis, I propose to say that this new phenomenon, appellation, also contains the place of attestation engraved within itself. This forces us to question ourselves about its possible link with the 'strange status of one's own body' (*OA*: 55/72), which Ricoeur himself, in the conclusion of the second study, links to the phenomenon of anchorage.

2 Attestation and the ability to do

When we approach the analysis of the ability to do, we find ourselves faced with another enigma, that 'of the relation between the action and its agent' (*OA*: 56/73). Here, the indications of a problematic of attestation become more perceptible. To understand the extent and the limits of this analysis, which takes up the third and fourth studies, we should keep in mind that it 'is confined in principle to describing and analyzing utterances in which individuals state their actions' (*OA*: 57/74), and that it therefore wants to be a simple analysis of the conceptual network of action. So 'action' is still not synonymous with 'practice', far from it! On the other hand, it is important to recognize that the analytic theory of action represents a short cut in relation to the Heideggerian hermeneutics of the self, precipitating directly towards the exploration of the ontological status of the self by immediately bringing about the link with attestation. What characterizes the Heideggerian hermeneutics of the self is that it is totally driven by the question *who?* Now the theory of action puts the stress on the *what?* and the *why?* of action. Ricoeur's bold wager here is that this detour can be turned to advantage against Heidegger's undue haste (*OA*: 59–60/76–7). One could fear that the phenomenon of attestation is simply lost from view for the benefit of other objectives, for example, the struggle against an ontology of the impersonal event.

Now this is not the case. For it is precisely as a result of the debate on the nature of intentional action carried on with and against G. E. M. Anscombe that we again meet the problem of attestation, in a passage where for the first time we see attestation go from laconic notes at the bottom of the page into the body of the text itself (*OA*: 72–3/91–3). After having shown that Anscombe destroys the question of the transfer of an (intentional) action to its agent in favor of the mutual implication of the questions *what? why?*, Ricoeur stresses that this transfer raises a problem of truthfulness, and no longer just of the simple truth. Now this problem of truthfulness is derived from a broader problematic of attestation, which analytic philosophy, borne exclusively by the concern for accuracy and objectivity of description, risks at least partially hiding. In order to remove this handicap we require nothing less than a change of philosophical method: 'the problem posed belongs to a phenomenology of attestation, which cannot be reduced to a criteriology suited to description' (OA: 72/91). This all takes place as if we must call phenomenology to the rescue in order to resolve this problem. Ricoeur is well aware that he is reading the work of Anscombe with the clearer eyes of another tradition. 'What Anscombe calls knowledge without observation belongs, it seems to me – and this in opposition to the author's will – to this order of attestation' (OA: 72/92). Moreover, the phenomenological inadequacy of the Anscombian analysis of intentional action is shown in the fact that it eliminates 'the one who, in intending, places this intention on the path of promising' (OA: 73/92). It is this forward-looking impulse, which has been left in the background by a conceptual analysis in the service of a semantics of action, that phenomenological analysis must put in the foreground.

Much more of this path has to be explored before the attestation of intention can be transformed into 'attestation *of* self'. The future-oriented promise forces us right away to incorporate the temporal parameter, which will play a decisive role in the definition of narrative identity, into the analysis of intention. But before we get there, we must take note that the phenomenology of intention which was just touched on, already calls for a change in the ontological course. Against the ontology of the impersonal event in Donald Davidson, which does not go outside the framework of sameness, Ricoeur proclaims the necessity of a 'different ontology', in harmony with the phenomenology of intention and with teleological causality (OA: 86/107). It is only on the grounds of this *different ontology* that the ontological function of attestation will be able to be analyzed.

First of all, the aporias of ascription, which are considered from the first study onwards, have to be reincorporated into the framework of the theory of action, which corresponds to the old and new problem (OA: 89/110) of an agent: a principle of action which is a self, and a self which is a principle (OA: 91/113). The enigmatic character of this relationship between the action and the agent goes back to a simple fact: the 'power to act' (OA: 101/124) for which the specific expression in the practical domain is *initiative*[5] (OA: 109/133). But this simple fact is simple only insofar as it is rooted in a phenomenology of 'I can', which itself goes back ultimately to an ontology of one's own body (OA: 111/135). The confidence which characterizes the initiatives of the agents belong therefore to the region of attestation. The type of certainty which goes along with the ability-to-do shows to an equal extent an ontological aspect which it is the aim of the tenth study to clarify.

3 Narrative attestation

By coining the expression 'narrative attestation', which is not to be found in Ricoeur, I would like to stress the exceptionally strong bond between the concept of narrative identity and the phenomenon of attestation. If it is true that 'action is that aspect of human doing that calls for narration' (*OA*: 58/76), it is equally true that the action recounted shows a face different from the one expressed by the simple semantics of action. Up to this point we have had to deal only with isolated actions; now we have to deal with 'practices' ranging from the most elementary to the most elaborate. Again, we must begin with a negative fact: in the two studies devoted to the concept of narrative identity, the *expression* attestation is not mentioned. However, this is not to say that the *phenomenon* itself is out of sight, or that it does not affect the concept of narrative identity with which we advance in the formulation of a hermeneutics of the self. Henceforth, we are dealing with two contrasting models of personal identity through time: the perseverance of character under the sign of identity-*sameness* and the perseverance of faithfulness to the word under the sign of identity-*ipseity* (*OA*: 123/148). The task of narrative identity is to fill the gap in meaning between these two significations, where the second obviously and immediately appeals to attestation and even to testimony. Who else but the witness says 'I will uphold' and affirms the maintenance of oneself in the act of assurance?

Insofar as the narrative plot succeeds in articulating these two dimensions, it involves the same type of certainty. Again we rediscover the epistemic aspect of attestation: the fact of relating (or reading) the history of a person is inseparable from the certainty that the narrative attests to a certain cohesiveness of life, sometimes weak, at other times very strong. But to be able to arrive at this type of certainty, we must first free ourselves from the suspicion that personal identity could be only a simple illusion, the result of a misplaced belief. We can then understand the importance of the debate with Derek Parfit who, drawing support from the *puzzling cases* of the literature of science fiction, systematically deconstructs the beliefs which establish the idea of personal identity before concluding that, even from an ethical point of view, personal identity is not of any consequence.

In his encounter with this formidable adversary, Ricoeur brings to light the irreducibility of a *mineness* which cannot be observed as factual event (*OA*: 131–2/158), in other words, a mineness which can only be attested. But Parfit is not just an obstacle on the road leading to narrative identity. The debate, and the perplexities it raises, allows us to specify in advance what must be understood by narrative identity: not a 'synthesis of the heterogeneous' sheltered from doubt and suspicion – the untroubled strength of a self-possession attained once and for all – but the precarious balance between possession and dispossession of the self. If it is true that the narrative plot develops a dynamic concept of identity (*OA*: 143/170), it also puts the acting and suffering person into the plot (*OA*: 144–5/172) by holding both ends of the chain together, the temporal permanence of character and that of the preservation of self (*OA*: 166/196). No doubt it is the idea of attestation that causes Ricoeur to state at the end of his analysis of the narrative self, 'In a philosophy of ipseity like my own, one must be able to say that ownership is not what matters' (*OA*: 168/198; translation altered). In fact everything takes place as if the narrative plot, at the same time that it allows us to articulate (or that it 'shapes') the identity of the self, makes it equally problematic. It not only presents an answer to the question *Who am I?*, it allows it to be applied equally to the self in its nakedness.

No doubt it is in this perspective that it is useful to reread the long analysis of the 'imaginative variations' that contemporary literature presents with regard to the idea of the self. If we begin with Robert Musil's *The Man Without Qualities*, we have some eloquent examples – perhaps we should say 'testimonies' – of the instability of the narrative self, which in no way prevent us from presenting a poetic reply to the aporias of ascription. What should particularly hold our attention in this context is the thesis maintained at length against Alasdair MacIntyre that 'literary narratives and life histories, far from being mutually exclusive, are complementary, despite, or even because of, their contrast' (*OA*: 163/193). If it is true that the notion of narrative unity of life makes of the self an 'unstable mixture of fabulation and actual experience' (*OA*: 162/191), in spite of everything we are surprised at the significance Ricoeur attaches to the possibility of a reshaping of life by fiction, to such an extent that it is precisely the narratives of fiction which most effectively contribute to the examination of oneself in real life. Of course we can call up, as Ricoeur does, the ability to identify oneself with the hero of a fictional narrative; but we must moreover agree to reverse completely the relationship of imaginary/real that the very notion of 'fiction' suggests – escapism does not lie where we think it does. It is not fiction which encourages escapism from the concerns of real life; on the contrary, it is fiction which holds out to us the promise of a possible cohesiveness of life, notwithstanding the 'elusive character of real life' (*OA*:

162/191). And it is no doubt only on these terms that fictional narratives themselves gain the value of attestation: they attest possibilities of cohesiveness not actualized in our real life; sometimes – and here we glimpse the connections between narrativity and ethics – they even let us hold out when everything else urges us to give up. That is what Chtaranski writes of when telling how during his long months of isolation in the KGB prisons he prepared himself for his interrogations not only by remembering the actions of biblical characters, Abraham or Moses, but also by imagining himself to be Don Quixote, or Ulysses in Cyclops's cave.

Let us add a final remark. In his important work *Les puissances de l'expérience*, Jean-Marc Ferry warns against the attempt to absolutize the concept of narrative identity by recalling that not all identities are narratives, since besides narrative identity there is also interpretative, argumentative and reconstructive identity.[6] I dare say we could not accuse Ricoeur of wanting to absolutize the notion of narrative identity, for he clearly states in the conclusions of *Time and Narrative III* that 'narrative identity does not exhaust the question of the ipseity of a subject, whether it be a particular individual or a community of individuals'.[7] But even with this proviso, the concept of narrative identity does not in any way have the same status for the two authors. To be brief, we can say that Ferry considers it mainly under the aspect of *stasis*, while Ricoeur inserts the aspect of *envoy*. With Ferry, the narrative activity is defined as 'reflective thematization which produces the *first symbolic texture of the surrounding world*'.[8] On this basis, narrative activity already brings us into the order of recognition, but its power is limited in two ways. On the one hand, it is limited by its closeness to actual experience, particularly when it concerns a traumatic actual experience – the role of narration then being the 'cauterization of a psychic wound'.[9] On the other hand, it is limited by insertion into a narrative tradition; the process of recognition then consists of 'repeating the narrative, of passing it from generation to generation'.[10] Here the narrative seems more likely to refuse an identity which is confused with a *belonging* ('I belong, therefore I am') than to *attest* to the constantly fragile identity, never permanently acquired, of a singular self seeking to discover the cohesion of its life. If on the other hand we declare, as Paul Ricoeur does, that 'narrative identity, constitutive of ipseity, can include change and mutability within the cohesion of one lifetime' (*TN*: 246/355; translation altered), we should take an interest in the modes of attestation which are specific to such an identity.

4 Attestation and moral accusation

To the precise extent that we allow ourselves to be guided by the dialectic of stasis and envoy, we will be better prepared to recognize in 'ethical responsibility the highest factor in ipseity' (*TN*: 249/359). A language game borrowed from Lévinas calls attention from the outset to the importance that the phenomenon of attestation takes on for the 'little ethics' that Ricoeur puts forward in the seventh, eighth and ninth studies of *Oneself as Another*: the 'Here I stand' of responsibility which is the necessary complement of *Who am I?* which the narrative plot brings into play. But here again we must examine in a more precise way the presence of attestation in this conception of ethics. We know that this ethic unfolds in three moments – the self and the ethical intention; the self and the moral standard; and the self and practical wisdom (itself inseparable from tragic wisdom) – and that this ethic lets itself be guided by another three-part formula: '*aiming at the "good life," with and for others, in just institutions*' (*OA*: 171/202).

Where does attestation fit into this framework? The hermeneutics of the self here displays ipseity along the two lines of *self-esteem* (the ethical aspect) and *self-respect* (the deontological aspect) (*OA*: 171/201). So it is at the level of this complementarity that we must try to uncover *attestation*. But in order to properly understand this complementarity we must pass through the threefold course just mentioned. This means that the hermeneutics of the self must prevent the concept of self-esteem (and its moral equivalent, self-respect) from closing in on the purely egological focus of a self-sufficient ego – an ego which is *not* in search of the good life, open to others in solicitude, and inhabited by a sense of right and wrong which creates the meaning of the idea of self-esteem. Or, to put the same thesis in more 'hermeneutic' language, 'self-esteem follows the fate of interpretation'; 'on the ethical plane, self-interpretation becomes self-esteem' (*OA*: 179/211). Self-esteem is not immediately obvious; it is the result of a labor of interpretation about our actions, our ideals and our accomplishments, our successes and our failures. So it is never observable from the outside, but is a matter of conviction more or less supported by experience: in this sense, self-esteem presents itself from the outset as 'the new figure in which attestation appears' (*OA*: 180/211).

The appearance of others, under the form of different faces of solicitude, mutual friendship, ethical responsibility in Lévinas's sense, which makes us say: 'Here I stand', faced with the appeal which arises from the face of others which puts us in the accusative, far from putting this structure into danger, only reinforces it to the extent that the labor of interpretation passes through the 'affective flesh of feelings' (*OA*:

192/224) – feelings which convey certainties that a more impartial judgment may ignore. This reinforcement here takes the paradoxical form 'of the exchange at the very scene of the irreplaceable' which allows us to suppose the basic equivalence between 'the esteem of the *other as a oneself* and the esteem of *oneself as an other*' (OA: 194/226). The inclusion of a third person who has no face completes the hermeneutical construction of self-esteem by a 'distributive interpretation of the [social] institution' (OA: 201/234) which finds its expression in the meaning of justice which is inseparable from the meaning of equality. The hermeneutical point of view shows itself here in the fact that the ethical aim is to rediscover, particularly in situations of social crisis, the underlying principle which constitutes the 'will to live and act together' (OA: 197/230; translation altered).

When subjected to the test of the moral standard with its characteristic requirement of universalization, self-esteem becomes self-respect, which offers the same complex triadic structure as the former (OA: 204/238). We might well say that the dimension of attestation that the analysis of self-esteem has discovered is not repudiated, despite the change of perspective that the idea of law brings. Even if the opposition between autonomy and heteronomy constitutes moral ipseity, the 'positing of a legislating self must not be confused with an egological thesis' (OA: 211/246). Ricoeur recognizes 'the specific form taken by the attestation of *who?* in the. moral dimension' (OA: 212/248) in the 'fact of reason', which constitutes the self-legislating capacity of the moral subject. But we must raise a problem that Kant did not face: what relation obtains 'between the quasi-positing character of the self by itself in autonomy and the virtual nature of affection by the other implied by the status of respect as a motive?' (OA: 214/249). If respect represents 'the variable of self-esteem which has successfully passed the test of the criterion of universalization' (OA: 214–15/250), it is a matter of great concern to analyze 'its strange nature' according to its threefold framework.

The demand for universalization which characterizes the morals of obligation necessarily creates situations of conflict which practical wisdom should learn to appropriately manage through moral judgment, by producing *convictions* which have their origins in the aims of real life. 'Conviction', and more precisely 'considered conviction', such is the final face that attestation presents at the conclusion of Ricoeur's 'little ethics'. There is conviction where there is first the admission of unavoidable conflicts which force us to speak of an authentic 'tragedy of action'. But would we be in a position to speak of it if we had not already been instructed by the voice of great tragedies, even before philosophy? 'Tragedy teaches us'; it says something fundamental about the inevitable nature of conflict in moral life (*OA*: 243/283). This in no way means that tragic wisdom can come to be a substitute for ethics. Even if the same word '*phronein/phronesis*' appears on both sides, the distance between tragic and practical wisdom remains. We could also say that practical wisdom increases the aporias of narrative identity which ethics and morals tend to neutralize.

So it is in the light of the tragedy of action that Sophocles' *Antigone* in particular illustrates that the three faces of the moral self – which the detour through Kant has allowed us to sort out – will have to be reread: the autonomy of the universal self, the plurality of persons as objects of respect, and the rule of justice in its procedural form. Specific unsurpassable conflicts, which are so many manifestations of the tragedy of action, appear on each of these levels. With regard to respect, this forces us to push reflection to the point where another is set up before us in his irreplaceable singularity (*OA*: 264/308). Faced with the exception which is another person, respect becomes availability (*OA*: 267–8/311). Practical wisdom here consists in 'inventing conduct that will best satisfy the exception required by solicitude, by betraying the rule to the smallest extent possible' (*OA*: 269/312). Such solicitude will therefore be a '*critical solicitude*' (*OA*: 273/318).

But above all it is the principle of autonomy which is reinterpreted in light of the tragedy of action. Far from purely and simply being opposed to heteronomy, autonomy is a tributary of the latter in two ways. First, the moral self encloses 'the other of freedom in the figure of the law, which freedom nevertheless gives itself; the other of feeling in the figure of respect; [and] the other of evil in the figure of the penchant toward evil' (*OA*: 275/320). Second, 'this threefold otherness within the self joins the properly dialogical otherness that makes autonomy part and parcel of, and dependent on, . . . the rule of reciprocity' (*OA*: 275–76/320).

Finally, practical wisdom seeks a resolution to the conflict between contextualist and universalist ethics, by distinguishing the level of *justification* from that of *fulfillment*. In the regressive order of justification, the universalism of an ethics of discussion, conceived in the manner of Jürgen Habermas and Karl-Otto Apel, triumphs. In the progressive order of fulfillment of the moral life, the last word belongs to the convictions which receive the stamp of a specific culture and historical context. But the dichotomy between argumentation and convention should be replaced by a 'subtle dialectic between *argumentation* and *conviction*' (*OA*: 287/334). It is '*the reflective equilibrium between the ethics of argumentation and considered convictions*' (*OA*: 289/335) which lets us mediate the conflict between universality and historicity. In this sense, attestation – this time under the name of 'considered conviction' – has the last word in the different determinations of the self, which the 'hermeneutical-phenomenological cycle' (*OA*: 291/338) that we have just gone through lets us sort out.

5 Being oneself: the ontological commitment of attestation

Taken together, these nine studies have determined the epistemic function of attestation, even as on several occasions they have also allowed us to glimpse its possible ontological function. It remains for the tenth study to state clearly the ontological commitment of attestation. Indeed, if the hermeneutics of the self cannot straightaway rush into an ontological investigation of the status of the self – if, as always with Ricoeur, ontology is for him a promised land rather than a conquered one – it can no longer restrict itself to characterizing attestation in terms of certainty, as a specific mode of credence and trust (*OA*: 299/347); it must be defined as a specific *mode of being* of the self. Then it becomes 'the assurance – the credence and the trust – of *existing* in the mode of ipseity' (*OA*: 302/351; translation slightly altered). To tell the truth, this simple declaration results in an extremely ambitious ontological inquiry. On the one hand, an ontology of ipseity should bring into play – but with profound modification – the resources of the Aristotelian ontology of act and potency. It is on a '*ground of being at once potentiality and actuality*' (*OA*: 308/357) that the mode of being that we have in mind when we speak of attestation, is to be understood. On the other hand, it is a matter of making intelligible the 'slight difference' (*OA*: 308/358) which separates Ricoeur's approach to attestation from its thematization within the framework of Heidegger's existential analytics. In fact, the debate is twofold; it relates as much to the interpretation of Aristotle as to the guiding concepts of *Being and Time*.

In regard to the first perspective, Ricoeur seeks to break the monolithic aspect of the concept of Being-in-the-world: 'oneself, care and Being-within-the-world are to be determined together' (*OA*: 311/360; translation modified). In regard to the second, it is the concept of facticity, considered as a synonym of *energeia*, which presents a problem (*OA*: 314/364). Is the difference between the two approaches so 'slight'? This is not certain, given the fact that it is the Spinozist *conatus* which is brought into play for a better understanding of the connection between a phenomenology of the acting and suffering self and the actual and potential ground against which ipseity stands out (*OA*: 315–17/365–7).

There remains a last thesis to be introduced, which this time engages in a dialogue with Lévinas. As it is a matter of describing the labor of otherness at the heart of ipseity, we must start from the 'polysemic character of otherness' (*OA*: 317/368) which prevents us from reducing the Other to the otherness of others. In this case, 'passivity becomes *the* attestation of otherness' (*OA*: 318/368) spread over three irreducible sources of otherness which are all different faces of passivity: one's own body, the otherness of others, and the relationship of the self to itself in *conscience* (in the sense of *Gewissen*). Does this 'tripod' exhaust all the possible phenomenological representations of passivity-otherness? It is not certain! Should not the unconscious, to mention only one representation of otherness, also be part of the picture?

However it may be with this question, we can conclude by asking ourselves if there is not a hidden complicity between the threefold unfolding of the hermeneutics of testimony on which the first part of our study ended and the assertion that the three basic modes of *otherness* should not be confused; because in the final analysis they are, in their very difference, in accord with the speculative idea of otherness.

Institut Catholique de Paris, France
[Translated by Steve Rothnie]

Notes

1 Paul Ricoeur, 'L'herméneutique du témoignage', in *Le Témoignage*, ed. Enrico Castelli (Paris: Aubier, 1972), pp. 35–61; English translation published David Stewart and Charles E. Reagan, trans. as 'The Hermeneutics of Testimony', in *Essays on Biblical Interpretation*, ed. Lewis S. Mudge (Philadelphia, PA: Fortress Press, 1980), pp. 119–54. Subsequently cited in the text as *HT*, with both English and French pagination.
2 Paul Ricoeur, 'Herméneutique de l'idée de Révélation', in *La Révélation* (Brussels: Facultés universitaires Saint-Louis, 1977), pp. 15–54, especially pp. 47–54; English translation published as 'Toward a Hermeneutic of the Idea of Revelation', trans. David Pellauer, in *Essays on Biblical Interpretation*, ed. Mudge, pp. 73–118, especially pp. 110–18.
3 Paul Ricoeur, 'Emmanuel Lévinas, penseur du témoignage', in *Répondre d'autrui: Emmanuel Lévinas*, ed. Jean-Christophe Aeschlimann (Neuchâtel: De la Bâconnière, 1989), pp. 17–40; subsequently cited in the text as *EL*.

4 Paul Ricoeur, *Soi-même comme un autre* (Paris: Editions du Seuil, 1990); English translation published as *Oneself as Another*, trans. Kathleen Blamey (Chicago, IL: University of Chicago Press, 1992); subsequently cited in the text as *OA*, with both English and French pagination.

5 On the concept of initiative, see also Paul Ricoeur, *Du texte à l'action: Essais d'herméneutique II* (Paris: Editions du Seuil, 1986), pp. 261–80; English translation published as *From Text to Action: Essays in Hermeneutics, II*, trans. Kathleen Blamey and John B. Thompson (Evanston, IL: Northwestern University Press, 1991).

6 Jean-Marc Ferry, *Les puissances de l'expérience, essai sur l'identité contemporaine, Vol. 1, Le sujet et le verbe* (Paris: Editions du Cerf, 1991), p. 104.

7 Paul Ricoeur, *Temps et récit III* (Paris: Editions du Seuil, 1985), p. 358; English translation published as *Time and Narrative III*, trans. Kathleen Blamey and David Pellauer (Chicago, IL and London: University of Chicago Press, 1988), p. 249; translation altered. Subsequently cited in the text as *TN*, with both English and French pagination.

8 Ferry, *Les puissances*, p. 107.

9 ibid.

10 ibid., p. 109.

Mara Rainwater

Refiguring Ricoeur: narrative force and communicative ethics

Paul Ricoeur has long been recognized for his major contributions to hermeneutics, phenomenology and ideological critique in the human sciences. Yet, despite Ricoeur's persistent focus on language, self and narrativity, his name has been notably absent from the domain of communicative ethics. The expressed aim here is to 're-figure' Ricoeur in order to highlight the importance of his work for the ethics of discourse and to interpret it accordingly.

Much of the contemporary debate in discourse ethics has centered on the possibility of claiming universal validity for norms justified in the context of 'an episode of argumentation.[1] Contributions to this debate on procedural justification from both universalists and communitarians alike have been provocative and fruitful, but in this article I shall invoke an enlarged sense of communicative ethics that includes a discursive 'narrative force' as well as a performative 'illocutionary force' of arguing or asserting. It is here that the philosophical project of Paul Ricoeur provides valuable insights to those who are already exploring the ethics of discourse.

In his ongoing hermeneutic inquiries, Ricoeur has consistently focused on such complexities of language as semantic innovation and narrative structuration. Ricoeur clearly distinguishes between static synchronic structure and the dynamic structuration which 'is an oriented activity that is only completed in the spectator or reader'.[2] He has thematically attempted to examine and elucidate these linguistic features at the level of *extended* discourse, rather than within the confines of mere lexical boundaries or sentential propositions. Given the centrality of language to his enterprise, Ricoeur has thereby also engaged an entire network of concerns that G. H. von Wright has marked as 'language-oriented notions, such as meaning, intentionality, interpretation, and understanding'.[3]

This attention to discursive language has also led Ricoeur to develop a model of selfhood that privileges a narrative (*ipse*) identity emerging cumulatively and intersubjectively, always mediated by others.[4] He rejects the alternative of an isolated, disembedded cogito that remains safely and hermetically incubated within its sameness or *idem*-identity. Such an idem perspective on 'personal identity' establishes a paradigm that finds its philosophically interesting questions arising from the aporia of substantial duration through time. On Ricoeur's account, selfhood understood as ipse-identity prioritizes the issues of agency, praxis and intervention, all vitally important to critical theory and its offshoot, communicative ethics.

A final thematic in Ricoeur's work, his continuing dialogue with the human sciences, supplements his concern with language, selfhood and narrativity. Ricoeur has broadened the horizon of hermeneutic inquiry by engaging both *Verstehen* and *Erklären* in a dialectic which privileges neither.[5] By allowing 'explanation' to function within the hermeneutic context, he resists what von Wright has called 'positivism's idea of the unity of science', i.e. the methodological monism that refuses to acknowledge the methods of the *Geisteswissenschaften* as 'science'.[6] He therefore brings the 'narrative function' to bear on critical methodological implications, beyond simply aesthetic significance, in psychoanalytical and historical discourse.

These issues of language, narrativity, selfhood and interpretation within the human sciences have all permeated Ricoeur's work. It is with this in mind that we can proceed to examine his relevance to communicative ethics, particularly in the direction taken by Seyla Benhabib.

I

Artisans who work with words produce not things but quasi-things; they invent the as-if.[7] (Paul Ricoeur)

Certain problems immediately surface when an attempt is made to incorporate narrativity explicitly within the program of discourse ethics. Most importantly, it is claimed that a primary genre distinction exists between the 'literary' character of narrative and the 'pragmatic' character of daily communication in the life-world. Despite the contributions of philosophers like Ricoeur, Danto and Mink to a general theory of narrative that transcends such genre distinctions, the epistemological implications of their work have been largely ignored.[8] Thomas McCarthy has elaborated the prevailing viewpoint in the following way:

> In the communicative practice of everyday life, language functions as a medium for dealing with problems that arise within the world. It is thus subject to an ongoing test and tied to processes of learning. In poetic discourse, by contrast, the everyday pressure to decide and to act is lifted, and the way is free for displaying the world-disclosive power of innovative language. . . . *Language's capacity to solve problems disappears behind its world-creating capacity.*[9] (emphasis added)

McCarthy's 'disinterested' perspective, which isolates narrative discourse in a purely aesthetic domain, is perhaps his reaction to what is perceived as an irresponsible attempt 'to uproot propositional truth and devalue discursive, argumentative thought'.[10] However, we must also admit that the very premises which are asserted (or inductively speaking, the examples which are submitted during argumentative episodes) are often grounded in narrative accounts that claim to state the case first and prove it only subsequently. In Book III of the *Rhetoric*, Aristotle notes that 'one must say all that will make the facts clear, or create the belief that they have happened or have done injury or wrong, or that they are as important as you wish to make them'.[11] We are meant to understand the act of narrating as the Greek term *diēgeomai* (διηγέομαι) should be translated: setting out in detail or describing.

Moreover, in the effort 'to resist the leveling of the genre distinction between philosophy and literature and the reversal of the primacy of logic over rhetoric with which it is linked', McCarthy assumes a rather debased understanding of what constitutes the rhetorical strategies that underlie argumentative encounters.[12] In fact, it is not in Aristotle's *Rhetoric*, but in Book II of his *Prior Analytics* – which aims to establish the most general procedures of inference – that we find rhetorical strategies firmly entrenched:

> In order to avoid having a syllogism drawn against us, we must take care, whenever an opponent asks us to admit the reason without the conclusions, not to grant him the same term twice over in his premisses, since we know that a syllogism cannot be drawn without a middle term, and that term which is stated more than once is the middle. How we ought to watch the middle in reference to each conclusion, is evident from our knowing what kind of thesis is proved in each figure. This will not escape us since we know how we are maintaining the argument.[13]

While such strategies need not be seen as blatantly and solely eristic in design, nor about to deteriorate into the worst demagoguery, they are still solidly *rhetorical*, and they depend on the temporal development of an 'argumentative episode' subject to its own emplotment. The ability to foresee the trajectory an opponent's argument will follow is analogous to having the ability to predict a rival's probable sequence of moves in chess. Both rely on an understanding of the adversarial relation that frames and presupposes these encounters at a primordial level. Aristotle is quite frank about the acceptability of an interlocutor's using even strategic *silence* in a way that 'will most likely deceive his opponent'.[14] He recommends:

> That which we urge men to beware of in their admissions, they ought in attack to try to conceal. This will be possible first, if, instead of drawing the conclusions of preliminary syllogisms, they take the necessary premises and leave the conclusions in the dark; secondly, if instead of inviting assent to propositions which are closely connected, they take as far as possible those that are not connected by middle terms. For example, suppose that A is to be inferred to be true of F; B, C, D, and E being made middle terms. One ought then to ask whether A belongs to B, and next whether D belongs to E, instead of whether B belongs to C, and so on.[15]

Thus, these preliminary considerations regarding strict 'genre' distinctions and the primacy of logic over rhetoric that McCarthy has claimed suggest the need for at least a mild skepticism. How are we to locate the contribution of narrativity to a more comprehensive understanding of communicative ethics? Or even in a more limited sense, can narrative form be completely divorced from idealized 'argumentative episodes'? It seems not. Our faith in the purity of truth claims and the deserved victory of the disembodied 'illocutionary force of the better argument' must be tempered by pragmatic and contextual considerations as well. Participants in an argumentative episode must appreciate a rhetorical ground that includes narrative input as well as enthymemic deduction. Illocutionary force at the wrong time or in the wrong place is wasted. As Donald Davidson has remarked, 'Truth (in a given natural language) is not a property of sentences; it is a relation between sentences, speakers, and dates'.[16] Contingencies abound.

II

Ricoeur himself, however, recognizes that *historical* claims posited in a narrative mode still presuppose and remain committed to an extended

argumentative context. He notes that 'poets begin with form: historians argue from it. . . . And they argue because they know we can
explain in other ways.'[17] These features of selection and configuration
are unpacked in Ricoeur's general theory of narrative discourse, a
theory which delineates a common ground for both historical and
fictional narratives at the level of emplotment and human temporality.

For Ricoeur, it is the ontological condition of human being as
'being-in-time' that fuels all narrative constructs. There always exists a
temporal aporia arising from the discordant experience of our
inscription of lived-phenomenological time in cosmological time, an
aporia that finds some resolution in our effort to 'humanize our
experience of time' in narrative activity.[18] It is here that we can locate
the intersection 'between the private time of our mortality and the
public time of language'.[19] Thus, on Ricoeur's account, all narrative
form shares this temporal belonging and cognitively expresses the
experience of our historicity.

Since his project rejects the Husserlian notion of an unmediated
consciousness transparent to itself, Ricoeur stresses the need for
mediations via language, symbol, culture and history. In short, we
always proceed by interpretation: nothing is simply 'given' to consciousness. Narrative discourse confronts us with a 'thick' interpretive
matrix already offering to mediate and to explain. Indeed, 'on the level
of procedures, history is born as inquiry out of the specific use it makes
of explanation'.[20] But how is this matrix itself to be approached and
articulated?

Ricoeur deploys and elaborates two concepts from Aristotle's
Poetics, emplotment (*muthos*) and *mimēsis*, which he suggests provide
the dual structure for all narrative understanding. However, this
'making' (*poēisis*) of narratives is to be realized as a productive and
dynamic process that synoptically orders its material under a model of
concordance. The logical and dramatic unity of beginning, middle and
end provides the ordered background from which discordance
emerges. The overall intelligibility of emplotment requires a grasping
together of actions and events that resembles reflective judgment rather
than determinative judgment in the Kantian sense. Ricoeur notes:

> By means of the plot, goals, causes, and chance are brought together
> within the temporal unity of a whole and complete action. It is this
> synthesis of the heterogeneous that brings narrative close to meta-
> phor. In both cases the new thing – the as yet unsaid, the unwritten –
> springs up in the language.[21]

A certain directedness in the narrative itself moves the listener or reader to conclusions that seem probable and acceptable in the given framework, rather than predictable.

Whereas Ricoeur is able simultaneously to recuperate emplotment and to extricate it from Aristotle's narrower emphasis on tragedy, the task of rehabilitating *mimēsis* is somewhat more difficult. The representation of action (*mimēsis praxeōs*) cannot be understood as merely static imitation or illusory copying in the Platonic sense. Ricoeur establishes a tripartite model of *mimēsis* to expand this concept. He designates the prefigured world of action as *mimēsis 1*; the creative act of configuration as *mimēsis 2*; and the receptive act of refiguration back into the world by spectators or readers as *mimēsis 3*. Mimetic activity thus acquires an ethical and political significance that generates further action through recognition and persuasion. The power of narrative configuration to 'affect' us (*catharsis*) is also the power to persuade us. Whether based on the historical evidence of archive, trace and memory, or more freely configured as fiction, narrative links with praxis. The invasive dissonance of surprise, misfortune, chance and reversals of all kinds within the concordance of emplotment generate the tension that persuades:

> Hence, by its very nature, the intelligibility characteristic of dissonant consonance – what Aristotle puts under the term 'probable' – is the common product of the work and the public. The persuasive is born at their intersection.[22]

This characteristic attribute of narrative discourse to explain, and thereby to synoptically provide reasons which justify and *persuade*, has implications – both methodological and substantive – for any critical social theory. The human sciences as we know them were born in the crucible of the *Methodenstreit* that has raged intermittently throughout the past century.[23] One of the results of these skirmishes has been that narrativity, like *Verstehen*, could not be accommodated within new paradigms that affiliated themselves with the deductive-nomological model appropriate to the natural sciences.

Narrative claims were deemed to have no explanatory force beyond the most subjective level, and historical understanding was reappropriated by Hempel's Covering Law model.[24] The claim that any historical 'event' could be deductively subsumed under the larger umbrella of universal laws offering predictability as reliable as any empirical research conducted in the natural sciences proved attractive to many social theorists. Even those who resisted the hegemony of nomothetic methodology faced the challenge of devising more 'objective' tools for accessing their domain than the particularized (idiographic) methodologies of *Verstehen* and narrativity seemed to offer. It is only by recognizing the impact of this methodological dispute on critical theory that the overall *neglect* of narrativity as a respectably legitimate 'mode of comprehension' can be fully appreciated.[25]

III

Actions are identified narratively.[26] (Seyla Benhabib)

Ricoeur's project of philosophically grounding a general theory of narrative assumes added importance vis-a-vis communicative ethics as the issues of *agency* and *selfhood* become a vital node in the debate. His reflections in *Oneself as Another* revolve around the question 'Who?':

> In introducing the problematic of the self by the question 'who?', we have in the same stroke opened the way for the genuine polysemy inherent in this question itself: Who is speaking of what? Who does what? About whom and about what does one construct a narrative? Who is morally responsible for what? These are but so many different ways in which 'who?' is stated.[27]

In a series of 'studies' that work through the question of selfhood from an initial inquiry into the identifying reference of 'person' itself to his critique of Davidson's 'agentless semantics of action', Ricoeur is most concerned with leading us towards a construction of narrative identity that never loses sight of the ethical intention of 'aiming at the good life with and for others, in just institutions'.[28]

Ricoeur avoids the pitfall of identifying the 'good life' solely with Hegelian *Sittlichkeit*, and thus cannot be tagged with the label 'communitarian' or neo-Aristotelian *tout court* in terms of the current debate. In fact, what is most 'inadmissible in Hegel is the thesis of the objective mind and its corollary, the thesis of the state erected as a superior agency endowed with self-knowledge'.[29] The emphasis placed by Ricoeur on the critical importance of deliberation and discussion emerging from *conflict* rather than consensus is noteworthy. It is in and through such deliberation that the detour to self-understanding is negotiated by participants in dialogue.

The importance of narrative claims within the context of communicative ethics has recently been highlighted in the work of Seyla Benhabib, whose explorations of self and 'the phenomenology of moral judgment' have enlarged our understanding of what constitutes an adequate ethics of discourse.[30] There is a hermeneutic import implicit in her definition of 'the immersion of action in a web of interpretation which I shall call "narrativity"'.[31] The construction of a narrative identity plays a crucial role in an approach to communicative ethics that privileges the *process* of ongoing dialogue rather than the chimerical and somewhat rigid goal of total consensus. Benhabib maintains:

> And if I am correct that it is the process of such dialogue, conversation, and mutual understanding, and not consensus which is our goal, discourse theory can represent the moral point of view without having to invoke the fiction of the *homo economicus* or *homo politicus*. To know how to sustain an ongoing human relationship means to know what it means to be an 'I' and a 'me', to know that I am an 'other' to you and that likewise, you are an 'I' to yourself but an 'other' to me. Hegel had named this structure that of 'reciprocal recognition'.[32]

It is thus the ability to reverse perspectives and deploy 'moral imagination' that is presupposed by her claim that 'judgment involves certain "interpretive" and "narrative" skills, which, in turn, entail the capacity for exercising an "enlarged mentality"'.[33] Benhabib takes care to emphasize in her work that dialogue and conversation are *cooperative* models for communication that can certainly be as effective as purely argumentative strategies in fostering mutual understanding. In fact, the incorporation of Hegelian 'reciprocal recognition' permits moral conversation to continue in exchanges where openly adversarial postures may privilege sedimented and prejudicial 'paradigms of argumentation accepted as authoritative in adjudicating conflicting claims'.[34] Here Benhabib recuperates the suspicions of feminist critics like Nancy Fraser who oppose the narrow ethical rationalism that pervades less flexible models of discourse ethics. Consequently, we highlight the significance in moral dialogue of recognizing the self as constituted by *ipse* narrative identity rather than the ego-centered sameness of an *idem*-identity of necessarily limited perspective. Benhabib notes:

> In conversation, I must know how to listen, I must know how to understand your point of view, I must learn to represent to myself the world and the other as you see them. If I cannot listen, if I cannot understand, and if I cannot represent, the conversation stops, develops into an *argument*, or maybe never gets started. Discourse ethics projects such moral conversations, in which reciprocal recognition is exercised, onto a utopian community of humankind.[35]

We can see that Benhabib's expansion of the 'public sphere' (*Öffentlichkeit*) of discourse ethics to include diverse issues beyond narrowly construed forensic and political debate vitally engages many of Paul Ricoeur's insights on narrative identity. He similarly contends that 'narrative mediation underlines this remarkable characteristic of self-knowledge – that it is self-interpretation'.[36] The question of narrativity thus bears heavily upon the self-definition that evolves through time in a complex network of human relationships. In order to make the move from mere *ascription* of an act to actual *judgments* of moral imputation, Benhabib agrees that we must exercise 'moral imagination of possible act descriptions and narratives under which they fall', while any interpretation of one's own project 'entails comprehension of narrative histories – both one's own and those of others'.[37] The process of individuation can never be negotiated by an isolated *cogito* without solipsistic consequences, for 'narrativity is the mode through which actions are individuated and the identity of the self constituted'.[38]

IV

Recognition introduces the dyad and plurality in the very constitution of the self.[39] (Paul Ricoeur)

In re-reading and re-figuring Ricoeur, we are reminded throughout his work that all communicative action must be *hermeneutically* grounded because it is always intersubjectively mediated. Yet, Ricoeur keeps the distinctive phenomenological emphasis on 'reflexivity' at the core of an ethics of discourse. In his words, the hermeneutical variation of 'this reflexive philosophy considers the most radical philosophical problems to be those which concern the possibility of *self-understanding* as the subject of the operations of knowing, willing, evaluating, etc.'.[40] Reflexivity is never to be construed as a process leading to identity as sameness, but rather requires the 'moment of intellectual clarity and moral responsibility, the unifying principle of the operations among which it is dispersed and forgets itself as subject'.[41]

It is this dispersion, forgetting and retrieval, this construction of a self through *time*, that thematizes the crucial function of narrativity in communicative ethics. Certainly, Ricoeur's significant contribution has been to provide a philosophical and theoretical framework that enables us to critically examine narrative as a protean mode of discourse. We have seen that narrativity pervades even the most rigorous 'argumentative episodes' that must always constitute at least *one* aspect of our communicative interactions as deliberation. However, we have also seen that narrativity has the power to evoke moral imagination and thereby motivate actions which surpass the minimal requirements of mere duty and justification alone. This insight enlarges the very horizon of communicative ethics itself. Such an appreciation of narrative force has long been heralded by Paul Ricoeur. Participants in the communicative ethics debate, whatever their stance or persuasion, owe Ricoeur their recognition and gratitude for bringing the complexities of narrative discourse into sharper philosophical focus.

University College Dublin, Ireland

Notes

1 For the use of this specific terminology, see Matthias Kettner, 'Consensus Formation in the Public Domain', in E. Winkler and J. Coombs, *Applied Ethics* (Oxford: Blackwell, 1993), p. 42. There has naturally been a vast amount of literature generated on this topic, but for an exploration of both sides of the debate also see the following volumes: S. Benhabib and F. Dallmayr (eds) *The Communicative Ethics Controversy* (Cambridge, MA: MIT Press, 1990); M. Kelly (ed.) *Hermeneutics and Critical Theory in Ethics and Politics* (Cambridge, MA: MIT Press, 1990); and D. Rasmussen (ed.) *Universalism vs. Communitarianism* (Cambridge, MA: MIT Press, 1990).

2 See Paul Ricoeur, *Time and Narrative* Vol. I, trans. K. McLaughlin and D. Pellauer (Chicago, IL: University of Chicago Press, 1984), p. 48; hereafter cited as *TN*.

3 G. H. von Wright, *Explanation and Understanding* (London: Routledge & Kegan Paul, 1971), p. 29; hereafter cited as *Explanation*. Von Wright's reassessment of teleological explanation has proven of great interest to both Ricoeur and Karl-Otto Apel.

4 Ricoeur has elaborated upon this model of narrative identity and its ethical implications most extensively in *Oneself as Another*, trans. Kathleen Blamey (Chicago, IL: University of Chicago Press, 1992), especially pp. 113–168; hereafter cited as *Oneself*.

5 See Paul Ricoeur, 'The Narrative Function', in *Hermeneutics and the Human Sciences: Essays on Language, Action and Interpretation*, ed. and trans. John B. Thompson (Cambridge: Cambridge University Press, 1981), pp. 274–96; see also Paul Ricoeur, 'The Question of Proof in Freud's Writings', in ibid., pp. 247–73.

6 Von Wright, *Explanation*, p. 30.

7 Ricoeur, *TN*, I, p. 45.

8 See Arthur Danto, *Analytical Philosophy of History* (Cambridge: Cambridge University Press, 1965); also Louis Mink, 'Narrative Form as a Cognitive Instrument', in *Historical Understanding* ed. B. Fay, E. O. Golob and R. T. Vann (Ithaca, NY: Cornell University Press, 1987), pp. 182–203; hereafter cited as *Understanding*.

9 See Thomas McCarthy, 'Introduction', in Jürgen Habermas, *The Philosophical Discourse of Modernity* (Cambridge: Polity, 1987), p. xiii; hereafter cited as *Discourse*.

10 ibid., p. xi.

11 Aristotle, *The 'Art' of Rhetoric*, trans. J. H. Freese, Loeb Classical Library (Cambridge, MA: Harvard University Press, 1932), 1417a, 1 ff.

12 McCarthy, in *Discourse*, p. xii.

13 Aristotle, *Prior Analytics*, 66a, 25 ff., in *The Basic Works of Aristotle*, ed. Richard McKeon (New York: Random House, 1941).

14 ibid., 66b, 1–3.

15 ibid., 66a, 33 ff.

16 Donald Davidson, *Inquiries into Truth and Interpretation* (Oxford: Clarendon Press, 1984), p. 43.

17 Ricoeur, *TN*, I, p. 186.

18 Ricoeur, *TN*, I, p. 6. For an extended discussion of temporal aporia as Augustine's *distentio animi*, see ibid., pp. 5–30.

19 Paul Ricoeur, 'The Creativity of Language', in *Dialogues with Contemporary Continental Thinkers*, ed. R. Kearney (Manchester: Manchester University Press, 1984), p. 20.

20 Ricoeur, *TN*, I, p. 175.

21 ibid., p. ix.

22 ibid., p. 50.

23 For an overview of the background and influence of this methodological debate, see Theodor Adorno et al., *The Positivist Dispute in German Sociology*, trans. Glyn Adey and David Frisby (London: Heinemann, 1976).

24 Karl Hempel, 'The Function of General Laws in History', *Journal of Philosophy* 39(1942): 35–48.

25 See Louis Mink, 'History and Fiction as Modes of Comprehension', in *Understanding*, pp. 42–60; and Louis Mink, 'The Divergence of History and Sociology in Recent Philosophy of History', in ibid., pp. 163–81.

26 Seyla Benhabib, 'Judgment and the Moral Foundations of Politics in Hannah Arendt's Thought', in *Situating the Self* (Cambridge: Polity, 1992), p. 127.

27 Ricoeur, *Oneself*, p. 19.

28 ibid., p. 172.

29 ibid., p. 256. For an extended discussion of moving beyond *Sittlich-keit*, see ibid., pp. 250–62.
30 Benhabib, *Situating the Self*, p. 129.
31 ibid., p. 126.
32 See Seyla Benhabib, 'Afterword: Communicative Ethics and Current Controversies in Practical Philosophy', in Benhabib and Dallmayr (eds) *The Communicative Ethics Controversy*, p. 359.
33 ibid., p. 361.
34 ibid., p. 353.
35 ibid., p. 359.
36 Paul Ricoeur, 'Narrative Identity', in *On Paul Ricoeur: Narrative and Interpretation*, ed. David Wood (London: Routledge, 1991), p. 198.
37 Benhabib, *Situating the Self*, p. 129.
38 ibid., p. 127.
39 Ricoeur, *Oneself*, p. 296.
40 Paul Ricoeur, 'On Interpretation', in *Philosophy in France Today*, ed. Alan Montefiore (Cambridge: Cambridge Universtiy Press, 1983), p. 188.
41 ibid.

Bernhard Waldenfels

The other and the foreign

The most recent major work of Paul Ricoeur profoundly examines the 'work of alterity in the heart of selfhood' (p. 368).[1] This 'hermeneutic of the self' sets out to provide the self-explication that stands under the sign of an originary alterity. It results not in a self-certitude, but rather in a fallible self-assurance and self-attestation (*attestation de soi*). The 'school of suspicion' is again present as it was in his earlier work on Freud, this time represented particularly by Nietzsche. Now the cogito proves to be not only wounded, but crushed and shattered (*brisé*) with a rupture unable to be mended by any reflection. To cite Lévinas, whose thought is present in this work as a continual challenge, we can say that the positing and the self-positing of the cogito, its 'position', is undermined by an 'ex-position', an originary being-abandoned-to-the-other. I am not master in my own house, because I am not master of myself. Like Lacan, Foucault and Lévinas, Ricoeur rethinks the conception of the subject without entangling himself in mortal combat. The great 'subject' simply breaks apart.[2]

I Selfhood as alterity

Now the key word is 'self' (*soi*), which designates more what we see in Plato's 'care for self', 'care for the soul' (*Apology* 29d ff., 36c) and in Aristotle's friend as the 'other self' (*allos* or *heteros autos*), than an expression of an ego that is all too ready to make itself a substance and to centre itself in itself – though Rimbaud's famous dictum is easily evoked. Does 'I *is* an other', already in an aggramatically dislocated formulation, allow itself to be dislocated again, by introducing something like 'as myself I *am* an other'?

The exceptionally refined architectonic of Ricoeur's text gives rise to a three-part harmony announced in the title itself: self-reflexivity (*soi*), selfhood/sameness (*soi-même*), otherness (*un autre*). As for self-reflexivity, without the 'reflection' which – as Husserl and Merleau-Ponty have shown – is already equipped with a corporeal ground[3] and which is found, before all objectivizing and predicative self-reference, in the oblique use of reflexive verbs and pronouns, self-identification and self-imputation are as empty as every demand of the other which addresses me. After reflexivity, the next 'note' of the harmony forms a double register: *mêmeté* and *ipséité*, *idem* and *ipse*, *Selbes* and *Selbst*, or same and self. For Ricoeur there emerges from this a vast 'dialectic' of sameness and selfhood. The second 'dialectic', which introduces the third note of the harmony, ranges between selfhood (*ipséité*) and alterity (*altérité*). Only in this fashion does the announced theme develop itself fully. The connecting *as* forms the critical point: *as the others*. As Ricoeur stresses several times, this particle allows itself to be doubled as both a comparative 'as' (*wie*) and an implicative 'as' (*als*). Since alterity does not augment selfhood from without, but rather eats away at it from within, the stress is placed on the implicative nuance: 'the self as [*als*] an other' (cf. pp. 14, 37).

My reflections will focus on the tension between selfhood and alterity. According to Ricoeur, alterity exhibits the following primary features. 1) The other stands in contrast to *the self*, not to the same; the other is another self, not simply another entity (pp. 13 f.). 2) The ontological meta-category of alterity, situated on the Platonic level of 'major kinds' without reducing itself to a simple copy of *heteron* (p. 346), finds its phenomenological counterpart in *passivity* (p. 368). This means that we experience and encounter alterity in the form of suffering and endurance that either limits or precedes our initiative. 3) Like passivity, alterity takes *three different forms* as the alterity of one's own life, of the other and of conscience. An Aristotelian style of treatment is evident in Ricoeur's orientation towards polysemia, which presents a plurality of saying without looking for a single architectonic meaning. The open form of the dialectic that results can be designated as a mediation without a middle. The middle is not suppressed, but simply omitted.

The alterity of the other, upon which I will concentrate, is a central issue in three of Ricoeur's discussions: in his study of ethics (seventh study) morals (eighth study) and ontology (tenth study). The goal of his ethical project, which takes on an Aristotelian structure, is 'to aim for the "good life," with and for the other, within just institutions' (p. 202). In this way self-appreciation and self-love, without which the good life is no longer *my* life, unite both with friendship, in which I share my life with certain others, and with justice, which is institutionally derived from the point of view of a third. The same threefold division is found in a Kantian morality. Starting from self-respect, with which I sense myself submissive to the moral law, a concern for others develops that is sustained by principles of justice that oblige me as well as all subjects. In both cases we are justified in speaking of a 'search for equality through inequality' (p. 255). Finally, in the last chapter where Ricoeur exposes the ontological implications of phenomenological-hermeneutic studies of the self, the otherness of the other situates itself between the alterity of one's own body and the alterity of one's conscience, such that the triad of self–other–universality remains preserved throughout.

This vision links the Aristotelian moments of self-love, friendship and rectifying justice both with the Kantian motives of respect and unconditional duty and with the Heideggerian themes of concern and the summons of *Dasein*. It finds its critical counterpart in all attempts which aim to derive either alterity from selfhood or selfhood from alterity, and which thus disturb the equilibrium between acting and suffering, and between giving and receiving. This means that Ricoeur's critique directs itself from one side against Husserl's *ego*logical approach and from another side against Lévinas's approach, which we can designate as *hetero*logical since it emerges not from the ego, but in reverse manner from the other.[4]

II Alterity vs foreignness

It is surprising that Ricoeur bestows great importance on the doubling of identity in sameness (*identité-idem*) and in selfhood (*identité-ipse*) and draws extraordinary consequences from both of them, whereas he mentions the doubling of alterity in other-as-sameness and other-as-selfhood only in passing (p. 13) (although even the latter is no less threatened by continual contamination and reduction than the former). We shall put aside for the moment the question as to what extent Ricoeur himself runs this danger of reduction, and concentrate instead upon the distinction itself.

Linguistically we can differentiate between otherness as diversity (*diversité/Verschiedenheit*) whose opposite is sameness, and otherness as foreignness (*étrangeté/Fremdheit*) whose opposite would be ownness. It is well known that the usage of the German words *fremd* or *Fremdheit* is not unusual in situations where French prefers *autre, autrui*, or *alterité* and English uses 'other' or 'otherness'. Thus we find in Husserl expressions such as *Fremderfahrung, Fremdich, Fremdwelt*, or *fremder Körper. Fremdheit* does not limit itself thus to a foreign language, or even to a foreigner or a foreign land. In the background lie German words such as *Entfremdung* or *Verfremdung*, or a child's *Fremdeln*. In a few passages, when following the leads of Husserl and Heidegger in fact, Ricoeur does use *étranger* and *étrang(èr)eté*, but only in order to distinguish the '*alterité de l'étranger*' from both other forms of alterity (cf. pp. 369, 374, 378, 402, 408) and thus without attributing great importance to the concept generally. The far more common use of the corresponding word group in German results in something quite different, since the concept *fremd* exhibits several diverse nuances of meaning. As *fremd* we denote first what happens outside of our own domain (*externum, peregrinum, étranger*, stranger), second what belongs to another (*alienum*, alien), and third what is heterogeneous, such as the exotic, the unusual and the extraordinary (*insolitum, mirum, étrange, hétérogène* and so on). Thus the categories of place, possession and manner bestow on the *fremd* its diverse meanings.

Obviously we can investigate in the usual way in what the distinction between difference and foreignness consists, in order to find *what* the foreign is. But even in posing such a question, we enmesh ourselves more deeply in the realm of the same and the other, within which the foreign defines itself as an other and, as an other of a same, also as a same. The gap between difference and foreignness thus begins to disappear. If something is identified as identically the same, then the identity of identity and non-identity are at the threshold of acquiring the form of a comprehensive and distinctive identity. If we want to show that foreignness is more than a simple difference within a process and a system of determination, then the formulation of the question must change, somewhat in the sense evoked by Wittgenstein's famous situation: I don't know my way around. In such a situation, neither a simple description of facts nor a determination of essence helps at all.

The crucial importance of this formulation of the question emerges if we re-examine three previously mentioned aspects of the foreign. The first is the locational aspect that refers to a process of *establishing limits*. Since this entails that an external region stands apart from an inner region, the question of proper access arises. In this process two methods of establishing limits must be distinguished.[5] On the one hand, we have the possibility of *demarcation* which refers to the point of view of a third that distinguishes *a* from *b* and can just as well distinguish *b* from *a*. The comparison '*a* is (not) as *b*' is reversible in principle. The identification presupposes a comparability which in turn presupposes a point of view from which the comparison is made as well as a scale of the comparison *c*. From this perspective, whether it is a matter of an image, a concept, or a principle, there is always an 'equalization of the unequal';[6] a homogenization and homologization take place. The first, or last, viewpoint would be that which distinguishes itself from no other viewpoint, it would not distinguish itself from anything except the shadows of the pure nothing, the irrational, or evil. On the other hand, a double process of *inclusion* and *exclusion* distinguishes itself from simple demarcation. Here *a* detaches itself from *b* in such a way that what detaches itself from the other owes its origin and its continued existence to the processes of detachment itself. There is nothing that precedes the inclusion and exclusion. The inner realm is separated from the outer realm by a threshold, such as is present in cases of waking and sleeping, health and illness, youth and old age, man and woman. The foreign is not only distinct from ownness, but cut off from it.[7] To traverse the threshold would mean that one would at least momentarily become an other, as in the case of falling asleep.

The second aspect of the foreign signifies that the place that includes me and excludes the other is appropriated at the same moment. It is occupied as *my* point of view, my residence, my habits. The unity of these forms of possession is one's own body as anchorage in the world. Just as in the double process of inclusion and exclusion, here *possession* and *dispossession* are two sides of a single process. In this way the acquisition of a mother tongue is accompanied by the emergence of various foreign languages that become foreign to me inasmuch as they are languages.

The third aspect concerns forms of experience, forms of life and the order of things. What is foreign to us, as inaccessible and belonging to others, is not limited to factical contents of experience that still belong to one's own order, such as unfamiliar expressions of one's own language or of the unknown person in the street. Foreignness rather encroaches upon what finds itself outside of a determinate order, such as the words and grammatical forms of a foreign language. The *everyday foreign* that belongs to the realm of the orderly and normal must therefore be distinguished from the *structurally foreign* in the sense of the extra-ordinary. In this sense it is the formation of the peculiar (*Eigenartigen*) that goes hand in hand with the formation of the heterogeneous (*Fremdartigen*). Using a contemporary expression, we can speak of a simultaneous process of *normalization* and *anomalization*. The *radically foreign*, on the other hand, would be that which eluded every order and broke all standards. If a comprehensive or fundamental order were to stand behind the factical order, every heterogeneity would be relativized to a final affinity that would bridge the gap between homogeneity and heterogeneity. But this would mean that the foreign would be transformed back into alterity and the separation between ownness and the foreign would be only temporary. The borderline between ownness and foreignness would be designated as 'pre-liminary' but not as 'liminary' in the proper sense of the word.

In this context it is essential that the strange and the heterogeneous presuppose a certain *topology* that prevents the questions *what?* and *who?* from being detached from the question *where?* as the locus of the questioning itself. Following Husserl, who defined the experience of the foreign – with a rarely reached radicality – as 'verifiable access to what is originally inaccessible' (Hua, Vol. I, p. 144), we can thus consider inaccessibility a key characteristic of the foreign. As essentially inaccessible, the foreign differs radically from what is still not, or is no longer, familiar or understandable, even though a way of familiarizing or comprehension remains possible in principle. Absence, distance, separation, and withdrawal, which constitute the foreign itself, are not attributable to a simple lack or deficit. In this way the foreign resembles the depth of the past or the shades of perception, except that it definitively exceeds the realm of one's possibilities. But then the foreign would no longer be derivable from a unilateral alienation (*Entfremdung*) of ownness, as Husserl tried to do (Hua, Vol. VI, p. 189). Ownness and foreignness come from a 'primary division' (*Urscheidung*), as Husserl himself maintains elsewhere (Hua, Vol. VI, p. 260), which is a division that resists all unification. But it must be emphasized that if ownness is understood as accessibility and foreignness as inaccessibility, then the foreignness extends not only to the foreignness *of the other* but also to the strangeness *of myself*. Self-appropriation already presupposes self-alienation, a distance of the self from itself, and a non-coincidence.[8] At this point we meet up with Ricoeur. Taking up in his tenth study the familiar work of the phenomenology of the body, he establishes the division between one's flesh (*chair*) and body (*corps*) as the primordial form of alterity and designates this, citing Didier Franck, as my own alterity (*altérité propre*) (p. 375).[9]

Now the question arises as to how one can deal with the foreign without taking away its foreignness and silencing its claims. A xenology, which would establish itself as the standard science of the foreign, would stand before the paradox that the more it would make progress into the definition, understanding and explanation of its object, the more it would undermine it. The foreign, thus understood and explained, would cease to exist.[10] The sublimating forms of appropriation and surpassing of the foreign consist in reducing the foreign to ownness or in subordinating both ownness and the foreign to a universal. In this way egocentric and logocentric perspectives form no unconditioned opposition. If ownness is treated *as the foreign* and the foreign treated *as ownness*, ownness raises itself to the universal such that the difference between ownness and foreignness weakens and tends to abolish itself. If I myself and the other strive for the same goal or if we subordinate ourselves to the same norm, then the difference between ownness and foreignness balances out. The foreign survives as relatively foreign, as a particular variant within a teleological or normative order; it loses its definitive character. If the contextuality of the goals and the circumstances of the action bind themselves with the universality of unconditional norms, as Ricoeur suggests (pp. 329–36), the foreign is reduced either to a part of a whole or an instance of a rule, or to both at once. The other in the sense of the foreign would approximate the other in the sense of the diverse, not because the self would be reduced to a something or a someone to be identified, but because one's own self and one's alien self would be reunited through common goals and universal norms – despite all tragic conflicts for which Ricoeur takes pains to account. To bridge the distance between ownness and the foreign, Ricoeur, like Kant, always has a third term at hand which he calls similarity (p. 226), recognition (p. 344), or something similar. Even if this third term does not reach the level of an intermediate moment, as in the case of Hegel's ethical (p. 279), he still promises what Kant calls a 'disguised unity' (KrV B 679). Foreignness receives only the next to last word.

III Reciprocity between ownness and the foreign

Reciprocity forms the point of reversal from ownness to the universal.[11] Initially separate, the viewpoints of ownness and the foreign merge with each other in a process that one can denote with a contemporary term such as 'solidaritizing'. They lead to the characterization of 'one another' (*Einander/allelous*). Ricoeur derives the paradigm of this solidaritizing from Aristotle's teaching on friendship and justice. I seek for that which is good for me and leads to a good life – a seeking that reflexively finds expression in self-esteem. As a result of the striving towards that which is good *for me*, I become saved by a need for friends who help me with the attainment of my own good. In this way the good for me enlarges into a good *for us*, and one's own striving takes on the form of concern for the other[12] that transforms self-esteem into esteem for the other (*Fremdschätzung*). Using an interlocutionary model, Ricoeur demonstrates that this reciprocity contains three elements: reversibility, irreplaceability and similarity. The *roles* of addressant and addressed, which express themselves with the pronouns 'I' and 'you', are reversible: the *persons* that play the respective roles are irreplaceable. Similarity results from our reciprocal *exchange* between self-esteem and concern for the other (*Fremdfür-sorge*). The similar is not an effect of an external comparison, which views its own interests on the same level as those of the other; we assimilate to one another inasmuch as we participate with one another. Adopting the Platonic *homoiosis to theo*, we could speak of a *homoiosis allelois* that has as its common goal the approximation to the good *in itself and for all* (cf. p. 214). The reversal of ownness and the foreign thus completes itself in the way in which one both appreciates the other *as oneself* and, by means of this appreciation, conceives oneself *as an other among others*. From this a double movement results, which is subsequently designated as a 'crossover dialectic between oneself and the other than oneself' (*dialectique croisée de soi-même et de l'autre que soi*, p. 393). 'The appreciation of *the other as oneself* and the appreciation *of oneself as an other*' are fundamentally equivalent (p. 226). As in the case of the golden rule that – above all other values – obliges one to love one's neighbor *as oneself* (p. 255), the transition from ownness to the foreign also takes place at the level of norms as the transition from self-respect to respect for the other and for the law. Reciprocal concern and love transform themselves into justice, as long as this means not that one regards the other as oneself but that the interests of one's own and of the other are directed to the viewpoint of a third. From this viewpoint it matters not whether I view the other as myself or the other views me as him- or herself. From the viewpoint of justice, the reciprocity of two view-points converts them into two sides of one and the same thing. In the framework of the 'one another' of justice, each is just as much the one as the other. The judge, who judges without consideration of the person, knows only third persons; the first person remains reserved for the voice of the law itself. If the viewpoint of the third does not become fixed, but is imbedded in the 'dialectic' of selfhood and otherness, a threefold process of recognition emerges.

> The recognition is a structure of the self that reflects over the movement with which the self esteem is carried over to concern for others and this to justice. Recognition introduces the dyad and plurality into the constitution of the self. The mutuality in friendship and the equal proportionality in justice reflect themselves in the consciousness of myself, transforming the appreciation of myself itself into a form of recognition. (p. 344)

In the light of a reciprocity that produces a commonality in which aspirations both my own and foreign to me are interchanged, and in light of a justice that protects a commonality that distributes rights and duties among the members of an institution, every form of unilaterality and inequality appears in one of three ways: as preliminary, as in unavoidable stages in rational and moral development; as temporary, as in extreme cases of necessity and suffering; or as reprehensible, as in cases where it is imposed on individuals or determinant groups as immutable.[13] Thus human relationships, inasmuch as they concern the human person as such, are oriented to symmetrical relations. This implies that the border between ownness and the foreign becomes increasingly permeable in the course of understanding and socializ-ation.[14] The realm of the tragic, to which Ricoeur attaches an extraordinary importance in his ninth study, appears under this reflection as an insuperable *remnant of foreignness* that depends on the factical unilaterality of character and of moral principle (p. 290). In the end there remains only a foreignness de facto, not de jure.

IV Alterity, foreignness and passivity

We can wonder whether this ethical-tragic vision does justice to the radical foreignness of the other or whether unilaterality and inequality are the key components of the foreign. We can further define this question by focusing on the phenomenon of passivity, where Ricoeur situates the central locus of the phenomenological experience-form of alterity. It plays a central role in his debate with Lévinas.[15]

Following Aristotle, Ricoeur conceives action and passion, acting and suffering, agent and patient, as forms of *polarity and correlation*. In the relationship of myself to the other this means that the one does what the other suffers, and conversely that the one suffers what the other does. Acting and suffering are interconnected. Reciprocity entails that the role of agent and patient are in principle reversible: 'every agent is the recipient patient of the other' (p. 382). In the intersubjective realm acting and suffering take on the forms of giving and receiving; acting (*Tun*) turns into affecting (*Antun*) and suffering turns into receiving in such a way that acting and suffering are very close to giving and receiving in a dialogic interchange.

The polarity does not exclude the possibility that initiative, in the sense of a being able to do (p. 212), is unilaterally distributed. Ricoeur considers two extreme cases in much detail: the command that enjoins me and designates me as its recipient,[16] and the suffering of the other that appeals to my initiative, my compassion and my help, thus enabling me to become a benefactor. The unilaterality finds its limit inasmuch as there falls to the recipient of the command at least a minimal initiative in its reception of the directive, by determining the spirit of the command (for example, the spirit of a teacher's commands differ from those of an executioner) and by recognizing the authority of the one who commands. Inversely, the sufferer teaches the benefactor a lesson inasmuch as he demands from him – as in tragedy – the confession of his own frailness and mortality. The quest for equality thus maintains itself through all circumstances of inequality, whether the initiative comes more from the self or from the other. Friendship, where we associate with one another on the same terms, thus appears as 'means' (p. 225) between extremes. It is true that Ricoeur does not limit passivity and passion to the simple incurring (*pâtir*) of something, but brings them to the abyss of a suffering (*souffrir*), in which the suffering of myself, grasped as the 'intimate passivity' of my own body, binds with the suffering of the other. Nevertheless, even violent victimization still represents a 'reverse of passivity that plunges the glory of action into mourning' (p. 371).

Since this profound passivity is begun through one's own initiative and is counterbalanced to a certain degree, the title *Soi-même comme un autre* expresses the fundamental orientation of this work in a way that neither the title *Le même et l'autre* of Vincent Descombes's work nor the title *Moi et l'autre* would. The self does not oppose the other, but passes into the other, since it cannot be thought without the other (p. 14). The self passes into the other as 'subject of discourse, of action, of narrative, and of ethical engagement' (p. 387), drawn from the 'resources of goodness' and guided by a 'benevolent spontaneity' (*spontanéité bienveillante*) (p. 222). The principal reproach against Lévinas is thus that he abruptly opposes the 'otherness of the other' to the 'identity of the self' such that he blocks the pathway from the ego (*Ich*) to the self, enclosing the ego in an ontological totality and separating it from the other, who thus becomes exiled in an absolute exteriority. For Lévinas it follows that the initiative of the ego is replaced by the initiative of the other, and the original nominative of the formulation '*I* am' is replaced by an accusative 'it's *me*' (*me voici*). Ricoeur avoids this impasse, as the whole work attests, by his 'different philosophy of the same' (p. 391), different from the philosophy that Lévinas would view as an ontology of totality. This different philosophy would be his proposed philosophy of the self. What in Lévinas would have to be repudiated by a direct reading as a descriptive misrepresentation of the phenomena, Ricoeur preserves by a 'hyperbolic' reading. This reading confirms that Lévinas, through a systematic *exceeding* (*excès*) evidenced by his deliberate overemphasis of both the otherness of the other and the identity of the ego, produces the effect of rupture through which an egological 'philosophy of the same' inevitably has to pass. As Lévinas himself says, 'in separation the ego ignores the other' (Ricoeur, p. 389).

This interpretation of Lévinas raises many questions. I shall limit myself to a few remarks that will bring us back to the problem of otherness and foreignness.

(1) From a methodological point of view, one could ask in a general fashion whether Lévinas simply reverses the position of the ego into the 'ex-position' for the other, so that the initiative is displaced simply from within Being to a region beyond Being. It must be acknowledged that Lévinas repeatedly speaks, albeit not without some hesitation, of an inversion, particularly of an inversion of intentionality.[17] Nevertheless, he also uses other formulations, speaking of a 'reverse side without a front' (*envers sans endroit*) and of how this inversion includes a turning-away towards the other (*envers l'autre*).[18] We are far away from a simple inversion that replaces one member of a relation by another. The inversion is guided by a *reversal of the relations* that does not merely displace old weight but posits new.

(2) We come nearer to the heart of the matter if we ask ourselves whether one can conceive of a passivity that in no way forms the polar opposition to activity. Such a passivity would be situated in the very core of activity, and in a certain sense would be coextensive with it.[19] Lévinas's search for an *originary passivity*, which precedes the difference between action and passion, must be taken seriously. Moreover, Ricoeur himself confirms that 'the flesh ontologically precedes the difference between the voluntary and the involuntary' (p. 375).

(3) A particularly incisive example of this problem is found in the phenomenon of *responding*. Indeed we must distinguish between the answer which we give or do not give and the giving of the answer itself: the response. The response is a speech-event that is never absorbed by what is actually said. We begin with a situation in which an other addresses me, with or without words, such that a demand or request arises to which I cannot but respond. *How* I should answer, or what I give as an answer, depends on me; *whether* I answer does not depend on me. Not to respond is to respond. Watzlawick's 'We cannot not communicate' could be reformulated as 'I cannot not respond'. One's own initiative emerges from an other's demand or request, thus it is in a certain way *not* my initiative. The response is an *event* comparable to the comprehension of something which strikes me (*einfällt*) or I come upon (*auffällt*): a thought comes 'when "it" wants, not when "I" want'.[20]

Not only does the identification of the speaker and the doer of something come after the fact, but the attribution of words and actions to someone does as well. It already presupposes an event of responding that is neither an act that I accomplish nor an act that happens to me.

Just as consciousness has its blind spot, so freedom has its weak point. Once again it is helpful to distinguish between alterity as diversity and alterity as foreignness. The response which I give is comparable with the latter, resembling it more or less. But, on the other hand, the event of responding meets up with a demand or request that, being neither similar nor dissimilar, is foreign to it since that about which and that to whom we respond both elude our grasp. No conjunction can bridge the gap between demand and response.[21]

(4) The linguistic formula '*me voici*' is not limited to a grammatically accented accusative because it is *I* who speak: '*me* voici'. In the nominative the ego co-appears, but either as 'subject of the enunciation' and not 'subject of the enunciated', or as an 'operant' ego and not a thematized ego, as Husserl would say. The ego appears *as respondent*, thus as in a certain obliquity. Anyone who answers without simply giving a pre-existent response thus plays not only a role in saying 'I'; in a certain way she *is* her role. The symmetry we meet on the level of comparison is preceded by an asymmetry that is situated beyond every comparison. Since this asymmetry occurs in the plural, every 'seeking for equality' effectively gets entangled in an inequality that originates from a profound incomparability.

(5) There is a phrase in this work of Ricoeur's that particularly amazed me. In reference to Lévinas's 'ontology of totality', Ricoeur writes that his own investigation neither assumed nor even was prompted by it (p. 387). This can explain the fact that, by jumping over Hobbes and steering wide of Foucault as Gadamer does, Ricoeur decisively returns to Aristotle, trusting his 'benevolent spontaneity'.[22] This explains how foreignness – as in both classical Greek and modern thought – belongs as a relative foreignness not to a first but to a second philosophy. The radically foreign is conceivable only as an 'elsewhere', as an *extra-ordinary*.[23] Where a sole order stands on the horizon, and even if it is still indeterminate and concealed, in the final analysis the 'universal' prevails. But if every order is limited, selectively as well as exclusively,[24] so every socialization that promises reconciliation between ownness and the foreign appears as a sublime act of violence that does injustice to the foreign. What is *foreign to me* is not only *other than me*, but evades me in making demands on me.

Ruhr-Universität Bochum, Germany
[Translated by James Swindal]

Notes

1 Paul Ricoeur, *Soi-même comme un autre* (Paris: Editions du Seuil, 1990), cited with page numbers only.

2 Concerning the question of the subject, which accompanies all of the works of Ricoeur, see the lengthy monograph by D. Jervolino, *Il cogito e l'ermeneutica: La questione del soggetto in Ricoeur*, 2nd edn (Genova: Marietti, 1993).

3 See Husserl, *Husserliana* (The Hague: Martinus Nijhoff, 1950), Vol. I, p. 128; hereafter cited as Hua. For a similar treatment see Merleau-Ponty, 'Le philosophe et son ombre', *Signes* (Paris 1960): 210. This same theme is also taken up by Merleau-Ponty in *Le visible et l'invisible* (Paris: Gallimard, 1964).

4 See Ricoeur, *Soi-même*, pp. 221–5, 382–93. The supposed opposition between Husserl's 'gnoseology of meaning' and Lévinas's 'ethic of command' is not pertinent, since in a certain way it weakens the two positions. While for Husserl the common event of meaning implicitly aims towards a goal of ethical self-responsibility, for Lévinas ethics itself becomes first philosophy with the consequence that the bestowal of meaning through consciousness transforms itself into an originary gift for the other.

5 See Bernhard Waldenfels, *Der Stachel des Fremden* (Frankfurt: Suhrkamp, 1990), Ch. 2.

6 *Wahrheit und Lüge im außermoralischen Sinne*, KSA, Vol. I, p. 880 (Berlin: de Gruyter, 1967).

7 If here we want to speak with Lévinas of a certain 'separation', we would need to distinguish between the constitution and the fixing of ownness in the way that Rousseau, for example, distinguished between *amour de soi* and *amour propre*. Here Ricoeur's critique touches a precarious aspect of Lévinas's theory (cf. p. 389).

8 See Merleau-Ponty, *Le visible et l'invisible*, pp. 162 ff.

9 It seems unfair to me to accuse Husserl of conceiving of the other only as an alter ego and not also of the self as an other (p. 377), given the alteration and multiplication of the self through time in these explicit forms. See my 'Erfahrung des Fremden in Husserls Phänomenologie', in *Profile der Phänomenologie* (Phänomenologische Forschungen 22) (Freiburg and Munich: Alber, 1989; [English translation published as 'Experience of the Alien in Husserl's Phenomenology', *Research in Phenomenology* 20 (1990): 19–33].

10 See my 'Eigenkultur und Fremdkultur: Das Paradox einer Wissenschaft vom Fremden', in *Studia Culturologica* 3 (1994): 7–26; [Italian translation published in *Paradigmi: Dialogo interculturale e Eurocentrismo* 30 (1992): 643–63].

11 In French the formalized expression *réciprocité* bears similarity to the expression *mutualité* which has a strong social connotation. See pp. 225 ff.

12 We can ask whether Heidegger's care, which takes the double meaning of a 'für den Anderen einspringenden' and 'seinen Möglichkeiten vorausspringenden Fürsorge' (*Sein und Zeit*, §26) can truly be integrated into an Aristotelian framework. But I shall leave this intertextual question aside.

13 Aristotle concluded by excluding the relationship between master and slave from the domain of friendship. The supposed coincidence between misery and suffering says nothing about their frequency and does not exclude an essential vulnerability (see Ricoeur, pp. 223–225), it only excludes the possibility that someone could be a sufferer by nature.

14 This is true also for Gadamer's hermeneutical method that starts from the experience of the foreign, and yet aims 'die Fremdheit aufzuheben and Aneignung zu ermöglichen'; see *Wahrheit und Methode*, 2nd edn (Tübingen: Mohr [Siebeck], 1965), pp. 508, 365, 368.

15 See also Ricoeur *Soi-même*, pp. 221–6, 382–93.

16 According to Husserl, receptivity in its orientation-towards and turning-away-from is the lowest form of spontaneity.

17 For example, see his *Autrement qu'être ou au-delà de l'essence* (The Hague: Martinus Nijhoff, 1978), pp. 60 ff.

18 ibid., p. 63.

19 Husserl already spoke of a 'passivity in activity' in his *Erfahrung und Urteil* (Hamburg: Meiner, 1948), p. 119, yet it remains an open question whether and to what extent passivity retains, following Aristotle, its importance as a limitation of activity inasmuch as it is thought as its opposite, and to what extent it holds its own weight as, for example, in Husserl's theory of time.

20 Nietzsche, *Beyond Good and Evil*, §17, KSA, Vol. V, pp. 30 ff.

21 See Blanchot, *Entretien infini* (Paris: Gallimard, 1969), pp. 106 ff: 'L'interruption'.

22 For more on the critical distance Lévinas takes vis-a-vis a 'natural benevolence', see his *Autrement qu'être*, pp. 142, 160.

23 Relevant here is the semantic affinity between the French adjectives *étrange* and *étranger* and the English adjectives 'strange' and 'stranger'; foreign manner and foreign place meet.

24 For a further treatment of this problem, see my *Ordnung im Zwielicht* (Frankfurt am Main: Suhrkamp, 1987).

Edi Pucci

History and the question of identity: Kant, Arendt, Ricoeur

The unmasking of the illusions lying at the core of philosophies of history challenges contemporary thought to respond to the questions concerning historical judgement, and the identity we can appropriate within the finite condition of human existence. Since in Paul Ricoeur's ontology of finitude the question of personal identity cannot be detached from the historical present and past, I will try to link the question of identity with that of history. To be a self, a finite cogito, and to grasp one's own way of being in time are inseparable tasks. Becoming aware of oneself occurs within the reappropriation of the past, while the future discloses new possibilities. Such interplay between past and future takes place at the level of individuals and of communities.

I will therefore develop three themes – history, judgement and identity – on the basis of some suggestions offered by Paul Ricoeur on the problem of personal identity in *Oneself as Another*[1] and in a seminar he gave in Naples in May 1993 on Kant's *Critique of Judgement*.[2] As the seminar deals with Arendt's interpretation of Kant, I will frequently refer to her work as well. I do not intend to summarize Ricoeur's arguments in full, but rather to offer a tentative treatment of the themes in order to indicate avenues of thinking which could be explored later.

I The problem of historical narrative and judgement

Hegel's speculative construction of history, in which everything is prefigured, proves untenable on account of its contradictions and its metaphysical justification of whatever violent path history takes. According to Ricoeur, Hegel's fundamental error, which makes his philosophy of history *passé*, lies in a blurring of the distinction between past and present. Ricoeur recalls that the historical past remains alive and preserves itself only in traces. The 'trace', Ricoeur writes, 'signified without making something appear. With Hegel, this restriction is abolished. To persist in the present, for the past, is to remain. And to remain is to have repose in the eternal present of speculative thought'.[3]

Since the past proves inaccessible to speculative intuition, we can hope to reconstruct it only through traces and documents. What is the true place of the historical past? Does it consist in the irreducibility to the present of an historical consciousness, in its reactualization of what has been? Or is the past an enigma which marks an insurmountable boundary to our comprehension? This question rephrases, in the larger context of our common life-world, what we face in our everyday existence as singular persons, namely, the question of our identity: *who are we?* Are we a singularity with a unique personal destiny and, as such, irreplaceable and meaningful; or, are we a recollection of scattered and heterogeneous fragments of life, incapable of sustaining self-constancy? The theory of narrative already shapes the problem of personal identity as Ricoeur pursues it, making the search for the narrative dimension of history a search for the sense of identity. For Ricoeur, recalling Arendt's work, 'the story told tells about the action. of the "who". And the identity of this "who" therefore itself must be a narrative identity.'[4]

Ricoeur considers narrating to be irreducible to self-knowledge, for it is a reproposing of life-experience in which we find ourselves exposed to an original passivity. Any action presupposes suffering and the state of subjection; this is what it means to be involved in situations in which events do not depend upon our will. Ricoeur acknowledges the instability of narrative identity. Narrative identity can be made and then unmade, since it is possible to weave different plots through the same personage, even if these plots oppose one another. If we grant this, narrative identity cannot say the last word on the identity of the subject, neither as a particular individuality, nor as part of a community of individuals. Furthermore, this approach to identity still permits the easy speculative binding of the present to the past, a binding always taking the form of a narrative.

Is there, within the dimension of narrative itself, an approach which defers to the fragmentary and particular and avoids the violence of unifying identification? It would be fruitful at this juncture to introduce an interpretive opposition offered in the work of Jacques Taminiaux.[5] This is the opposition between speculation and judgement. As an example of these two opposite approaches, we could cite Hegel as a speculative thinker and Kant as a philosopher of judgement. The mirror-like circularity of Hegelian thought would be opposed to Kant's emphasis, in the *Critique of Judgement*,[6] upon the exemplary particular, the judgement of which refers to the idea of an agreement among persons who are both alike and different. One can easily see that the narrative sense of the historical past admits of these two approaches. Hegel offered us a speculative narrative. Here I would like to examine the writings of Kant in order to explore the possibility of a narrative sense of history which would start from the particular and the fragmentary in order to understand history in the light of the problem of identity, which appears, as Ricoeur himself finally admits, as a task and therefore an Idea in the Kantian sense.

The problem of historical judgement begins to be framed by Kant in his writings on the philosophy of history, in essays such as 'Idea for a Universal History with a Cosmopolitan Intent'[7] and 'Perpetual Peace'.[8] In his Naples seminar, Ricoeur examines the possibility of extending Kant's conception of reflective judgement to the problem of narrative and history. Along the way, he often appeals to Hannah Arendt's interpretation of the *Critique of Judgement* in her book *Lectures on Kant's Political Philosophy*.[9] I would like to pursue the theme of judgement along the lines Ricoeur delineates, and I will refer directly to Kant's own writings as well as Arendt's analysis in order to develop my discussion.

II Arendt's reading of Kant's political and historical judgement

In the Naples seminar Ricoeur takes up Arendt's attempt to interpret Kant's political writings in the light of reflective judgement in order to suggest the idea that fragmentary histories may receive intelligibility from this kind of judgement.

Arendt attempts to apply political judgement to exemplary events of history and to provide a model for political judgement by invoking the judgement of taste. By appealing to the exemplary validity carried within the judgement of taste, she tries to prevent a relapse into teleological judgement. Favouring the exemplariness of the judgement of taste, Arendt excludes Kant's second way of grounding judgement, i.e. in the purposiveness of nature. For to appeal to purposiveness would reintroduce a hidden teleology which Arendt believes would seriously risk a rebirth of a speculative philosophy of history. Arendt also excludes the possibility of replacing Kant's unwritten political philosophy with a philosophy of history. Since history is part of nature, the historical subject is understood by Kant as the human species where creation accomplishes its highest point. While perceiving the melancholy arising from the causality and contingency of history, Kant shapes the idea of a 'universal history' as the secret plan of nature which makes possible the progress of the species. Since the life of the individual is too short to allow the accomplishment of all human possibilities, nature by exploiting humans initiates history along its course, whether it be called 'progress', 'culture', or 'freedom'. The notion of progress appears to Arendt to be extremely problematic. Historical progress, whether its outcome is culture or freedom, always implies a denial of human dignity. For Arendt, Kant himself did not escape 'this contradiction: infinite Progress is the law of the human species; at the same time man's dignity demands that he be seen (every single one of us) in his particularity, and, as such, be seen – but without any comparison and independent of time – as reflecting mankind in general'.[10] If the notion of progress becomes the teleological idea guiding the course of history, we are left once again with the Hegelian statement that *die Weltgeschichte ist das Weltgericht*. But there is more involved in the idea of progress: were progress the criterion of history, then history as narrative plot would never reach an end. For, as Arendt notes, there is no point where we could pause and look back, with the 'backward glance' of the historian.[11] Arendt rejects the view that progress, whether it belongs to nature or to a metaphysical force, may be transformed into an effective reality. For the notion of progress is still tied up with that of success, which places a judging criterion of history within history itself. Arendt questions a teleological judgement of history and therefore expects any historical judgement to be external to history.

Unlike any philosophy of history, Kantian political philosophy is, according to Arendt, free from teleological judgement. Thus, political thought is not part of the philosophy of nature present in the 'Critique of Teleological Judgement'. To verify this detachment let us look at Kant's comments on past history. These observations proceed retrospectively, making the global finality of history problematic. Arendt's own distrust of every philosophy of history appears in her preference for the notion of exemplariness as the key to the reflective judgement concerning the particular for which a universal is sought. She therefore turns to the 'Critique of Aesthetic Judgement', in which Kant develops a theory of the exemplary and the particular, which does not insist upon a subordination to some purpose, even if it be human dignity itself. According to Arendt, two fundamental questions left open in Kant's philosophy are taken up again in the *Critique of Judgement*. The first concerns the peculiar sociability of humanity. To be among others is the sign of being human. Kant recognizes this necessity as peculiar to the life of thinking beings. Arendt considers the reciprocity of humans, the need to be in society, as a key to the first part of the *Critique of Judgement*. The second question is raised in §67 of the third *Critique*, the question of the necessity of the existence of human beings. Arendt sees the second part of the third *Critique* as answering this question. We ask about the purpose of nature simply because we are teleological beings and in our purposive orientation we belong in our intentionality to nature.

Clearly, our problem is the following: can we make a judgement upon history without recourse to teleology? Cannot the notion of a communicability of thought, the public aspect of thought, be linked to that of history? While Kant introduces a criterion for judging the morality of political actions, Arendt separates the judgement of the spectator from that of the actor. Our question, concerning the judgement of the historian, clearly requires an account of the judgement of the spectator. What could be the criterion for the spectator's and therefore the historian's judgement? Here, Arendt appeals to §40 of the 'Critique of Aesthetic Judgement' where Kant introduces the idea of a *sensus communis*, which he defines as 'the idea of a sense common to all, i.e., of a faculty of judgement which, in its reflection, takes into account (a priori) . . . the mode of representation of all other humans in thought, in order as it were to compare its judgment with the collective reason of humanity'.[12] Impartiality is reached by taking into account the point of view of others. The power of the mind which enables us to broaden our thinking through a comparison with the idea of a *sensus communis* is the imagination. Imaginative broadening of one's perspective is the key to world-citizenship, according to Kant. Here, Arendt leaves aside the perspective Kant put forward in 'Speculative Beginning of Human History',[13] where sociability is seen as the final destination of humanity, and turns instead to that contained in the 'Critique of Aesthetic Judgement', where sociability is the authentic essence of the human, an origin and not an end. This is a radical turn, which is indeed relevant to the problem of personal and community identity. For membership in a worldly community would then be grounded simply on the very fact of being human. Citizenship ceases to be a given reality to become a regulative idea, a state that must be constructed rather than taken as an existing fact. Would this not entail an abandoning of the old concepts of nationality, race, nativism, in favour of a sense of identity, which is never pure, original, or fully developed, but rather an ongoing process, one towards which humanity is simply oriented? While criteria such as race, nation, roots recede to less significant levels, other aspects and values emerging from the human search for consensus would come to the foreground. To this question – which Arendt never states explicitly but which we may infer from her arguments – I will return later, after examining Ricoeur's reading of the problem of historical judgement.

III Ricoeur's reading of Kant and Arendt concerning historical judgement

In his Naples seminar, Ricoeur draws attention to two approaches: the attempt to arrive at a conception of political judgement from the *Conjectural Beginning of Human History*, and the attempt to interpret political judgement in the light of the theory of aesthetic judgement in the third *Critique*. In the wake of Arendt, Ricoeur likens political judgement to the judgement of taste, suggesting the presence of an unwritten political philosophy in Kant's work. First of all, Ricoeur finds in the peculiar *communicability* of the judgement of taste a parallel with the vision of a *plurality* of humans living together in similarity and difference. Second, he agrees with Arendt's insights concerning the *particularity* that the judgement of taste preserves. Third, the primacy of the spectator over the agent of history reminds him of the *tension* between taste and genius.

For Ricoeur, to ground political judgement upon the exemplariness of the particular, together with an ideal of human communicability, is a remarkable philosophical project, yet one which requires the addition of a moral thematic. Ricoeur considers Arendt's attempt as flawed by an excessive aestheticization of human affairs: 'the Kantian citizen of the world is actually a *Weltbetrachter*, a spectator of the world.'[14] What is left, Ricoeur asks, of the morally judging and active citizen invoked in 'Perpetual Peace'? According to Ricoeur, before us lies the task of developing Kant's unwritten political philosophy in its double relation with the *Metaphysics of Morals*[15] and with the *Critique of Judgement*.

For Ricoeur, the reflective, that is, the regulative, status of Kant's essays on history would protect his embryonic philosophy of history from the risk of being absorbed by Hegel's explicitly speculative philosophy of history. However, Ricoeur seems to favour an agreement between the works of nature which he takes as regulative, i.e. he favours indirectly the social aspect of human beings and more explicitly the political dimension of the communicability of aesthetic judgement. Ricoeur writes: 'It is above all the extraordinary notion of unsocial sociability which is equal to a cunning of nature and extorts from humanity the task of establishing a well-ordered society. This notion should be placed close to that of the communicability of aesthetic judgement, although it does not depend on its sphere of competence. . . . Furthermore, the problem which a parsimonious nature set cannot be solved only within the frame of the civil constitution of the State, but on the level of international re- lations. . . .'[16] Ricoeur thus sees a bridge drawn towards 'Perpetual Peace': only a citizen of the world can solve the problem left open by nature. Whereas Ricoeur sees a complementarity among political, aesthetical and ethical discourses, Arendt is extremely concerned to keep the political and aesthetic separated from the ethical. Ricoeur suggests that we consider Kant's ideas as rules guiding the relationship between nature and history, i.e. the progress of the human species in history. By emphasizing the search for the rule, under which to subsume historical fact, Ricoeur privileges the critical aspect of Kant's philosophy of history rather than the speculative aspect. He thus attempts to rescue the teleology arising from the finality of nature by reinscribing it into a regulative dimension.

IV The idea of fragmentary history

With respect to the preservation of local histories, several relevant points emerge. The historian is a spectator with a particular point of view, a perspective which, insofar as the historian tries to understand foreign times or places, proves limiting in its particularity. The limitations of the historian's perspective are, in the worst case, sanctified as universal and orientational. Thus, Hegel viewed Asian cultures as preludes to European civilization. Overcoming this vio- lently teleological construction of historical narrative requires a broadening of perspective through which the historian does not arrogate to himself or herself automatic universal status, but recog- nizes his or her particularity and need for imaginative enlargement of perspective. The comparison of one's own perspective with that of humanity in general, together with a recognition of the particularity and situatedness of every point of view, is a non-teleological reflective judgement, similar in structure to the judgement of taste as Kant explains it. There is no point of view which is superior to others, none without a possible debate concerning its legitimacy. However, in fragmentary histories, this point seems more problematic, for histories of different peoples seem to demand such a great difference in perspective as to be incommunicable. Perhaps in this circumstance the criterion of impartiality which takes into account the other point of view is a relevant criterion. This is what Kant means by enlargement of thinking which he defines as 'comparing our judgements with others, and . . . putting ourselves in the place of any other man, by abstracting from the limitations which contingently attach to our own judgement'.[17]

Yet, many questions remain. First of all, how can the spectator of the fragmentary narrative be as disinterested as the act of judgement requires? Does not such an act already involve the violence of discrimination and the subsumption of the universal spectator? In order to reach a detached position, is one not compelled to lose one's own perspective, one's own particular history and identity? How can we avoid a totalizing vision of history without falling into moral relativism, finally reducing judgement to the estimate of the validity of historical action on the basis of cultural tastes or personal emotional tendencies, criteria lacking any objective validity? Ricoeur accords to the maintenance of historical memory in narratives the moral dimension of historical judgement. The delicate task of dealing with the moral concern of historical judgement is assigned to the art of narrating. Were there no narrative of human actions, there would be no cultural transmission of what merits remembrance to subsequent generations. We should remember here our earlier reservation that a narrative approach to history may go hand in hand with totalizing speculation.

What kind of history emerges in the light of the above reflections? History as fragmentary resists the temptation to metaphysical unity and import. A limit to the fragmentary arises, however, in the very remembrance of the historian or storyteller who reflectively relates a narrative to the present situation, whether the present be unique and unprecedented or a moment in an ever recurring cycle. Since this reflective relation of narrative is an act of judgement, we are invited to compare such a judgement in which the remembered past and the lived present are placed side by side with the judgement of the universal historian in which the past becomes intelligible within the scope of a grand and meaningful narrative encompassing every worthwhile human pursuit. The judgement of the fragmentary narrative remains situational, limited to the local significance of the remembered narrative, constitutive of a local sense of identity and perspective. The problem we face with this local and situational judgement which makes the past significant for a person or a community is that there remains within it a violence towards the past, since memory is put into the service of identity. Put otherwise, the problem is that even a fragmentary constitution of identity employs metaphysical force in the light of which the past must be not only constitutive but at the same time something to be mastered. Significance must be imported into memory in order to serve the function of identity, whether cultural or personal. The constitutive force of the past involves this act of violence as soon as the past rises into memory for the sake of bestowing sense upon the present.

But a truly fragmentary history might take other forms. One could imagine historical fragments not as merely local identity-functions, but as exemplary within a wider field. The Greek historians practised history as a remembrance of exemplary persons and events in order to make them visible to the human audience. In this sense, history provided examples to emulate and preserved the memory of actions to celebrate or condemn. The exemplariness of the fragmentary narratives refers to the opportunity which a trace, remembrance, or testimony offers for thought. The fragmentary narrative need not be tied to its identity function, but can serve as a work of art does, for example, offering an artefact or a performance for the thoughtful engagement of whomever wishes to be a spectator, with as little or as much significance as the spectator can cull from it, but without any pretension to a grand universal identity-function. It seems that only in this way could the indeterminate diversity of cultural manifestations be preserved against the universal identity to which a philosophy of history pretends and without the local, yet still violent, identity-functions of the isolated community which must protect its own heritage, even at the cost of violence done to its own past. Since Kant has developed a theory of judgement (which is not to say 'whim', caprice, or 'subjective fancy') in order to explain the manner in which the beautiful offers itself to all human spectators, and precisely insofar as they overcome their idiosyncratic tastes, we need not fear considering history in a similar light, offering to all human spectators something to think about, a way to broaden their imaginations, and open themselves to the past.

V Identity and history in the perspective of fragility and responsibility

We must clearly distinguish between the universality which the speculative historian arrogates to his or her viewpoint and the enlargement of thinking which guides the reflective yet non-teleological approach to history. The difference between speculation and judgement is the difference between the illusion of transparently pure reason and the recognition of plurality. According to Ricoeur, the plurality of persons is more important than the idea of pure rationality, because 'with the person alone comes plurality'.[18] In plurality alterity appears, and the respect which the moral law imposes is the expression of this relation with alterity, as the accomplishment of solicitude. The Other has primacy with respect to the law. Moral judgement is exercised only in concrete situations. This does not overrule the morality of obligation but only subordinates it to a practical wisdom of which the more authentic rules are solicitude, respect, reciprocity and justice. The universality of law ought not to limit the right of singularity and difference.[19]

Ricoeur is aware that the ontology he pursues cannot be expressed in the categorical language of predicative judgement, i.e. apophantic discourse, where truth and falsehood are defined in terms of objective verification. This is because apophantic discourse entails no personal commitment to the authenticity of the experience of attestation and *témoignage*. At this juncture, we can wed the act of bearing witness with the act of reflective judgement by a spectator. The spectator, in passing judgement, bears witness to what has been seen and to the perspective from which it was viewed. Such an act of reflective judgement, requiring a comparison of one's own viewpoint with that of all other possible spectators, invokes the notion of the witness: when I judge, I bear witness to what I have seen, inviting others to look also and placing the value and impartiality of my own judgement upon the appeal to all possible spectators. Bearing witness to something is like saying: 'This is what I saw and I wish you were there to see it too. Had you seen what I saw, you would feel and judge as I do.' Even while recognizing that every spectator will be perspectively situated as I myself am, I appeal to the idea of a *sensus communis*, which is to say that whatever appears stands under the judgement of all possible witnesses.

Conclusions

From the above considerations emerge three different levels of philosophical reflection on history. For Kant, the moral and rational destination prevails. For Arendt, aesthetics and communicability alone grant the possibility of a meaningful human history. Finally, for Ricoeur, the search for self and communal identity strengthens the ethical dimension of history.

However, in Arendt's attempt I also see the overcoming of Kant's and Ricoeur's aporetic efforts to ground politics upon morality. Indeed, for Arendt, politics is not grounded upon a pre-established agreement, but points to the necessity for human differences to be communicated, for consensus as something to be sought after. While the differences of points of view maintain plurality, politics becomes the shared territory for a possible mediation of human conflicts.

Gonzaga-in-Florence, Italy

Notes

This paper was originally presented at the annual meeting for the Society for Phenomenology and Existential Philosophy (SPEP) in Seattle, Washington, October 1994.

1 Paul Ricoeur, *Oneself as Another*, trans. Kathleen Blamey (Chicago, IL: University of Chicago Press, 1992).
2 Paul Ricoeur, 'L'acte de juger', Seminar given at Istituto Italiano per gli Studi Filosofici in Naples, May 1993 (unpublished résumé).
3 Paul Ricoeur, *Time and Narrative*, Vol. III, trans. Kathleen Blamey and David Pellauer (Chicago, IL: University of Chicago Press, 1988), p. 202.
4 ibid., p. 246.
5 Jacques Taminiaux, *Poetics, Speculation and Judgement*, trans. Michel Gendre (Albany: State University of New York Press, 1993).
6 Immanuel Kant, *Critique of Judgement*, trans. J. H. Bernard (New York: Hafner Press, 1951).
7 Immanuel Kant, 'Idea for a Universal History with a Cosmopolitan Intent', in *Perpetual Peace and Other Essays*, trans. Ted Humphrey (Indianapolis, IN: Hackett Publishing, 1983).
8 Immanuel Kant, 'Perpetual Peace', in *Perpetual Peace and Other Essays*.
9 Hannah Arendt, *Lectures on Kant's Political Philosophy*, ed. Ronald Beiner (Brighton, Sx: Harvester Press, 1982).
10 ibid., p. 77.
11 ibid.
12 Kant, *Critique of Judgement*, §40, p. 136.
13 Immanuel Kant, 'Speculative Beginning of Human History', in *Perpetual Peace and Other Essays*.
14 Ricoeur, 'L'acte de juger', p. 6.
15 Immanuel Kant, *Metaphysics of Morals*, trans. Mary Gregor (Cambridge: Cambridge University Press, 1991).

16 Ricoeur, 'L'acte de juger', p. 5.
17 Kant, *Critique of Judgement*, §40, p. 136.
18 Ricoeur, *Oneself as Another*, p. 224.
19 ibid., pp. 218 ff.

Joseph Dunne

Beyond sovereignty and deconstruction: the storied self

No topic is more central or contested in contemporary philosophy than
'the self'; it is a main stake, for instance, in debates between 'liberals'
and 'communitarians' as well as between defenders of modernity and
the Enlightenment against its postmodernist critics. In addressing this
topic in the present article my procedure is schematic. I first outline a
classic modern notion of the self and then a more recent perspective
which comprehensively negates it. Interesting creases in each of these
two views are ironed out only because I intend them to serve a
dialectical purpose in clarifying a third – and, I believe, more adequate
– view of the self, which I go on to explore in the main part of the
article. A preliminary intimation of the terms of this dialectic is offered
by Paul Ricoeur when he writes of 'a hermeneutics of the self [that] can
claim to hold itself at an equal distance from the cogito exalted by
Descartes and from the cogito that Nietzsche proclaimed forfeit'.[1]

I The sovereign self and the deconstructed self

1

The sovereign self (as I shall use the term)[2] represents an idea with deep
roots in modern philosophy, which, as an ideal, has permeated much of
modern culture and perhaps, to a greater or lesser degree, has shaped
the self-image of everyone now living in advanced industrial societies.

The sovereign self conveys, first of all, a sense of secure location or anchorage – though the metaphor misleads by suggesting a sense of surrounding space or ground-bed: an inapt sense since this self seems so much to be *its own* ground. One source of this notion of the self is Descartes's 'I' or 'ego', which is immediately, transparently and irrefutably present to itself as a pure extensionless consciousness, already established in being, without a body and with no acknowledged complicity in language, culture, or community. Another source, as drastic politically as Descartes's picture is epistemologically, is Hobbes's notion of the self as a passionate centre of assertion – though one defined in the midst of, or rather over against, a plurality of other like centres. While arising in two different and in some respects rival traditions of philosophy, both of these pictures of the self proved capable of combining, particularly through the incorporation by each of them of an ideal of knowledge which, contemporaneously with their own emergence, was becoming newly available: knowledge as explanatory and predictive with respect to its object and as residing in this newly masterful self as subject or knower – a subject, moreover, which could decisively extend its mastery by incorporating anything *in itself* which was not a pure faculty of knowing into the object-domain of knowledge.

In its separateness and mastery, this self presents an invulnerable front. But in fact it emerged in response to a profound vulnerability: in Descartes's case, an omnivorous doubt supercharged by the spectre of a deceitful cosmic genius and, in Hobbes's case, the incursions of fellow-creatures driven by the predatory and acquisitive instincts that are common to all. The drive for certainty and security of this self is related, then, to a fallibility and precariousness which are experienced or hyperbolically imagined (to the point of entirely obliterating any sense of an affinity – natural or transcendental – between our cognitive powers and the world in which we are placed, or of our having been cared for by our elders long before we were capable of reciprocation or even of having a proper sense of danger). The self is a citadel in which a lucid reason is at the service of a naked will. Reason and will are instruments first of self-preservation and then of self-advancement. The fabric of selves is not constituted by shared qualities springing from their joint participation in communal engagements; there is no substantial web or mediating context which might come to characterize them. Still, if they lack as single selves any commonly shaped characteristics they are not, on that account, singular; the materials which might make up a particular identity or destiny for any individual do not appear within the dominant philosophical articulations of this notion of the self. What can be attributed to any self is the generalized endowment of every other self – disengaged reason, an amalgam of basic instincts, and will as an executive agency combining the calculative ability of the former with the inclinations and energies of the latter; there is nothing here to give variety or texture to lives, singly or together.

This self, I have suggested, is originally posited in isolation. Self-enclosure cannot be maintained, of course, if life is to be lived; action, which is at the same time interaction and commerce with others, is unavoidable. If ultimate self-sufficiency is impossible, the engagement with others implied by this impossibility is tolerable, however, only if it involves no loss of self-ownership. And this condition is met only if action springs from choice, where this term has a rather particular sense. Through choice I contract to do something or consent to undergo something solely on the basis of consulting my own interests and desires and calculating how their satisfaction is to be maximized. These interests and desires are *mine* in that they reside within me in such a way that even if the mode of their satisfaction is not brutely predetermined but leaves room for discretionary interpretation on my part, still interpretation is something of which I alone am arbiter: no one else can be in a relationship with me of a kind that would enable her or him to interpret for me where my interest or 'good' might lie; nor can any prior relationship in which I stand have any constitutive role in shaping what my preferences will be. My self and the other are impermeable then in the sense that not only do our respective interests make us adversaries, when we are not simply indifferent to each other, but also that any communication between us can in no way be transformative of either of us. I can never come to discover or realize myself in a new way through interaction with the other; for I am already securely given to myself as my self prior to interaction and all that can be at stake in the latter is success or failure in realizing my antecedently established ends. Also excluded from this picture of course is the possibility of a common good between us, which is more than simply a coincidence of our separate interests – a good, in other words, which is not just instrumentally dependent on coordinated action (so that it might be achieved through some other alliance) but which simply could not exist as *this* good, without this particular form of collaboration.

2

If the sovereign self presents a picture of a stable centre incorrigibly present to itself and negotiating with its surrounding world from within its own securely established powers of knowing and willing, a picture which is almost the reverse of this has come increasingly to the fore in recent philosophy. While the first picture occludes any sense of an encompassing context that might have a mediating or constitutive role with respect to the self, the second picture brings such a context into relief – to the point where it engulfs, if not annihilates, the self.

A tendency in this direction was already apparent in two major movements of the 19th century which (also hugely influential, sometimes in fusion with each other, in our own century) had already greatly encroached on the sovereignty of the self, namely Marxism and psychoanalysis. Not just its efficacy in pursuing its interests but, more fundamentally, even its supposed transparency to itself in knowing where these interests lie, was very much put in question. For Marx, false consciousness or a state of ideological mystification – and not rational access to oneself and the world – is the *given* posture of the self in a society compelled to conceal or suppress basic contradictions in its productive and wealth-distributing processes. And a somewhat similar alienation is depicted by Freud: the self which consciously determines its life-projects and tries to keep them afloat is compromised by (unconscious) forces already operative on, or even resident within, this same self as given in consciousness and revealed through speech and action. If Marxism and psychoanalysis point up the illusions of the sovereign self they do not, however, on that account, renounce the ideal of selfhood or indeed of a certain kind of sovereignty. To the contrary, their recognition of what they analyse as *alienation* presupposes some notion of unalienated self-possession; and in each case the analysis is in the service of a therapeutics through which human subjects can be enabled to regain this self-possession. The structures of oppression and repression are not in principle opaque to intelligent subjects; the intrepid therapist and revolutionary theorist, at least, can decode them – and help others to a kind of agency which will break their thrall over their lives. Insofar as they assume a notion of liberation, then, albeit one that can be achieved only through the ordeals of a dialectical struggle, neither Marxism nor psychoanalysis is committed to the 'demise of the subject'. Both remain within the horizon of 'humanism' in its classic modern form. For despite the deeply critical impulse which animates them – or rather *because* of the *kind* of critique to which they are committed – both retain a sense of the possibility of attaining truth about the human condition (in general, and in particular historical or biographical formations) and a sense of a good that is to be brought about through a practice of this truth. This truth is available to undeceived subjectivity; and it can become efficacious to the extent that a strategic form of communication mediates between the subjectivity of the original theoretician, that of the resourceful therapist/leader and that of the suffering patient/proletariat.

It is commonplace to regard psychoanalysis as a further stage of a decentring of the person that began with Copernicus's heleocentric hypothesis and continued through Darwin's evolutionary one. To speak of the decentred self now, however, is to refer to something different from that essentially modern displacement of the spiritual person from the centre of a providentially ordered cosmos. For this displacement, and the disenchantment that went with it, could be appropriated into its self-consciousness by the subject: as a tribute to its own capacity for disinterested inquiry and as a challenge to its moral power stoically to transcend these successive blows to its narcissism. The new decentring is more radical in that it does not allow an ascetic contraction (which can after all lead to a certain intensification) of subjectivity; rather, it tends to abolish subjectivity altogether – so that even the theorist who propounds it can find no easy way of reconciling *what* he or she propounds with notions of selfhood, truth-claiming and agency that seem to be implicit in *his or her own act* of propounding. There is a common structuralist (or poststructuralist) impulse in the most influential variants of this position which I shall briefly characterize.

A first 'site' is language. Much good philosophy in the continental and analytical traditions had already exposed the untenability of the Cartesian and empiricist conceptions of the self as immediately present to its own ideas: ignored in both views was the role of language in constructing these ideas before they could become available to consciousness. This 'linguistic turn' certainly required an altered understanding of the self; but it did not require that the self should be sacrificed to an entirely autonomous and impersonal language system. This is what structuralism implies when it conceives language as being neither responsive to those who speak it nor bound to a world beyond itself. Instead, language is a great self-referential system where individual signs get their meaning entirely through their relationships – of similarity but more especially of difference – with other signs within the system. Words are emptied of any referential power which we might have supposed them to have with respect to extralinguistic reality and, instead, are drawn ever outwards in relationships with other signs, the 'traces' of which they silently bear and which enforce on them, by the multiple networks in which they enmesh them, an indefinite deferral of their 'meaning'. Every local use of language then – no matter how sharply delineated the topic to which it is apparently addressed – suffers this dispersal into the totality, which has its own systemic codes and laws and which functions anonymously beyond the control of every speaker. Indeed, it now appears illusory to suppose that a person speaks the language, for through her utterance it is the language itself which speaks. Moreover, speech is to be depreciated in favour of writing, which is more obedient to the linguistic system itself and in particular entertains fewer illusions about 'presence' – the presence of reality to a speaker or of one speaker to another. Whether as writer or as speaker, the individual is in any case eclipsed by language. There remains no personal centre of experience that can assert itself against the great monolith of language; at best what the 'self' can do – when it is not just conditioned and constructed by anonymous codes beyond its awareness – is to be a medium through which the play of language, and the jouissance that springs from its superabundance, can appear.

There are other influential ways of deconstructing the self which do not succumb to linguistic monism or the hypostatization of language, 'discourse', or 'textuality' as the only reality. Another viewpoint, with a similar effect, postulates pervasive social practices which exercise systematic power or domination over those who are caught up in them. Even the modern 'normal', 'autonomous' self is not a source of responsible agency (as it takes itself to be, when even its frequent sense of being perplexed or in the dark makes sense only on the assumption that it *is* such a source) but, rather, the paradoxical product of an amalgam of socially entrenched practices (or technologies). These 'practices' are the more entrenched in that they are not vulnerable to being identified, analysed, or exposed by some critical knowledge or theoretical discourse. For knowledges and discourses are themselves pre-empted as codifiers of the 'discipline' imposed by these practices; they are 'regimes of truth' which give the latter sense and legitimacy, while keeping individuals captive within the constructed identities they make available to them.

But what about the (meta-) theory which presents this picture? Surely it escapes the status of being merely one more coercive regime of truth and, because it does so, can open a space for a critique with emancipatory potential? But here the screw is turned tighter. For the meta-theory (whether it be 'archaeology' or 'genealogy') is one which seeks simply to affirm the fact and indeed the inevitability of power – which subordinates 'truth' to itself – while disavowing epistemological or moral implications which might seem to follow from this affirmation. One such implication is that there is a regime-independent truth, after all, a recognition of which might suggest and *justify* resistance to the encompassing domination. But to respond to the theory in such a way, we are to understand, is not to gain a liberationist perspective from which we might reconfigure the dystopian picture but is, rather, simply to confirm this picture. For, by doing so, we should only show ourselves to be still captive to the fiction of an autonomous agency and selfhood – a fiction which is itself simply the product of a certain constellation of modern technologies and regimes. It is of course notoriously unclear what kind of truth can be claimed by a theory which proposes that truth is no more than a device of power. And indeed it is no more clear how this power can be regarded as *domination* if there are no potentially free agents over whom it is exercised. But, whatever their force, these reservations point in any case to something which the deconstructive project itself would scarcely deny: that the casualty list of this project includes not just the self but truth and freedom, too.

II The storied self

1

The previous section has provided negative pointers for the task of the present section: how to characterize a self whose intrication with its life-world denies it sovereignty without thereby depriving it of selfhood. This task is greatly complicated by the fact that the self lacks the substantiality and discreteness of an object which is amenable to direct description or explanation. Nor can it be captured privately by an internal act of introspection or self-perception. Its reality is peculiarly dispersed, it is always partly outside or beyond itself, receding from focal presence into background penumbra, implicated in and formed by relationships, permeated by otherness. It seems very difficult to do justice to this dispossession and still save the identity of the self. Indeed, at the very outset (and using terms offered by Ricoeur), we have to renounce the normal sense of identity as *sameness* (Latin: *idem*), which we ascribe to a thing when we attribute to it numerical identity, or uniqueness as this thing rather than that, and also – especially significant in the case of beings which develop through successive stages – permanence over time; although a person can of course be regarded as a thing, the identity of *selfhood* (Latin: *ipse*) is of a different order from that of sameness.[3]

In setting out to trace this other form of identity, we need to resist the picture of a pristine core of selfhood, coated as it were with accumulated experiences but always capable of withdrawing itself from the latter into a transcendental point, an antecedent 'I'. Insofar as this picture can accommodate an 'empirical' self which is more or less the product of a life-history, it supposes that the original 'I' orchestrates the course of this history and so constructs the empirical self – or at least that this would be the case did it not sometimes unfortunately lapse from transcendental alertness and so forfeit its authorial role to some other force. If this picture is rejected, the whole self is as it were brought inside its history so that there is no original detached self to be author of the process of self-construction from the outside. Within a life-history, an infant begins to use 'I', or 'my' or 'mine' – evidence of her distinguishing her individual location in the world and sensing a proper coherence of her own – usually in the second half of her second year. But this use is primarily indexical and hardly indicates possession of a substantial self-concept. At this stage the self is, rather, in-construction, largely in response to those around the infant who invest it with love and care (or fail to do so), who speak and act towards it in focused ways, modelling to it modes of thinking, feeling and acting, and eliciting similar modes from it, treating it – in quite specific ways that come to be modified by the infant's own developing responses and initiatives – as a 'you', and thus evoking in it a sense of 'I'.

The self, then, is historical through and through, and is enfolded *ab initio* within a web of relationships. At least in its formative stage (i.e. in childhood) these relationships are overwhelmingly significant and are ones not just of material and emotional nurturance but also (though this is not something entirely distinct) of meaning. Basic senses of himself or herself – as worthy of love or respect, as capable or incapable – are mediated by 'significant others' and deeply internalized by the child. Here indeed is original heteronomy; but without the responses to her of others the child could have no coherent sense of herself at all.[4] It is in interaction, in confrontation with and con-firmation by others, and especially in being drawn by them into language, that a child can begin to deepen awareness and orientation as a self. This is not in the first place a directly reflexive process. To be sure, humans are 'self-interpreting animals' (which they can be only insofar as they are 'languaged' beings) and their self-interpretations are constitutive – are to great extent what they *are*. Still, the primary experience for a child is one of finding himself in a world which draws his energies and attention outward and which becomes more mean-ingful as he comes to share in the language in which it is interpreted by those around him who speak to him – so that it becomes for him in large part a world-in-common with these others, his main partners in speech. And his self-understanding is always as it were routed through this world-understanding. An understanding of himself as being physically strong, puzzled, dissatisfied, interested, brave, generous, being of a sunny disposition or frequently miserable, being a bright student or a member of an unhappy family – all such self-identifications are mediated through a language of description and appraisal which is firmly his only insofar as he understands it as mapping this world-in-common with others.

It would be a mistake to think of this language simply as a grid, already shaped, which is thrown over his experiences by others. For his development crucially depends on the kind of interlocutory stances he is enabled to take in significant conversational settings (and hence in his own inner reflections). A stance we may think of as natural to a child is one of questioning, rooted in a still elemental wonder. Even though – or perhaps because – her grasp of the language is precarious by comparison with that of her elders, she may still be more attentive to words and their meanings than the latter, more earnest in wanting them to fit.[5] A child combines this open, interrogative stance, which puts her in an active mode, with a continuing need to learn from others and to accumulate linguistic stocks and repertoires, which puts her in a receptive, dependent mode. And she is vulnerable to the possibility that (for a variety of reasons) the adults in her world will accentuate the second mode at the expense of the first. If this should happen, emphasis on the social construction of the self should not lead us to deny that there is a *loss* to the child – even if we do not want to postulate a transcendental I in order to make sense of this loss. For a child may *not* find in the language and roles available to her an adequate way of expressing some of her significant experiences (or, rather, she may not be able properly to *experience* something that she is nonetheless undergoing)[6] and hence if she is limited to this language and these roles she may suffer an estrangement: not just expressible and hence comprehensible unhappiness, but rather an inarticulate ache or a vague sense of missing or lost meaning. If this is very strong, as touching a basic need, it will continue to haunt the socialized self, rendering it chronically insecure (here is the terrain of psychotherapy). But if it concerns only the making of fine discriminations or the realization of subtle possibilities it may simply 'disappear', leaving a comfortably integrated self. Here too, however (which is perhaps the proper terrain of education), we should be able to recognize a loss. It is part of our being-in-time that what has become substantial and actual, fixed in our habits, can erase all trace of momentary but missed opportunities along the way. Against this inexorable work of time the educator works pre-emptively – by a constant awareness of what is *at stake* for children in her characteristic interactions with them.

2

It is in its negative aspect – that of 'roads not taken' – that we have just adverted to the temporal dimension of a life. But we need to take fuller account of this dimension in the constitution of the self – a self, moreover, who is not only a speaker in a field of meaning but also an agent seeking bearings in relation to value, or the good. Through action, or rather through its inescapability – the fact that we cannot not act – time eats into the self. When we act, we disclose who we are or (what amounts to the same thing) who we have become – most recognizably when our actions are 'in character'; that is to say, shaped by the history of previous actions which have left a sediment in what is now our character. If past actions have a force, however, so too have present actions; and so, through what I do now, I not only disclose who I have become but expose myself (through the opportunities and risks of new experiences which I do not know how I shall respond to or integrate) to becoming *different*. Chance plays its ineliminable part here, but also the fact that I act in relation to others whose reactions, with their effects on myself, cannot be predicted or counted on in advance.[7] Action has this double aspect, then, in one respect carrying a pull from the past, but in another respect pushing me into a future which, through it, may be made different from the past.

In this overspill of action in both temporal directions, we see the severe abstractness of talking about 'an action' as if it were an isolatable, self-contained event – and the need, then, to invoke the more encompassing notion of a *narrative*. Moreover this need presents itself not only in relation to 'an action' but also in relation to 'the agent'. The point is forcefully made by MacIntyre: 'Just as a history is not a sequence of actions, but the concept of an action is that of a moment in an actual or possible history abstracted for some purpose from that history, so the characters in a history are not a collection of persons, but the concept of a person is that of a character abstracted from a history.'[8] The notion of a history or narrative seems to be necessary in order to make sense of the notion of 'self'; for we make sense – or fail to make sense – of our lives by the kind of story we can – or cannot – tell about it. It is always true of course that others may tell a more meaningful story of my life than I myself can tell – if only because, outliving me, they are in a position to relate it to my death.[9] Still, narrativity is integral to my life – and not just at the level of retrospective articulation. Kierkegaard's point surely stands: that while we articulate backward we must live forward. Still, living is *itself* the *enactment* of a narrative, and MacIntyre's point also stands: 'Stories are lived before they are told – except in the case of fiction.'[10]

There are two distinctions here: one between living and telling in real lives, and the other between real lives and fictional ones. The second distinction reminds us that no one can have the privileged perspective on his own life that an author has on her fictional creations; the enacted narrative of my life meshes too finely with the narratives of other lives (themselves similarly meshed) for it to be subject to my sole construction: I am the main protagonist in but not the author of it.[11] Notwithstanding this distinction between them, however, there is a significant mediation between real lives and fictional ones – a point I will touch on later in adverting to fictions as construed by their readers rather than as constructed by their authors. But turning now to our first distinction, between living and telling, here too we are dealing with activities which are not discrete or parallel to each other. For while I may not strictly be the author of my life, still it is unexchangeably *my* life, it is at least partly shaped by intentions of mine, and I am accountable for it in a way that clearly no one else can be. Accountability is inherent in the very living; giving an account of it, to others or to myself, is not something discretionary, apart from the living, which I may or may not indulge in. If *no* account can be given of my life, it can scarcely be called a *human* life (this may be related to Aristotle's famously ascribing a life without *logos* either to a beast or a god);[12] and if *I* cannot give an account of it, it can scarcely be said to be *my* life – or, what perhaps amounts to the same thing, I can scarcely be considered a self.

What I am claiming here, of course, is not only that accountability is intrinsic to living a properly human life but that narrative (because of its responding to something already deeply inscribed in our living) is the paradigm form of giving an account. To be sure, there is a more limited form of accounting that we might designate as justification or reason-giving, which typically answers the question, 'Why did you do that?' However, if this question is posed persistently to a person in relation to a wide range of her actions over a considerable span of time – indeed ultimately her life-span – then it seems to give way to the wider question, 'Who are you?' And it is *this* question which is best answered in the form of a story. But perhaps one may wonder whether this question itself can be meaningfully asked, or whether it isn't the kind of limit-question which Kant has taught us to regard as pointing beyond the scope of possible knowledge. In a sense it *is* an impossible question, for it is impossible to answer it directly or definitively – while at the same time it is impossible that it not go on being asked. And this impossibility of its not being asked arises more in relation to living than to telling; even if the question is not explicitly posed either by oneself or by others, or if one's experience is precisely that one has *no* coherent story to tell, the question is still at least indirectly posed by life itself, and one's own life is an implicit attempt to answer it. For one is faced more directly with other questions which one answers through deeds – thereby implicitly and cumulatively answering this larger question, 'Who are you?' The other questions have to do with what matters to one, what one bothers with, admires, holds dear, or is prepared to commit oneself to. The point about these questions, which may be brought under the single rubric of questions about 'the good' – though they are unlikely to receive unequivocal or conflict-free answers – is that they allow neither escape nor indifference. To exist as a self is, in Charles Taylor's apt metaphor, to be situated in moral space, in which one can no more live without bearings than, as a being in physical space, one can avoid orienting oneself by basic senses of front or behind, left or right, above or below.[13]

Here the self does not subsist in itself but is 'ek-static', seeking direction by reference to what it senses, not simply as a function of its own desires or wishes, to be admirable or at least acceptable and thus worthy of pursuit (or reprehensible or unworthy and thus to be avoided) in action, feeling or way of life. This sense is always revisable – if not entirely reversible at least it can become more discriminating or acute – and hence remains open to questions actually or potentially put. Moreover, to be a self is to be involved not just in directional (i.e. ethical) questioning but also in a *quest*;[14] for one cannot but *care* about how one is situated or is moving relative to the direction one discerns. If this is care about oneself it is at the same time care for the goods which determine the direction. These goods, in other words, are the objects of love as well as of attention. 'Objects' is perhaps an unfortunate term insofar as it suggests that the power of the love comes from the self as subject or source – whereas it would be truer to say (with Taylor, following Iris Murdoch and of course Plato) that these goods empower the self, by arousing its love, and are thus *its* sources (or resources).

At this point we seem to have identified the self with its loves; but how, it may be asked, is this a move towards establishing the essential place of narrative – in the first place, as enacted – in the constitution of the self? Well, desire or aspiration has to be realized in actions, a realization which entails a translation from universals to particulars. Moreover, one's adherence to the goods undergoes change in this process of realization and translation. This is all the more the case when one must enact them in situations or circumstances where there may be deflecting or contrary pressures – so that one has to count real *costs* – and when, in any case, one feels other pulls (e.g. to comfort, vanity, or dominance) which may weaken not only one's response to but even one's perception of these goods. Aristotle's ideal of the good person as one in whom the passions are attuned to the doing of good betokens an attractively healthy moral psychology, but ethical living still seems to be realistically pictured when '[t]he self . . . is seen to live and travel between truth and falsehood, good and evil, appearance and reality'.[15] One may be drawn towards and moved by the good, but scarcely without conflict; hence a recognition that moral life is not only a quest but a *struggle*. Nor can this struggle simply be interiorized into the self. For it is played out at many different points of intersection with other lives and is shaped by 'environmental' (not to speak of 'hereditary') factors that may be stubbornly opaque both to will and to desire. When account is taken of the contingency of the scenes in which the self is entangled – the sheer givenness of early primary figures and the historical density of class, gender or national roles into which one is conscripted, the fortuitousness of influential meetings and the un-expected opportunities that may open up as well as the unsought trials (even disasters) that may befall one – then the notion of *plot* may come into focus with the notion of character in trying to comprehend the shape of a life.

3

With plot and character – as well as quest and struggle – we have key elements of narrative. And what I have been trying to show is that narrative is latent in one's living, that a life calls out for narrative recounting – is, as it were, a story waiting to be told. What, then, is *added* by the telling? A first answer might be: a kind of configuring which (studded with expressions such as 'and then . . .', 'because', 'in order to', 'for the sake of') introduces connectedness and thus reveals the *unity* of one's life. But here it may immediately be objected that the contemporary self is one that experiences – or even *embraces* – precisely fragmentation, discontinuity, disruption; and hence that any attempt to introduce coherence betrays only nostalgia for the more stable life of an earlier age as well as subjection to the dominating projects (or 'hegemonic', 'totalizing', 'logocentric' ones: the lexicon of pejoratives here is a rich one) which made this stability possible. Although, thus posed, the objection is tendentious – inviting us to adopt either some kind of romantic conservatism or a perhaps no less romantic (despite its irony and disillusion) postmodernism – there is still a real question here, which one may acknowledge to be greatly sharpened by our postmodern condition, even if one does not want to endorse a postmodern*ist* answer to it. (I take the former term to be a descriptive one now more or less applicable to all of us living in advanced capitalist societies and the latter to be a normative one canvassing a particular way of responding to life in such societies.)

To be sure, in relating the acts and events of a life, narrating seeks to supersede sheer succession, heterogeneity and discordance, and, moreover, in doing so, it has recourse to established genres and narrative conventions. However, it is not thereby committed either to a substantialist notion of the self *or* to a static notion of narration. The *historicity* of an individual self is something I have been stressing throughout this whole section. But there is also the historicity (i.e. the 'dialectic of sedimentation and innovation') of narrative genres themselves, as they have evolved from the earliest epic right up to the most experimental novel or anti-novel;[16] and indeed it seems plausible to suggest that this historical development of genres reflects the evolution of subjectivity itself, i.e. of significantly different modes of being constituted, or of constituting oneself, as a self. From this it seems to follow that strategies of fictional narration (which I have just been referring to) and 'real-life' narrative strategies are permeable to one another. This being the case, it seems unnecessary to presume that the latter must in principle presuppose seamless continuity and unambiguous closure. But if this is true of the act (or art) of narrating, it is no less true of what is narrated, i.e. the life as lived. For to speak of the unity of a life is by no means to imply that a life is unified by an overarching design or master project; it is, rather, to invoke the *whole* of a life, however fragmented and dislocated this whole may be. Nor is it to obscure the fact that a person is implicated not in one but in several stories – which, moreover, are not self-enclosed, since each may interlock with other stories belonging to one's own life or to the lives of others.

The second case may be illustrated by a person's story as a husband, which clearly interlocks with another person's story as his wife, or by a person's story as a teacher, which merges with others' stories as her pupils. In cases such as these, which are embedded in practices (family life, schooling), an established genre sustains the story-lines, while allowing to each agent a more or less wide range of improvisation or individual utterance. So long as both recognize themselves to be operating within the same genre, the conventions of which neither of them unduly strains, their stories may remain largely in the implicit zone of enactment. Serious discordance, however, may press one party into the explicitness of telling and, indeed, it may be that the discordance is brought about in the first place by the quite explicit telling by the other party of a new story (or the recasting of patterns and events of the old story in a new way). Through a growing feminist consciousness, for example, a woman may begin to reconfigure her ongoing story as a wife. Her husband then finds that certain utterances or gestures within his story fail to get their old purchase (flowers in certain situations lose their melting effect). And perhaps it is insofar as he is no longer able to enact this story that he is forced for the first time to really tell it. Telling, then, would arise in the face of anomaly or crisis. In the case just considered it would arise at the point where the story perhaps *cannot* continue, without a major reorientation. But we can envisage other cases where a story is chronically problematic but where a protagonist feels that, despite (or perhaps because of) this fact, it *must* continue. And here, too, a need to tell may arise precisely in response to difficulties or crises in enactment. We might think, for instance, of some afflicted or oppressed groups who sustain a struggle with the help of a story very explicitly told, perhaps one which incorporates their struggle into a larger historico-religious narrative (the continuing power or 'effective history' of the Exodus in this respect is mentioned by Charles Taylor and explored by Michael Waltzer).[17]

The first case mentioned above – where a story interlocks with other stories of *one's own* life – might be illustrated by the case of a married man with children whose widowed mother can no longer go on living alone: she must move in either with his family or his only sister's, or retire to a nursing home. Faced with this situation and with working out his own responsibility in it – with respect not just to his mother's wishes and tolerances but to those of the other persons close to him who will be intimately affected by whatever decision is made – this man may be confronted in a critical way with stories of himself as son, brother, husband and father. It may be that up to now he has been able to live some of these stories relatively discretely, thereby parcelling out, as it were, different parts of himself. Now, however, he faces a situation which is critical precisely insofar as it throws these stories together, demanding a decision which will relate them in some way to one another. Here, too, it is likely that the crisis will push him into a more explicit *telling*. But as the decision in this case cannot be confined within any one of his stories, so what will emerge in the telling which accompanies the deciding must be some larger story of his life *as a whole*.

4

Let us now take up again the question which first prompted my reference to the whole of a life: what does telling (or narrating) add to enacting (or living)? In the light of the examples just discussed, we might say that narration answers the challenge in the Socratic dictum that an unexamined life is not worth living, by offering a medium of reflection through which *self-understanding* can be achieved in an exemplary way.[18] Self-understanding is always an understanding of one's relatedness to others and to the good. As, in reading a fictional narrative, one's projection of the whole and one's understanding of each successive incident clarify and complete each other cumulatively (this is one aspect of the famous 'hermeneutical circle'), so, in enacting a real narrative, a similar dialectic mediates between one's overall, often vague, sense of the good (the good to be pursued, with and for others as well as for

oneself, e.g. as father, husband, teacher, son, or brother – and ultimately, though not separately, the good of one's life as a whole) and
one's particular responses in this or that situation. *Phronēsis*, which
Aristotle relates very explicitly with self-understanding in Book 6 of
the *Nicomachean Ethics*, has this dialectical structure – or so I have
argued in *Back to the Rough Ground*.[19] The dialectic can of course
close in on itself when particular responses become routine (clichéd)
and, correspondingly, background senses of good disappear into un-
reflective habit. Against such closure, tension-points in a narrative, of
the kind I have briefly adverted to, are invitations to self-understanding
– by disrupting a settled relatedness and putting in question the character of the goods implicit in it. *Phronēsis* provides insight into particular situations through a reflective concern with overall goods. Its
character as *concrete* wisdom is not well understood, however, if these
overall goods are seen simply as universals (which can provide terms
for major premises in practical syllogisms). For the agent must also
understand their texture as goods-for-her, that is to say, the way they
have become woven into the fabric of her life – so that reflection on
them really is self-reflection. And it is in pursuit of such reflective
understanding that the gathering or collecting proper to narrative is indispensable.

The significance of this added understanding is that it does not lie
alongside our living but is rather absorbed by and integrated into the
latter (this is the character of *phronēsis* as *practical* wisdom). It is not
that we have a self anyhow and that there is now an added
understanding of it which we happen to have acquired. Rather, the
new understanding (which will have modified an old one; we cannot
live without *some* self-understanding) to a considerable extent is
constitutive of us, is what we *are*. The stories we tell ourselves make a
difference. For the temporal arc of our lives is such that the past (as
collected in the present) throws a deep shadow over our future; and
so the primarily retrospective (or recollective) character of narrating
does not prevent it from having prospective, indeed truly self-
transformative, effect. Moreover, through this connection with what
one does and who one is, narrating is related not only to self-
understanding but also to a strong sense of accountability: the fact that
one not only can offer an account but also can be *counted* on by others.
It is only in the light of a story of oneself that one can own – in the sense
of *own up to* – that one emerges from an amorphous background of
circumstance and conditioning with the affirmation: 'Here I am,
answerable for myself – to and for others'.[20] There is a constancy[21] here
which implies a kind of self-possession (it is most strikingly absent in
someone who is living out – or, perhaps more accurately, being lived

out as – a part in someone else's story, so that his actions are scripted even though he himself has never recognized or appropriated, let alone composed, the script).[22]

Constancy does not imply that one has achieved final identity with oneself. To be sure, the accumulated weight of what one has done and undergone – now congealed in one's 'character' – exerts a determining effect. But it is part of the drama of narratives, real and fictional, that even though this is the case, *nonetheless* the story remains unpredictably open. And, rather than denying this openness, constancy has to be reconciled with it: even though my story remains open, *nonetheless* there is a fidelity of which I am capable. The openness – which cannot but render fragile all the self's undertakings – is related to the contingency already mentioned. But it is also related to the inexhaustible nature of the good – which is what gives life its character as a quest. Perhaps in the end all one can be faithful to is what one now apprehends of the good that one pursues – while recognizing the pursuit itself to be part of that good; in MacIntyre's words, 'the good life . . . is the life spent seeking for the good life'.[23]

The openness I have just been speaking of is primarily the openness of an enacted narrative, i.e. of a life. But there is good reason to insist, too, on the importance of keeping open the narrative through which a life is recounted. For this narrative may, of course, be *false* – not necessarily in the sense that the values portrayed in it are unworthy ones but rather in the sense that it may misrepresent who one actually is. This is the province of self-deception, which might be defined as a significant discrepancy between the story one lives and the story one tells. I have already suggested, of course, that the story one tells oneself influences one's actions and becomes part of who one *is* (or, in other words, that one's self-understanding becomes partly self-constitutive). The conflict involved in self-deception, therefore, is not in fact as simple as a conflict between who one is and who one represents oneself as being (this would be the kind of conflict involved in the much more straightforward cases where one deceives not oneself but others). It is, rather, a deeper conflict *within who one is*, when one part is lived out only at the cost of disowning another part which, though disowned, still continues to find disguised expression in one's life.

It will never be the case, of course, that everything that transpires in our lives will be faithfully recorded in our narratives; full self-transparency is angelic rather than human and, in any case, every story is edited.[24] Still, there is a great distance between a lack of total clairvoyance with respect to the self and serious self-deception. The latter, with the complacency or illusion that it most often sustains, distorts moral perception and precludes moral development (certain nationalist narratives, with heavy ideological loading, can have a parallel effect in the historical lives of peoples or polities). And self-deception, indeed, need not always flatter our living; for sometimes there may be a significant movement towards a new good in our lives, which remains unfulfilled, however, just because it will not fit a comfortable or conventional story of ourselves that we continue to adhere to. Even though I have presented narrating as a key to moral insight, then, it is no guarantee, in itself, of the achievement of this insight; to the contrary, it carries with it its own moral challenge. This challenge is, first, that our stories of ourselves do justice to what is actually going on in our lives (the good and the bad). But, beyond this, is there not a work of the narrative imagination that projects possibilities of life and action other than our own with such vividness and power that they come to inform our moral evaluations and thus to challenge the stories we are living? And might we look to a certain way of reading narrative fiction, especially novels, as the paradigm way of developing this mode of imagination? These questions lie beyond the scope of the present article. But perhaps I may conclude by suggesting that it is one of Paul Ricoeur's most significant achievements that he has both taught us to ask these questions and offered us very fruitful ways of answering them affirmatively.[25]

St Patrick's College, Dublin, Ireland

Notes

This is an abridged version of a keynote paper presented to the Philosophy of Education Society of Great Britain at New College, Oxford in April 1995. I am deeply indebted to my friends Fergal O'Connor OP and Frank Litton for many stimulating conversations in the course of writing it.

1 Paul Ricoeur, *Oneself as Another*, trans. K. Blamey (Chicago, IL: University of Chicago Press, 1992), p. 23.
2 The notion of the sovereign self here has obvious affinities with the 'unencumbered' self in Michael Sandel's *Liberalism and the Limits of Justice* (Cambridge: Cambridge University Press, 1982) and Charles Taylor's 'punctual' or 'disengaged' self in *Sources of the Self* (Cambridge: Cambridge University Press, 1989).
3 On this distinction between 'sameness' and 'selfhood', see Paul Ricoeur, *Oneself as Another* and "Narrative Identity", in David

Wood (ed.) *On Paul Ricoeur, Narrative and Interpretation* (London: Routledge, 1991).

4   This heteronomy represents a lack, an irremediable ontological fault, for monological philosophers such as – in their very different ways – Sartre (in *Being and Nothingness*) and Lacan (especially in the early work on the 'mirror stage'). On the other hand, a philosophical anthropology which sees personal life as essentially dialogical can regard it more benignly – while still being able to acknowledge that it remains susceptible to various kinds of deformation; see, for example, John MacMurray, *The Form of the Personal*, Vol. 1 *The Self as Agent* and Vol. 2, *Persons in Relation* (Gifford Lectures, 1953–1954; repr. New York: Humanities Press, 1991) and M. M. Bakhtin, *The Dialogic Imagination*, ed. M. Holquist, trans. C. Emerson and M. Holquist (Austin: University of Texas Press, 1981) and *Problems of Dostoevsky's Poetics*, ed. and trans. C. Emerson (Minneapolis: University of Minnesota Press, 1984).

5   For illuminating accounts by a philospher of what I attribute to children here, see G. Matthews, *Philosophy and the Young Child* (Cambridge, MA: Harvard University Press, 1980) and *Dialogues with Children* (Cambridge, MA: Harvard University Press, 1984).

6   For a way of construing the possibility of expression as intrinsic rather than as optionally added to experience, see the discussion of R. G. Collingwood's concept of 'imaginative expression' in Joseph Dunne, *Back to the Rough Ground: Phronesis and Techne in Modern Philosophy and in Aristotle* (Notre Dame: University of Notre Dame Press, 1993), pp. 60–3.

7   I echo here Hannah Arendt's concept of action, which encompasses notions of self-disclosure, natality (or initiative), unpredictability and plurality – as well as the notion of story or narrative which I take up in the next paragraph; see *The Human Condition* (New York: Anchor Books, 1959), pp. 155–78.

8   Alasdair MacIntyre, *After Virtue* (London: Duckworth, 1981), p. 202.

9   Arendt makes the point that '[a]ction reveals itself fully only to the storyteller, that is, to the backward glance of the historian, who indeed always knows better what it was all about than the participants' (*The Human Condition*, p. 171). This point about the disadvantaged position of the agent relative to the narrator finds a hermeneutical parallel in the position of the author relative to the interpreter. After Schleiermacher, the interpreter is seen to benefit from the 'temporal distance' separating him or her from the original writing and so (*pace* Plato, at *Phaedrus* 275) to be able to understand the text better than its author; see H. G. Gadamer, *Truth and Method*, trans. G. Barden and

J. Cumming (London: Sheed & Ward, 1975), pp. 169–73 and 263–7.

10 MacIntyre, *After Virtue*, p. 197.

11 This is a point forcefully made by Arendt; see *The Human Condition*, pp. 163–4.

12 Aristotle, *Politics*, 1, 2.

13 See Taylor, *Sources*, pp. 27–32.

14 Taylor, whom I am following closely here, borrows this term from MacIntyre; see *Sources*, pp. 17 and 48, and *After Virtue*, pp. 203–4.

15 Iris Murdoch, *Metaphysics as a Guide to Morals* (London: Chatto & Windus, 1992), p. 166.

16 See Paul Ricoeur, 'Life: a Story in Search of a Narrator', in M. J. Valdes, *A Ricoeur Reader* (Hemel Hempstead, Herts: Harvester Wheatsheaf, 1991), pp. 429–30. The point is well made by Bakhtin that the epic hero, represented as a distant image in an absolute past, fully coincides with his external social position and fate, so that he is a completed character, with no surplus of subjectivity unexhausted by what the plot decrees to him. By contrast, the temporality, subjectivity and possibility so well suppressed in the epic are given their fullest release in the novel, wherein the 'incongruity of a man with himself' is elaborated in 'the spontaneity of the inconclusive present'. Moreover, because of the openness of its subject-matter, the form of the novel itself remains open: its 'generic skeleton . . . is still far from having hardened, and we cannot foresee all its plastic possibilities'. Indeed, '[it] is plasticity itself. It is a genre that is ever questing, ever examining itself and subjecting its established forms to review' ('Epic and Novel: Towards a Methodology for the Study of the Novel', in *The Dialogic Imagination*).

17 See Taylor, *Sources*, pp. 96–7, and Michael Waltzer, *Exodus and Revolution* (New York: Basic Books, 1985).

18 See Ricoeur, 'Life: A Story', p. 435.

19 See Dunne, *Back to the Rough Ground*, especially Ch. 9; and, for analysis of the places in Book 6 of the *Ethics* where *phronēsis* is expressly related to self-understanding, pp. 269–70. It is noteworthy that Ricoeur assigns a central place to *phronēsis* in his study of ethical agency in *Oneself as Another* – a study, he does not mind acknowledging, 'whose tone is Aristotelian from start to finish' (see pp. 174–81 and 290–1).

20 In *Oneself as Another*, Ricoeur uses a formula similar to this at the point of reconciling a self formed by narrative contingencies with an ethical self which is nonetheless bound to aim at 'the good life with and for others in just institutions' (see pp. 167 and 172).

21 The need to find some way of specifying 'constancy' (a primary virtue

of heroines in Jane Austen's novels) is one of the factors that motivates MacIntyre's movement beyond 'practices' to 'narratives' in his cumulative account of the virtues. See MacIntyre, *After Virtue*, p. 189.

22 For an intriguing cross-generational account of an extreme example of this phenomenon – the case of a 'delinquent' boy who is 'absent from himself' because invaded by unconscious projections of a parent who has failed to mourn the loss inflicted by *his* parent – written, appropriately, by a novelist and a psychoanalyst, see A. Thomas Ellis and T. Pitt-Aikens, *Secrets of Strangers* (Harmondsworth, Mx: Penguin, 1986).

23 MacIntyre, *After Virtue*, p. 204.

24 The need for some transparency – through reflection or articulation – and at the same time the impossibility of anything like *full* transparency, which we meet here in terms of a dialectic between 'life' and 'narration', is elaborated (also in the context of an account of the self which assigns a key role to narrative) by Owen Flanagan in terms of a dialectic between 'actual full identity' and 'self-represented identity'; and (in the context of a wider reflection on being-in-time) by Gadamer in terms of a dialectic between 'effective history' (*Wirkungsgeschichte*) and 'effective-historical consciousness' (*wirkungsgeschichtliches Bewusstsein*). See Flanagan, *Varieties of Moral Personality* (Cambridge, MA: Harvard University Press, 1991), pp. 135–9 and *Consciousness Reconsidered* (Cambridge, MA: MIT Press, 1992), pp. 195–211; and Gadamer, *Truth and Method*, pp. 267–74

25 While a theorist such as Louis O. Mink restricts the concept of narrative to intentionally constructed histories or literary fictions and MacIntyre (arguing expressly against Mink) locates the primary arena of narrative in real lives, it is characteristic of Ricoeur that he can admire both of these thinkers while theorizing, in a way that neither of them attempts, precisely the *mediation* between literature and life. See *Oneself as Another*, pp. 157–68, 'Life: A Story', espec. pp. 436–7, and *Time and Narrative*, Vol. 3, trans. K. Blamey and D. Pellauer (Chicago, IL: Chicago University Press, 1988), pp. 244–9. Other recent works that interestingly explore the implications for ethical life (and for moral education) of the reading of fiction are Martha Nussbaum, *Love's Knowledge* (Oxford: Oxford University Press, 1990) and Robert Coles, *The Call of Story: Teaching and the Moral Imagination* (Boston, MA: Houghton Mifflin, 1989); Ricoeur's contribution to this topic is distinguished, however, by the whole hermeneutical preoccupation, and in particular the rich theory of reading, out of which it arises (see *Time and Narrative*, Vol. 3, section 2, espec. Ch. 7, 'The World of the Text and the World of the Reader').

David Rasmussen

Rethinking subjectivity: narrative identity and the self

In the following I want to consider whether or not it is possible to retrieve the concept, or better, the phenomenon of subjectivity under the category of the narrative identity of the self. In so doing, I will be considering the question regarding the re-emergence of subjectivity in a world of philosophical discourse which had conceived of itself as having overcome the perils of subjectivity, either in the form of the hermeneutic critique of early phenomenology or in the form of the analytical critique of skepticism. Conceived against the backdrop of the perceived achievements of a theory of interlocution, this will force us to reconsider the problem of the intersubjective achievement of valid knowledge one more time.[1]

In reflecting on the phenomenon of the re-emergence of subjectivity, I want to consider a number of arguments presented in Paul Ricoeur's recent book, *Oneself as Another*.[2] In so doing my task will be not simply to reduplicate Ricoeur's argument. Rather, my concern will be to attempt to consider the implications of the concept of narrative identity for the question of the re-emergence of subjectivity as it relates to a theory of interlocution. To anticipate the argument, I am particularly interested in the implications of Ricoeur's critique of the theory of interlocution from the point of view of self-identity. If Ricoeur's critique is correct, it would follow that the attempted overcoming of the problem of subjectivity through a theory of interlocution is achieved only by undermining an adequate concept of self-identity. In order adequately to reconstruct the problem as it develops in continental philosophy, it will be necessary to go back to Husserl.

For a certain form of European philosophy the dilemma associated with subjectivity reached its darkest moment in Edmund Husserl's 'Fifth Meditation',[3] where it was acknowledged that the phenomenological ego could not constitute the other in the same manner in which it could constitute itself. Husserl, through the use of apperception, appresentation and pairing attempted to find ways through which the other could be constituted by analogy to the self. In the end, his analysis appeared to pose an epistemological problem. Critics would point out that one could never know the other in the same way as one could know the self and, as such, the enigma of solipsism seemed to haunt Husserl's philosophy.

However, in retrospect, Husserl may have had a point. Perhaps there is a sense in which the other can never be known by the self in the same sense that the self can know itself. There is a certain duality at the heart of the problematic of self and other. According to Husserl, I can know the other only by analogy to myself. This is where apperception, analogical appresentation and pairing applied in Husserl's reflections eventually become clues to the way the phenomenological ego can develop a 'constitutional theory of the experience of someone else'. For Husserl, at the most basic level one intuits the other as the other's 'body' by a kind of 'analogizing apperception' to one's own body. At a somewhat higher level one can make a differentiation between 'ego' and 'alter ego' as given in 'an original pairing'. Thus, according to Husserl, we have an account of the manner in which the other enters into my field of perception. But the other never enters my field of perception with the same originality as does the ego, and in this sense Husserl characterizes the transcendental synthesis to which ego and alter ego belong as a 'passive synthesis' of 'association' and not of 'identification'. The distinction is important from an epistemological point of view because from the standpoint of subjectivity from which Husserl begins his analysis one can never reach an identification with the other. That is because the alter ego can never be present to the ego in the same way in which the ego is present to itself. Hence, the problem of the other, the other as 'mind' or as 'body', could never be resolved in an originary way. It is this dilemma that Husserl gave to the philosophy of language. The philosophy of language would resolve the dilemma of self and other, but only by undercutting the radical dichotomy that exists between them. Hence the problem becomes one of constructing a notion of intersubjectivity which preserves the uniqueness of self-identity while at the same time bridging the gap between self and other.

I From identity to self

At the heart of Ricoeur's reflections on the identity of the self is the thesis that identity can be conceived in the sense of either 'the Latin *ipse* or *idem*'. The latter term tends to emphasize sameness while the former term, and this is the interesting point, 'implies no assertion concerning some unchanging core of the personality'.[4] *Ipse* then can be used to articulate the experience of the self in time, the category under which subjectivity returns.

Ricoeur's initial strategy is to think through the process of identification by considering the basic analytic transitions from semantics to pragmatics, keeping in mind the relationship of the problem of identity to that of self-identity. Inasmuch as semantics and pragmatics both claim to overcome the philosophy of subjectivity, there is an underlying polemical thrust to Ricoeur's argument. Ideally, the argument, which could be conceived as a critique of the analytic theories of reference and reflexivity, would read as follows: 1) while semantics can conceive of identity only on the basis of a conception of *idem* or sameness, 2) pragmatics (speech-act theory) attempts to get beyond the question of identity to self-identity through a theory of interlocution. 3) However, theories of interlocution are limited by being able to consider identity only on the basis of the concept of sameness or *idem*. 4) Finally, the basic thrust of the movement from semantics to pragmatics is towards particularity, which should be towards a conception of self-identity based on *ipséité*. This, of course, is a matter of contention. Can the logic of the move from semantics to pragmatics include a transition from the concept of self based on identity to one that can acknowledge otherness and temporal particularity? If the movement from semantics to pragmatics cannot account for this latter development, then one is left to ponder the achievement of the reconceptualization of the self at the level of a theory of interlocution. While Ricoeur wants to reconceptualize the basic thrust of the analytic arguments as arguments which drive towards *ipséité*, it is not at all clear that the authors of those arguments either can or wish to do so. While the basic thrust of the analytic arguments may be towards a more particular conception, their fundamental limitation is that they are unable to conceive of the self as an entity that changes over time. Without loading the argument, I will simply assume for the moment that this is an inadequacy.

Taking Strawson's *Individuals*[5] as representative of the semantic form of argumentation, Ricoeur argues that the self is 'neutralized by being included within the same spatiotemporal schema as all the other particulars'. The concept of identity is thus expressed as 'sameness (*mêmeté*) and not as selfhood (*ipséité*)'.[6] Hence, 'in a problematic of identifying reference, the sameness of one's body conceals its self-hood'.[7] To be sure, Ricoeur acknowledges the uniqueness of Straw-son's strategy.

> The advantage of this new strategic decision is certain: to say that bodies are the first basic particulars is to eliminate, as possible candidates, mental events; that is, representations or thoughts, whose shortcoming is that they are private rather than public entities. Their lot, as specific predicates of persons, is simply postponed. They first had to be dislodged from the dominant position of ultimate reference, which they occupy in a subjectivist idealism.[8]

Given the great advantage of this approach, the consequence is that it tends to eliminate the problem of the so-called 'lived body', i.e. the body that is experienced as belonging to a particular self. Hence, the actuality of selfhood is really concealed in a kind of likeness of one particular body with all other bodies, i.e. as a predicate ascribed to an entity. And this is the overall point when it comes to the forms of ascription within the 'primitive' concept of the person. While being able to characterize selfhood by reference to sameness, this view overlooks the particularity associated with the self as an entity living through and within time.

The theory of interlocution (pragmatics) moves beyond the problematic of identifying reference by considering the 'speakers' who refer in specific ways. In this sense the 'illocutionary act' is joined to the act of 'predication' by concentration on the reflexive implications of the notion of utterance.

Ricoeur believes this concentration on the utterance of the speakers *could* lead to the notion of selfhood because the reference is to the event of utterance. 'In short, utterance equals interlocution.' But what of this utterance? It would appear that the very emphasis on the one who utters would allow for the expression of the self as a unique someone who makes this particular statement as a testament to her own identity. But that is precisely where speech-act theory becomes elusive. The very reflexivity which characterizes speech-act theory does not sustain the promise of highlighting the particularity of selfhood. Instead, it manifests itself as a form of sameness. 'Ultimately, one would have to say that reflexivity is not intrinsically bound up with a self in the strong sense of self-consciousness'.[9] As Ricoeur claims, the intersubjective character of speech-acts is derived by the fact that the utterance 'is mirrored' in the act of another. The result is a 'reflexivity without selfhood'. However, Ricoeur thinks that speech-act theory can drive beyond itself in the sense that by 'anchoring' interlocution in the 'speaking subjects' the particular experience of the speakers would have to be taken into account.

In any case, if one chooses to step beyond Ricoeur at this point a more general argument can begin to take shape. The move to speech-act theory has been taken to mean a step beyond the philosophy of the subject. Hence, the movement to the philosophy of language conceived in this sense was thought to overcome the dilemma of subjectivity. However, that step was achieved at a certain price. Only by reducing the phenomenon of subjectivity to sameness, and thereby sacrificing the temporality of the individual self, could speech-act theory achieve a rational explanation of interlocutionary activity. If one were to accept Ricoeur's argument, it would appear that the interlocutionary act taken as event would drive speech-act theory beyond itself. But even if it does not, it would still be impossible in purely illocutionary terms for one to account for the self as embodied and temporal. In other words, speech-act theory retains the Cartesian bias of the disembodied self. One might even go so far as to suggest that such an approach retains the traces of a philosophy of identity.

Here, one could make a further point about the manner in which continental philosophy has appropriated the philosophy of language, particularly in the form of speech-act theory. Immediate recourse to a theory of interlocution as the linguistic counterpart for a theory of intersubjectivity as, for example, in Jürgen Habermas's attempt to overcome the so-called dilemmas of the philosophy of consciousness by recourse to speech-act theory achieves its goal, but only at a certain price; namely, through a false reduction of self to other under the rubric of the identity of discourse. The problem is that the very philosophy of identity that such an attempt is tailored to overcome is suspect, inasmuch as it relies on another system of identities, namely, identical expression.[10]

Certainly, it is not possible simply to go back to Husserl. The wager is this: if we go forward remaining within the context of a philosophy of language, it is possible to reconceptualize self-identity as narrative identity. In brief, this is the potential for a theory of narrative.

II The self and personal identity

Thus far we have established that the problematic of subjectivity re-enters the philosophical scene because the analytic philosophies of language could only conceptualize an identity in terms of sameness. In order to take the next step in the argument it will be necessary to show, first, what it means to conceptualize an identity that can be character-ized temporally and, second, how one can achieve such characteriz-ation linguistically. Following Ricoeur, the first issue centers around personal identity while the second concerns narrative identity.

The conceptualization of sameness privileges similitude. The most radical form of similitude is, of course, numerical. We say of two different things that they represent one and the same thing; for example, *x* equals *p*, cognition equals recognition. The criterion of similitude begins to weaken when applied to a 'current perception' in relationship to a 'memory'. Ricoeur suggests that, in order to posit identity, one needs a category such as 'uninterrupted continuity' which would postulate a relationship between present and past. Hence, the concept of similitude should be widened to include various discon-tinuities or changes in identity. Ricoeur suggests that at the base of this widening of the concept of similitude is the 'principle of *permanence in time*'.[11] One can anticipate the argument in terms of the already posited dialectic between sameness and selfhood, between *idem* and *ipse*. It is not the case that one gives up on sameness. But, through the introduction of the category of temporality, the question becomes one of attempting to get beyond the reduction to sameness, which eliminates the different forms which self-identity takes over time. One will then have to find a way in which the self endures, in the sense that earlier forms of identity can be associated with later forms of identity without reduction to sameness. Ricoeur's solution is to designate identity through character.

In its most elemental form character is defined as a 'set of lasting dispositions by which a person is recognized'.[12] Of course, the Aristotelian origin of this designation is apparent. The self is known by its character. In its most originary sense, character announces itself and can be so designated through habit. As Ricoeur puts it, 'habit gives a history to character'.[13] Habits can manifest themselves as in process of being formed, and they can be already acquired. In terms of the dialectic between *idem* and *ipse*, they give the appearance of sameness to a changing self. In fact, habit tends to abolish the appearance of innovation by giving the appearance of sameness. In Ricoeur's terms it is here that *ipse* manifests itself as *idem*.

III Narrative identity: the dialectic of selfhood and sameness

A narrative can link the past with the future by giving a sense of continuity to an ever changing story of the self. Because narrative has this potentiality it is uniquely qualified to express the ongoing dialectic of selfhood and sameness while at the same time it can allow one to rethink the meaning of subjectivity. The way in which narrative identity is initially expressed is through fictional narratives. Fictional narratives disclose 'character' through 'emplotment'. In Ricoeur's words there is a kind of 'discordant concordance' which is conveyed through narrative which in philosophical terms may be conceived as a 'synthesis of the heterogeneous'.[14] The plot accounts for 'diverse mediations' between 'disparate components of the action – intentions, causes, and chance occurrences – and the sequence of the story' as well as mediations 'between pure succession and the unity of the temporal form'.[15] In other words, narratives link events together by giving account of the intentions of the actors so that the character appears to have a certain chronology. Narratives make sense out of self-identity in the context of time.

Narratives account for action. But they do so in complex ways. In the dialectic between plot and character narrative resolves the potential contradiction between the two by 'granting to the character an initiative . . . and . . . by assigning to the narrative as such the power of determining the beginning, the middle, and the end of an action'.[16]

This is, of course, the dilemma of tragedy. The protagonist appears to be the author of her own activity while spectator and chorus alike know that the narrative itself will eventually overwhelm the character in such a manner that she must succumb to the inevitable unfolding of events.

Ricoeur speculates that this dialectic between action and character produces a dialectic internal to the character. On the one hand the character draws her 'singularity' from the 'unity of life' which is, in turn, considered as 'a temporal totality which is itself singular and distinguished from all others'. This is the concordance side of the dialectic between concordance and discordance. On the other hand, '[f]ollowing the line of discordance, this temporal totality is threatened by the disruptive effect of the unforeseeable events that punctuate it'.[17] This forces the 'identity of character' to be summed up in the 'history of a life'. 'Thus chance is transmuted into fate'.[18] Freedom succumbs to necessity.

One of Ricoeur's most brilliant insights is to reconceive this dialectic of concordance and discordance on a higher level as the dialectic between sameness and selfhood thematized as a set of 'imaginative variations' entertained by the narrative. This is the very point of narrative. Narrative does not seek to conceal this dialectic but rather it seeks out the contradictions.

> In this sense, literature proves to consist in a vast laboratory for thought experiments in which the resources of variation encompassed by narrative identity are put to the test of narration.[19]

One can in fact generate a standard for the interpretation of fiction from this point of view. On the one hand, there is the kind of 19th-century literature which seeks to favor sameness of character, to which can be contrasted a kind of 20th-century literature which subjects selfhood to almost infinite variation. The latter would reflect a loss of identity while the former would concentrate on identity. Selfhood is defined by sameness as, for example, the character of Roskolnikov, in Dostoevsky's *Crime and Punishment*, to be contrasted with the protagonist in Musil's *Man Without Qualities*. In the latter, speculates Ricoeur, selfhood is exposed by 'taking away the support of sameness'.[20]

Equally, this reflection on the imaginative variations between selfhood and sameness can be used as a clue to the distinction between literary and technological (science fiction) forms of narrative. Here Ricoeur turns to his hermeneutic background to make the distinction. Literary fictions 'remain imaginative variations on an invariant, our corporeal condition experienced as the existential mediation between the self and the world'.[21] In literature we encounter beings like ourselves who are anchored to the world through their corporeal condition. One might even go so far as to state that, in literature, action is mediated through suffering. With science fiction the case is different. There the focus is upon technology. The brain is taken to be the equivalent of the person. The problematic for science fiction is the mediation of identity through sameness inasmuch as the resolution of identity is performed at the conceptual level. In contrast, the problematic of literary fiction can be said to be selfhood or 'selfhood in its dialectical relation to sameness'.[22]

IV Narration: between prescription and description

Seen against the backdrop of analytic philosophies of identity, the concept of narrative identity opens up the realm of the particular self, whose identity would have been subsumed under the category of sameness. As such, narrative can reopen the question of the self as a subjective and particular self, but on the basis of a form of linguistic expression. As narrative can thematize action, so it can be the bridge to ethical life. Or to put it specifically, it can bridge the gap between the 'ascription of action to an agent who has the capacity to act' and the 'imputation to an agent who has the obligation to act'.[23] Narrative has the unique capacity to conceive of that obligation mimetically. In this sense narrative provides an imaginative variation on practice. Hence, Aristotle could claim that 'tragedy' can be conceived mimetically in relationship to, not persons per se, but to 'action and life'. Here, through narrative we have the relationship between *mimesis, bios* and *praxis.*

However, fiction cannot be applied to life praxis without complications. To be sure, the organization of one's own life-history and a fictional account of a life are different. However, no one without the help of fiction can recount either their origin or death. Fiction complements life history by creating a framework where one's own life can be accounted for. It is in this sense that narrative identity has a relationship to ethical life. Hence, Ricoeur denies that the narration has a purely aesthetic dimension. Indeed, reflecting Kant's *Critique of Judgement*, one takes pleasure in following the destiny of a character through the narration, even to the extent that one can suspend the teleology of action itself. But this is just what narration contributes for ethics: namely, by analogy to the thought experiment, new ways to evaluate character and action.

> The thought experiments we conduct in the great laboratory of the imaginary are also explorations in the realm of good and evil. Transvaluing, even devaluing, is still evaluating. Moral judgment has not been abolished, it is rather itself subjected to the imaginative variations proper to fiction.[24]

Earlier, Ricoeur introduced the dialectic of selfhood and sameness under the categories of character and self-constancy. Self-constancy referred to 'keeping one's word' while character referred to the different moments in which selfhood expressed itself. Narrative not only poses the possible imaginative variations on the problematic of selfhood and sameness; it also, when applied to real life, invites difficulties. When one moves from fiction to real life the potential for loss of identity, as in the case of Musil's *Man Without Qualities*, is refigured as the self in reality 'confronted with the hypothesis of its own nothingness'.[25] On the ethical plane, the problem becomes one of conceiving how the self, which is confronted with the potentiality of its own nothingness, can assert itself as a moral or ethical agent.

V Time and narrative

I want to return now to a point made at the outset of this discussion. We began with the thesis that the failure of both a semantic theory of representation and a pragmatic theory of interlocution was that they were unable to render identity in any way other than through sameness. As such they were unable to render identity as selfhood which may be characterized by differentiation over time. Narrative identity has been able to overcome the dilemma which is at the heart of a theory of interlocution. Hence, the most important thing about narrative identity is its ability to make apparent the temporal dimension of selfhood, which must be obliterated if the theory of interlocution is said to be a triumph over the philosophy of the subject. In this sense it would be necessary to reconceive a theory of interlocution in the context of time. As Ricoeur suggests, 'every speech-act (or every act of discourse) commits the speaker and does so in the present'.[26] In this sense, 'assertions' are not mere empty identities. Rather, they are utterances in a temporal context which carry with them the tacit implication of 'sincerity'.

> I cannot assert something without introducing a tacit clause of sincerity into my saying it, in virtue of which I effectively signify what I am saying, any more than I can do so without holding as true what I affirm.[27]

If we conceive of a promise or a commitment in time, it is clear that it will carry with it the implication that one will be bound to it. In order to account for that one would have to bring back some form of subjectivity in the sense of the reference to the intentionality of a subject. 'By promising, I intentionally place myself under the obligation to do what I say I will do'.[28] And if one obligates oneself in the present it is also clear that one will have some obligation towards the future. Indeed, to make a promise has the implication of keeping it. The force of the statement 'I can' would then carry with it the implication of my initiative. If I say that I will do it, this implies, as Ricoeur suggests, not only that the statement 'becomes my act' but that I will inscribe 'my act in the course of things'. In this sense, the speech-act occurs at the juncture of internal and cosmological time. On the one hand it forms my commitment to the living present, while at the same time, commitment to such an act coordinates the activity of an individual within the course of things. Such an act then has an ethical signification which commits one to a certain form of participation in an historical present.

VI Narrative, subjectivity and validity

In *Time and Narrative* Ricoeur makes the claim that 'narrative' is the 'guardian of time, insofar as there can be no thought about time

without narrated time'.[29] Within this claim rests Ricoeur's fundamental reconstruction of the Husserlian thematic with regard to time,
which in Husserl's context raised fundamental questions regarding the
validity of intersubjective knowledge. In order to illustrate the problem
allow me to return to the 'Fifth Meditation' from which this discussion
began. When Husserl attempted to verify the experience of the other he
did so within the framework of internal time-consciousness. What is
shared between self and other is time, even though the other has to be
experienced 'somatically' in space. His claim is simply that 'what is
appresented by the "body" over there, in my primordial "surrounding
world", is not something psychic of mine, nor anything else in my
sphere of ownness. I am *here* somatically'.[30] In the terms of this spatial
metaphor, I can build up my experience of the other through my sphere
of ownness to include the otherness of the other but only through
appresentation, i.e. the indirect presentation of the other.

> My own ego however, the ego given in constant self-perception, is
> actual now with the content belonging to his Here. Therefore an ego is
> *appresented*, as *other* than mine.[31]

It is the bodily character of the other that raises real questions
regarding validity, in the sense that valid knowledge can only be
achieved at the appresentational level. How can one have valid
knowledge of the other as a body? In this sense it is the other as flesh
that forces one to raise the question of the validity of intersubjective
knowledge. If, of course, one could reduce selfhood to sameness the
problem would disappear.

When Husserl turns to temporality, which he actually presupposes
in the above analysis of the spatial and perceptual character of bodily
apprehension, he follows a similar pattern. Initially, of course, it is my
experience of myself that is experienced temporally. Following Husserl, one constructs a phenomenological account of the experience of
temporality as it effects knowledge by showing how, through experiences of past and future in an ever expanding now, temporality is at the
foundation of valid knowledge of the self. In other words the temporal
dimension of the experience of someone else follows a pattern similar
to the spatial dimension. Husserl refers to a '*common time form*' which
occurs as a consequence of the '*coexistence of my "polar" Ego and the
other Ego*, of my whole concrete ego and his, my intentional life and
his, my "realities" and his'.[32] For Husserl that leads to the following
proposition: 'every primordial temporality automatically acquires the
significance of being merely an original mode of appearance of
Objective temporality to a particular subject'.[33] This leads him to make

the claim, from the inside as it were, that internal time is related to objective time.

> In this connection we see that the temporal community of the constitutively interrelated monads is indissoluble, because it is tied up essentially with the constitution of *a world and a world time*.[34]

But 'world time' is not the same as the time of the phenomenological ego, with the result that knowledge of the other as it is mediated through the temporality of the phenomenological subject is discontinuous with knowledge of the self. Again, one returns to the question of how valid knowledge can be conceived on the level of intersubjectivity.

Ricoeur has shown how narrative identity resolves the discontinuity between calendar or cosmic time and internal time through its ability to integrate an account of the self within the context of a larger temporal framework. And the unique advantage of such an approach is that one can preserve the distinctive character of the experience of the self within the framework of the constancy of time. Clearly, with reference to the theory of interlocution, this reconfigures the role of the subject and subjectivity within a framework which attempts to establish validity. One might conclude that this contribution will force us to rethink the problem of the intersubjective achievement of valid knowledge one more time.

Boston College, Chestnut Hill, MA, USA

Notes

1 I refer to the numerous attempts to reconstruct a theory of intersubjectivity, from Hegel's concept of intersubjectivity as articulated through his critique of Kant's concept of autonomy, to Husserl's attempt to account for intersubjectivity in the context of his account of phenomenology, as well as the more recent attempts to account for intersubjectivity within the confines of language. To anticipate the argument of this article, Ricoeur's re-examination of the notion of the self opens up the question of subjectivity again after recent attempts to overcome the notion of subjectivity through a philosophy of language. In particular, I am interested in Ricoeur's attempt to force the 'theory of interlocution' associated with speech-act theory beyond the narrow confines of the 'identity' problematic which characterizes it.

2 Paul Ricoeur, *Oneself as Another*, trans. Kathleen Blamey (Chicago, IL: University of Chicago Press, 1992).
3 Edmund Husserl, *Cartesian Meditations*, trans. Dorion Cairns (The Hague: Martinus Nijhoff, 1960).
4 Ricoeur, *Oneself as Another*, p. 2.
5 Peter Strawson, *Individuals* (London: Methuen, 1957).
6 Ricoeur's critique is stated in the following way: 'In Strawson's strategy, however, the recourse to self-designation is intercepted, so to speak, from the very start because of the central thesis that determines the criterion for identifying anything as a basic particular. This criterion is the fact that individuals belong to a single spatiotemporal schema, which, it is stated from the start, contains *us*, in which *we ourselves* take place. The self is indeed mentioned in this passing remark, but it is immediately neutralized by being included within the same spatiotemporal schema as all the other particulars.' Ricoeur, *Oneself as Another*, p. 32.
7 ibid., p. 33.
8 ibid., pp. 33–4.
9 ibid., p. 47.
10 The theory of communicative action, relying as it does on speech-act theory, is unable to contextualize self-identity. A discourse theory with its overly atemporal reduction of self-identity to identical expression requires a narrative theory as its complement.
11 Ricoeur, *Oneself as Another*, p. 117.
12 ibid., p. 121.
13 ibid.
14 ibid., p. 141.
15 ibid.
16 ibid., p. 147.
17 ibid.
18 ibid.
19 ibid., p. 148.
20 ibid., p. 149.
21 ibid., p. 150.
22 ibid.
23 ibid., p. 152.
24 ibid., p. 164.
25 ibid., p. 166.
26 Paul Ricoeur, *Time and Narrative*, Vol. 3, trans. Kathleen Blamey and David Pellauer (Chicago, IL: University of Chicago Press, 1988), p. 232.
27 ibid.
28 ibid., p. 233.

29 ibid., p. 241.
30 Husserl, *Cartesian Meditations*, pp. 118–19; original emphasis.
31 ibid., p. 119; original emphasis.
32 ibid., p. 128; original emphasis.
33 ibid.
34 ibid.; original emphasis.

Richard Kearney

Narrative imagination: between ethics and poetics

Imagination has been an abiding, if often inconspicuous, preoccupation of Paul Ricoeur. In most of his works Ricoeur speaks less of imagination itself than of its multifarious expressions in symbol, metaphor, myth, dream, narrative and the social imaginary. This indirect approach is, I suspect, a scruple of hermeneutic detour inspired by the Kantian conviction that imagination is an 'art hidden in the depths of nature . . . a blind but indispensable faculty of the human soul'. If imagination indeed recurs in the dramatis personae of Ricoeur's work, it usually comes on stage masked, doffs a variety of costumes, and generally prefers the discreet voice of prompter to that of central performer.

In his conclusion to 'Metaphor and the Central Problem of Hermeneutics', first published in 1972, Ricoeur offers this hint of tacit agendas:

> Allow me to conclude in a way which would be consistent with a theory of interpretation which places the emphasis on 'opening up a world'. Our conclusion should also 'open up' some new perspectives, but on what? Perhaps on the old problem of the imagination which I have carefully put aside. Are we not ready to recognize in the power of the imagination, no longer simply the faculty of deriving 'images' from our sensory experience, but the capacity for letting new worlds shape our understanding of ourselves? This power would not be conveyed by images, but by the emergent meanings in our language. Imagination would thus be treated as a dimension of language. In this way, a new link would appear between imagination and metaphor. We shall, for the time being, refrain from entering this half-open door.[1]

In later works, from *The Rule of Metaphor* (1977) to *Lectures on Ideology and Utopia* (1986), *Du texte à l'action* (1986), and *Time and Narrative* (1984–8), Ricoeur returns at telling moments to this 'half-open door' and offers glimpses of what lies ahead. But, he has not yet pushed the door wide open. Perhaps his reserve expresses recognition that the passage from philosophical reflection to the 'hidden art' of imagination represents a hermeneutic threshold where philosophizing, in the strictly speculative sense, ends and poetics begins? Or perhaps there is a further sense of the limit at work here – a boundary marking a flexible but necessary divide between the *poetical* imagination (where all is permitted and 'passion for the possible' reigns supreme) and the *ethical* imagination (answerable to the suffering and action of real human beings)? Such a boundary would serve as a frontier post, where imagination exchanges the immunity of poetic license for a sense of responsibility to others – dead and living, present and past – towards whom we carry an irremissible debt. A critical hermeneutics of imagination functions accordingly as a *mentalité frontalière*, safeguarding the distinction between poetics and ethics while simultaneously invigilating moments of transition and interchange between them. That, at least, is a hypothesis I explore in what follows.

I have documented elsewhere the development of Ricoeur's theory of imagination from his early to later works.[2] Here I propose to concentrate on one aspect of this theory, narrative. I will confine most of my remarks to two – in my view crucial – passages in Volume 3, Part 2 of *Time and Narrative* (1984–8). The first features in the chapter 'The Interweaving of History and Fiction' and deals with the function of *historical imagination*. The second features in the 'Conclusion' and focuses on the problem of *narrative identity* in poetics and ethics.

I

In the first passage, Ricoeur argues that time is made human through the interweaving of history and fiction – or more precisely through the 'refiguration' of time in historical and fictional narrative. Imagination has a pivotal role here: 1) as a 'standing-in-for-the-past'; and, 2) as a return ticket from the world of the text to the world of the reader. Narrative imagination embraces both processes of refiguration – historical and fictional.

The interaction between historical and fictional narrative leads Ricoeur into an extended analysis of the function of imagination in *reading*. While history and fiction are clearly not the same ('historians argue, poets invent'), there is a convergence of the imaginative intentionalities of history and fiction at the level of the reader. Here history and fiction 'concretize' each other's intentionalities. For narrative theory this concretization corresponds to the phenomenon of 'seeing as' in metaphorical reference (analyzed in detail in *The Rule of the Metaphor*). It arises in relation to our historical consciousness's standing-for-the-past through the use of *analogy*; and, again in the actualization of a text considered as a work to be performed. But these 'concretizations' occur only when *history makes use of fiction* and *fiction makes use of history* – both for the same end, namely, the refiguration of time. 'This reciprocal concretization marks the triumph of the notion of figure in the form of "imaging that"; or more literally: "providing oneself with a figure of" [*se figurer que*] . . .'.[3]

Concerning the first of these modes of concretization – the fictionalization of history – Ricoeur makes it clear that he is not just talking about the role of narrative imagination in 'configuration' (i.e. emplotment/*mise-en-intrigue*). He is thinking more specifically of the way imagination intends the past 'as it actually was'. This latter intention does not mean denying the difference between a 'real past' and an 'unreal' one; rather, it requires that we demonstrate in *what unique way* the narrative imagination is interpolated into the 'intended having-been' of history.

What are the implications of such a claim? The specific character of historical reference to the past is that it seeks to reinscribe the time of narrative within the time of the universe. But, curiously, it is precisely in respect of this 'realist thesis' that imagination enters into the intending of what has been. It does so under three main rubrics: the *calendar*; the *succession of generations*; and the *trace*.

Already, at the level of a calendar, the 'reading of signs' involves an act of translation that brings together two perspectives on time – the natural/cosmic/physical motion of planets, on the one hand, and lived human time, on the other. The calendar enlists the schematizing power of the imagination in conjoining astronomical and social dimensions; and this schematizing clearly entails an interpretation of signs (similar to the reading of a sundial or clock). 'Dates are assigned to potential presents, to imagined presents', as Ricoeur puts it, and in this manner all memories accumulated by collective memory become dated events, due to their reinscription in calendar time.[4]

Amplifying the range of schematizing connectors between narrative and universal time, Ricoeur explains how the 'succession of generations' combines a biological component *and* an imaginative one:

It is always possible to extend recollection through the chain of ancestral memories, to move back in time by extending this regressive movement through imagination, just as it is possible for every one of us to situate our own temporality in the series of generations, with the more or less necessary help of calendar time. In this sense, the network of contemporaries, predecessors and successors schematizes – in the Kantian sense of the term – the relation between the more biological phenomenon of the succession of generations and the more intellectual phenomenon of the reconstruction of the realm of contemporaries, predecessors and successors. The *mixed* character of this threefold realm underscores its imaginary aspect.[5]

But is it in the phenomenon of the trace that the 'imaginary' character of connectors, founding historical time, finds its most fundamental expression. The imaginative mediation operative here is inscribed in the mixed structure of the trace as *sign-effect*. This structure takes the form of a synthetic function involving: 1) casual inferences applied to the trace as a mark left behind, and 2) acts of interpretation directed to the specifically signifying character of the trace as something *present* standing for something *past*. The synthetic activity of 'retracing' embraces diverse functions of selecting, preserving, collecting and reading archival documents which serve to schematize the traces as a *reinscription of lived time*.

Here Ricoeur opens out the analysis of the schematizing trace to the concrete workings of the 'historical imagination'. The imaginary character of the acts that mediate the trace is evidenced in the intellectual work of interpreting ruins, fossils, remains, monuments, museum pieces, and the like. However, these acquire the value of the trace – as agency of historical time – only when we provide ourselves, as readers, with a figure of the social and cultural context surrounding the relic that today is missing. With the expression 'to provide ourselves with a figure of', we again touch upon the activity of imagination.[6]

At this stage of the analysis Ricoeur supplements his poetics of historical narrative with an ethics of responsibility to the past – what he calls 'the debt we owe the dead'.[7] As soon as we genuinely address the question of the 'pastness of the past', the mediating/schematizing role of the imagination reaches a new urgency. The spontaneous 'realism' of the historians who lay claim to the past as it actually was (*wie es eigentlich gewesen*) cannot circumvent the difficult notion of 'standing-for'. This signals the ongoing ethical claim of 'something that happened' – a *Gegenüber* no longer existing today – on the ways we retrace or reread the past. Now we encounter the 'right of the past as it once was' to incite and rectify our narrative reconstructions of history, reminding us of our debt to those who have lived, suffered and died – reminding us that (contra Faurisson and other revisionists) the gas ovens *did* exist, Nagasaki and Cambodia *were* bombed, show trials and gulags *were* inflicted on countless innocent people.

The ostensible paradox here, however, is that it should be *imagination* which responds to the ethical summons to respect the reality of the past. It is poetics which comes to the service of ethics as a means of recalling our debt to the dead. It is the 'imaginary' which imposes itself once more as the indispensable servant of standing-for, providing us with a *figure of what was*.

The imaginative process of standing-for is complex. If re-enactment is a central goal of 'historical imagination', it is not its only goal. In addition to the imaginative act of reappropriating the past as present (under the category of the Same), historical imagination also has a duty to the otherness of the past by way of expressing the moment of what-is-no-more – what is absent in the narrative act of *standing-for*. 'It is still the imaginary', Ricoeur argues, 'that keeps otherness from slipping into the unsayable. It is always through some transfer from Same to Other, in empathy and imagination, that the Other that is foreign is brought closer.'[8] Thus, Ricoeur – in the tradition of Dilthey, Husserl and Gadamer – pursues the hermeneutic function of *transfer by analogy*; that is, the capacity of an interpreter to transport himself or herself into an alien psychic life.

It is this very transfer, moreover, that Lyotard and certain other postmodern advocates of the 'irrepresentable sublime' rule out in their critique of imagination. The following passage from Lyotard's essay, 'After the Sublime, the State of Aesthetics', exemplifies this stance: 'As every presentation consists in the "forming" of the matter . . . the disaster suffered by the imagination can be understood as the sign that the forms are not relevant to the sublime sentiment. But in that case, where does the matter stand, if the forms are no longer there to make it *presentable*?'[9] In the attempted subversion of imagination by devotees of the 'textual sublime', we may find not only 'Kant disfigured', but our ethical debt to the reality of what actually happened compromised.[10]

By contrast, what the hermeneutic recourse to analogizing imagination brings out in relation to the past-as-it-actually-was is the tropological nature of the term *as/wie*. The *as* comes to assume the value of '*such as* . . .' interpreted in metaphor, metonomy, synecdoche and irony. By the same token, the representative (as distinct from representational) function of historical imagination intensifies the act of 'providing ourselves with a figure of . . .'. In other words, the historical past is what I would have witnessed if I had been there (just as the other side of things is what I would see if I were standing over there rather than here). Tropology becomes the imaginary aspect of standing-for.[11]

Ricoeur takes an additional step that accentuates the rapport between poetical and ethical imagination; namely, the step beyond the dated past to the specifically *refigured* past. The modality of 'figurativeness' becomes now *explicitly* that of narrative imagination. Ricoeur resolves to show: 1) how specific imaginary features, made evident in fictional narrative, come to enrich diverse imaginary mediations (calendar, trace, etc.) mentioned above, and 2) how the actual interweaving of fiction and history operates in the *refiguration of time*.

Developing the metaphorical function of 'seeing as' into the more broadly imaginative function of 'providing oneself with a figure of', Ricoeur shows how the refiguration of the past in terms of quasi-intuitive fulfillment relates to history. Once we acknowledge that history is a refiguration of time, we can admit that the writing of history emulates and incorporates many types of narrative emplotment borrowed from literary practice. But what history-writing borrows from fiction-writing is not confined to the act of configuration (composition, emplotment, *muthos*). It also involves – and crucially so – what Ricoeur calls the 'representative function of the historical imagination'.[12] One and the same text can, for instance, be a great work of history *and* a great novel. It can relate the way things actually happened in the past and *at the same time* make us see, feel and live it 'as if' we were there. Moreover, this 'fiction-effect' of history actually enhances, rather than diminishes, the project of standing-for. That is why a history text can be read as powerful evocative narrative rather than mere unreliable fantasy. Fiction can serve history as well as subvert it. The two are potential allies. Michelet's picture of the French Revolution, for example, is also a literary work comparable with Tolstoy's *War and Peace*.

The above rests upon the supposition that the tropological/rhetorical/figural aspect of history-writing necessarily entails a fiction-effect upon the reader. As we move from configuration (text) to refiguration (reader), we understand better how the historical imagination produces an implicit pact of reading – a complicity between the narrative voice and the implied reader. The reader suspends disbelief and accords the historian the right to represent other minds.

The deployment of such novelistic strategies by historians, to place vividly before the reader's mind some long-past event or personage, was already recognized by Aristotle in the *Rhetoric* under *lexis* 'locution' – a manner of making things visible 'as if' they were present.

The danger is, of course, that the figural 'as if' might collapse into a literal belief, so that we would no longer merely *see-as* but make the mistake of *believing we are seeing*. The danger of such 'hallucination of presence' – easy prey to dogmatism or fundamentalism – is restricted by the critical vigilance of responsible historians, who combine strategies of presence *and* distance, belief *and* disbelief, engagement *and* estrangement, to produce a proper balance of 'controlled illusion'.[13]

Perhaps things are not so simple, however. If critical freedom from naive illusion is one aspect of the historical narrator's ethical responsibility, another is readiness to refigure certain events of deep ethical intensity. While in some cases it may seem appropriate for historians to put aside strong feelings of indignation, commemoration, or compassion in order to offer an 'objective' explanation of how things happened, in other cases, such as Auschwitz, it would appear that the ethical neutralization proper to such *setting-at-a-distance* is neither possible nor desirable. The biblical watchword *Zakhor*, 'Remember!', is more appropriate in such circumstances – something Primo Levi, a survivor of the Nazi camps, made hauntingly plain in his resolve to tell the story as it happened in the most vivid fashion imaginable. The recourse to tropes and narratives to this end is motivated throughout by an ethical imperative: *people must not be allowed to forget lest it happen again*. As Levi puts it in his conclusion to *Si c'est un Homme*: 'The need to recount to "others", to make the "others" participate, acquired in us before and after our liberation the vehemence of an immediate impulse . . . and it was in response to such a need that I wrote my book.'[14]

In such cases, rememoration takes on an ethical character of testimony quite distinct from the triumphalist commemoration of history's great and powerful. For if the latter often tends towards legitimating an ideology of domination, the former moves in the opposite direction – towards a *felt* reliving of past suffering, injustice, or horror *as if* we were there. The distinction is important. The *tremendum horrendum* needs narrative imagination to plead its cause lest it slip irrevocably into oblivion. 'Horror attaches to events that must never be forgotten', explains Ricoeur. 'It constitutes the ultimate ethical motivation for the history of victims. The victims of Auschwitz are, *par excellence*, the representatives in our memory of all history's victims. Victimization is the other side of history that no cunning of reason can ever justify and that, instead, reveals the scandal of every theodicy of history.'[15] In such instances, the refigurative powers of narrative imagination prevent abstract historiography from neutralizing injustice or explaining things away.

The role of imagination in remembering the horrible is tied to a specific function of individuation in our historical consciousness: namely, the need to respect the *uniquely unique* character of events such as the Holocaust, or Hiroshima, or the gulag. While historical explanation generally seeks to connect things together and see disparate events as part of a larger cohesive pattern, historical imagination is more responsive to the incomparable nature of events; it endeavors to isolate their singularity from sanitizing homogenization – from Hegel's 'Ruse of Reason' as much as from Heidegger's 'Destiny of *Techne*' (which puts gas chambers and combine harvesters into the same category).[16]

But Ricoeur issues a caveat here. He warns against the tension between 1) historical explanation that *connects*, and 2) historical imagination that *singularizes*, being pushed to the point of rupture. The latent conflict must not, he insists, lead to a 'ruinous dichotomy between a history that would dissolve the event in explanation and a purely emotional retort that would dispense us from thinking the unthinkable'.[17] To obviate such polarization, Ricoeur recommends that historical explanation *and* individuation be used to abet each other. In this scenario, the better the historical explanation the more indignant we become; the more struck we are by the narrative retelling of events, the more we strive to understand them. This is a way of saying that narrative imagination gives rise to thought (*le récit donne à penser*) just as thought gives rise to narrative imagination (*la pensée donne à raconter*).

All this amounts to endorsing the capacity of fictional narrative to provoke an illusion of quasi-presence controlled by critical distance. Without the quasi-intuitiveness of fiction, the horrible would be no more than 'blind feeling' (as no doubt it was, alas, for most of those who endured it at the time). The refigurative act of standing-for the past provides us with a 'figure' to see *and* to think about, to image *and* to respond to. 'Fiction gives eyes to the horrified narrator. Eyes to see and to weep. The present state of literature on the Holocaust provides ample proof of this. Either one counts the cadavers or one tells the story of the victims.'[18]

The interweaving of fiction and history reminds us, moreover, that both narrative modes share a common origin in *epic*. A particular characteristic of epic is that it preserves the memory of suffering (or glory in other contexts) on the collective scale of peoples. Placed in the service of the unforgettable, narrative fiction permits historiography to live up to the task of collective memory. For history-telling to lose this testimonial vocation is for it to risk becoming an idle game of curious exotica or, worse, a value-neutral positivism of dead facts. Such outcomes are not ethically permissible. 'There are perhaps crimes that must not be forgotten, victims whose suffering cries less for vengeance than for narration', writes Ricoeur. 'The will not to forget alone can prevent these crimes from ever occurring again.'[19] The ethical debt to the dead calls upon the poetical power to narrate.

II

The second and final passage I analyze from Ricoeur's *Time and Narrative*, Volume 3, concerns his discussion of narrative identity in his 'Conclusions'. Ricoeur ties the question of identity to narrative by suggesting that the best response to the question 'Who is the author or agent?' is to tell the story of a life. The permanent identity of a person, presupposed by the designation of a proper name, is provided by the conviction that it is the same subject who perdures through its diverse acts and words between birth and death. 'The story told tells about the "who." And the identity of this "who" therefore itself must be a narrative identity.'[20] Ricoeur even surmises that without recourse to narration, the problem of personal identity would be irresolvable.

He distinguishes, however, between this positive narrative identity of self (*ipse*) and a substantialist or formalist identity of sameness (*idem*). The narrative self constitutes an ongoing process of self-constancy and self-rectification which relies on poetic imagination to synthesize the different horizons of past, present and future. This self obviates the polar opposition between Same and Other to the extent that its identity as *soi-même* 'rests on a temporal structure that conforms to the model of dynamic identity arising from the poetic composition of a text.'[21]

Developing this textual analogy, Ricoeur argues that self-identity as *ipse* (*soi-même*) can include mutability and transformation within the cohesion of one lifetime. This means that the identity of human subjects (individual or collective) is recognized as a perpetual task of reinterpretation in the light of stories we tell ourselves and others. The subject becomes the reader and writer of its own life. The task of narrative imagination runs as follows: 'The story of a life continues to be refigured by all the truthful or fictive stories a subject tells about himself or herself. The refiguration makes this life itself a cloth woven of stories told.'[22]

Ricoeur's stance on narrative identity receives support from a number of contemporary quarters – including recent works by Charles Taylor, Alasdair MacIntyre and Seyla Benhabib. Benhabib, for example, states in her book *Situating the Self* that 'the Enlightenment conception of the disembedded cogito no less than the empiricist illusion of a substance-like self cannot do justice to those contingent processes of socialization through which an infant becomes a person . . . capable of projecting a narrative into the world of which she is not only the author but the actor as well'.[23] Ricoeur is clearly not on his own in promoting what Benhabib terms the 'narrative structure of personal identity'.

What particularly interests me here is the ethical import of narrative self-identity. First, it suggests that the age-old virtue of self-knowledge (first promoted by Socrates and Seneca) involves for us today not some egotistical or narcissistic ego but an examined life freed from infantile archaism and ideological dogmatism. The ethical subject of self-knowledge is purged and clarified by the 'cathartic effects of narrative, be they historical or fictional, conveyed by our culture. So, self-constancy refers to a self instructed by the works of a culture that it has applied to itself.'[24]

Narrative identity operates at the level of *both* individual *and* communal identity. With respect to the former, Ricoeur cites the example of psychoanalytical case-histories where the subject commits itself to a 'talking cure' – that is, a working-through (*Durcharbeitung*) of unintelligible and unbearable experiences until some narrative emerges by means of which the analysand can acknowledge its self-constancy in and through change. This model of analytical working-through also applies, with variations, to the collective stories told by historians. Psychoanalysis represents an instructive laboratory for understanding narrative identity in allowing us to grasp how the 'story of a life comes to be constituted through a series of rectifications applied to previous narratives, just as the history of a people, or a collectivity, or an institution proceeds from the series of corrections that new historians bring to their predecessors' descriptions and explanations, and, step by step, to the legends that preceded this genuinely historiographical work'.[25] Stories proceed from stories – just as histories proceed from histories.

Subjects, individual or communal, come to *imagine* and *know* themselves in the stories they tell about themselves. By way of exemplifying this role of narrative imagination in the history of a community, Ricoeur chooses biblical Israel. He considers this case particularly applicable since few communities have been so intrinsically mobilized by the narratives they have told about themselves. It was in telling the sacred narratives foundational to its history that biblical Israel formed the historical community that bears its name. In a typical hermeneutic circle we discover an historical Jewish community drawing its identity from the reinterpretation of those texts it has itself created.

The circle is not confined, however, to case-histories of individuals or collective histories of peoples. It is a basic narrative structure of human-being-in-the-world. Before we ever use narrative imagination to *configure* our lives into meaningful stories, we have already used it to *prefigure* our lives in terms of symbolically structured and temporally schematized action. The completion of the hermeneutic circle with the *refiguring* of time by narrative (writing and reading) is, according to Ricoeur, a 'wholesome' one. Refiguration (the third mimetic relation) is characterized by a narrative identity 'stemming from the endless rectification of a previous narrative by a subsequent one'.[26] Narrative identity proposes a 'poetic resolution' to a hermeneutic circle. It recognizes that life is in quest of narrative just as narrative is in quest of life.

But the picture is not yet complete. Poetical resolutions also have consequences (and not always positive ones) for ethics. It must be conceded that if narrative imagination does indeed provide the subject with a structure of self-constancy, its fictional power also exposes the subject to imaginative variations of self and other that can easily *destabilize* narrative identity. The recognition that self-identity presupposes narrative imagination requires, accordingly, the corollary recognition that narrative identity is something which perpetually makes and unmakes itself. In short, narrative identity poses itself ultimately not only as an answer but as a question. That is why we will never cease to be puzzled by the age-old interrogative challenge – 'Who do you say that I am?' There is a fundamental fluidity built into the principle of narrative identity by virtue of the fact that it is founded on narrative imagination.

At this crucial point in his thesis Ricoeur suggests adding an additional spoke to the wheel of self-identity – one last argument to negotiate the shifting subsoil of narrative imagination. Admitting that the imaginative component of narrative generally inhabits worlds and minds foreign to ourselves, Ricoeur proposes this be curtailed by a countervailing component of 'will' that impels us to ethical commitment. 'Narrative exercises imagination more than the will', continues Ricoeur, particularly in the moment of stasis when we submit to the 'as-if' illusion of the text; but reading also includes a moment of impetus which summons the will to act – to embark on the return journey from text to action. This occurs when a reader decides to respond to the persuasive call of the text by saying 'Here I stand!' Citing Lévinas's example of promise-keeping, Ricoeur confirms that narrative identity is not equivalent to 'true self-constancy except through this decisive moment, which makes ethical responsibility the *highest factor* in self-constancy'.[27]

The implication here is that narrative *imagination* needs to be supplemented by narrative *will* if an ethical notion of self-identity, constant in its commitments and promises to others, is to be sustained. As it happens, narrativity does carry within itself a certain evaluative or prescriptive dimension. The strategy of persuasion imposed by narrators on readers is never completely ethically neutral; it induces a re-evaluation of one's world. 'Change your life!' was the call of the Grecian statue to the readers of the poet Rilke; and Ricoeur would seem to agree that most narrative works share something of this summons.

So here at last, on the threshold of ethical action, Ricoeur counsels narrative imagination to seek further courts of appeal for the ultimate safeguarding of justice. Narrative can bring us to the door of ethical action but it cannot lead us through. It can do so much, but no more. Ricoeur concludes that while narrative can indeed *make claim* to ethical justice, it finally 'belongs to the reader, now an agent, an initiator of action, to choose among the multiple proposals of ethical justice brought forth by reading. It is at this point that the notion of narrative identity encounters its limit and has to link up with the non-narrative components in the formation of an acting subject.'[28]

III

A certain postmodern strand in philosophy – extending from Bataille and Foucault to Lyotard and Derrida – has, I believe, accorded priority to poetics over ethics. This may sometimes lead to an aesthetic of 'deliberate irresponsibility', as has been said of Foucault,[29] or to one of indecisive 'indifference', as has been suggested of Derrida.[30] Whatever the accuracy of such claims, they betray an anxiety that poetics left to itself can be a dangerous game. If it is true, as Ricoeur says, that imagination knows no censure *in itself*, then the summons of responsibility to others has to come from *beyond itself* – that is, *from* others. What narrative permits is the structuring of imagination in a way which propels it beyond its egotistical circle to a relation of analogy, empathy, or apperception (*Paarung*) with others. This involves an 'enlarged mentality' of imagining oneself in the place of everybody else – a mentality which Hannah Arendt also considers essential to ethical judgment. She writes:

> The power of judgment rests on a potential agreement with others, and the thinking process which is active in judging something is not, like the thought process of pure reasoning, a dialogue between me and

myself, but finds itself always and primarily, even if I am quite alone in making up my mind, in an anticipated communication with others with whom I know I must finally come to some agreement. From this potential agreement judgment derives its specific validity. . . . It needs the special presence of others 'in whose place' it must think, whose perspectives it must take into consideration, and without whom it never has the opportunity to operate at all.[31]

Arendt, like Ricoeur, sees this 'representative' mode of ethical deliberation as 'liberation from one's own private interests', but not necessarily as an exit from one's own sphere of identity. 'The more people's standpoints I have present in my mind while I am pondering a given issue, and the better I can imagine how I would think and feel if I were in their place, the stronger will be my capacity for representative thinking.'[32] The issue, therefore, it seems to me, is only partially resolved. Others' points of view are still being represented 'in my mind' and need not always challenge my sense of self-containment.

To state the problem differently: this movement of representation/ apperception, while potentially ethical, is still directed from the inside out, from the self towards the other. It opens us to the other but is not necessarily summoned by, or 'hostaged' to, the other (to use Lévinas's language). In this scenario the self is still in charge, though willing to imagine itself in another's shoes. Thus understood, it is susceptible to the suspicion that it may be responding to the other less as *other per se* than as *another self*, an alter ego (a position Husserl never got beyond in the fifth of his *Cartesian Meditations*).[33] While this may indeed constitute an act of altruistic *ascesis* or *kenosis* – wherein the self flows from itself towards the other through the free variation of imagination – it remains a unilateral declaration of intent. It is coming from the imaginative self towards the other rather than permitting the other to impinge upon the imaginative self. In this sense, it could be said that narrative imagination opens us to the foreign world of others by enabling us to tell or hear other stories, but it can never be sure of escaping the hermeneutic circle of interpretation, which ultimately strives to translate the foreign into the familiar, the discordant into the concordant, the different into the analogous, the other into the self (or, at best, the enlarged 'representative' self).

If we accept these lines of argument, Ricoeur is right to set a limit to the power of narrative imagination – the limit, in this instance, being the ethical limit of responsible action. People *can* do what they like in their fantasies; but they cannot act with impunity in the real world. *L'imaginaire ne connaît pas de censure*; but my responsibility to others does. Poetic license applies only to poetics, not to the ethical world of action beyond the text. Those who think otherwise, or simply refuse to acknowledge the distinction, have been known to make grave errors of ethical judgment – from Céline and Pound to Heidegger and Foucault.[34]

While I do not propose, by way of conclusion, to reimpose a dichotomy between poetics and ethics, I do believe we need to observe certain border controls. Otherwise the schematizing–synthesizing–fictionalizing impulses of narrative imagination run the risk of reducing otherness to selfhood (individual or collective). So doing, they run the risk of overlooking the primary principle of ethical responsibility to the other as other-than-self. I would agree, therefore, with Ricoeur that a poetics of narrative imagination is in many respects a condition of ethics, for (1) providing a base for a responsible self (with a perduring identity capable of making commitments, promises and pledges), and (2) transcending the self towards possible or alien worlds. But if such a poetics is a necessary condition, it is not a *sufficient* one. The condition for ethics only becomes sufficient when the other breaks across the narrative of the self and asks, 'Where are you?' – and the self responds, 'Here I am!'

'*Où êtes-vous? Me voici!*'

University College Dublin, Ireland

Notes

1 Paul Ricoeur, 'Metaphor and the Central Problem of Hermeneutics', *Revue philosophique de Louvain* 70 (1972): 93–112; trans. and ed. J. B. Thompson in *Hermeneutics and the Human Sciences* (Cambridge: Cambridge University Press, 1981), p. 181.

2 Paul Ricoeur, 'Paul Ricoeur and the Hermeneutic Imagination', in *The Narrative Path: The Later Work of Paul Ricoeur*, ed. David Rasmussen and Peter Kemp (Cambridge, MA: MIT Press, 1989), pp. 1–33; republished in a somewhat extended form as 'The Hermeneutical Imagination (Ricoeur)' in my *Poetics of Imagining* (London: Routledge, 1981), pp. 134–70. I also explore the poetical and ethical implications of Ricoeur's theory of narrative imagination in the conclusion to *The Wake of Imagination* (London: Hutchinson, 1988), pp. 392–439 and the more general ontological and eschatological implications of his hermeneutics of 'figuration' in *Poétique du Possible* (Paris: Beauchesne, 1984). Recent studies which explore the

crucial role of narrative in the refiguration of (Irish) political and cultural history include numerous publications of the Field Day Group (Heaney, Deane, Friel, Rea, Paulin), in particular the *Field Day Anthology of Irish Writing* (London: Faber, 1992–4); K. Rockett, L. Gibbons and J. Hill, *Cinema and Ireland* (London: Croom Helm, 1987); Helena Sheenan, *Irish Television Drama: A Society and Its Stories* (Dublin: RTE, 1987); *The Irish Mind: Exploring Intellectual Traditions*, ed. Richard Kearney (Dublin and Manchester: Wolfhound and Manchester University Press, 1984); and my *Transitions: Narratives in Modern Irish Culture* (Dublin and London: Wolfhound and Manchester University Press, 1987). Recent studies which challenge or repudiate the role of narrative in redefining cultural and political identity include Jean-François Lyotard's *The Postmodern Condition* (Minneapolis: University of Minnesota Press, 1979); *Nation and Narration*, ed. Homi Bhabha (London: Routledge, 1990); and Gayatri C. Spivak, *The Post-Colonial Critic* (London: Routledge, 1990).

3 Paul Ricoeur, *Time and Narrative*, Vol. 3, trans. K. Blamey and D. Pellauer (Chicago, IL: University of Chicago Press, 1988), p. 180.

4 ibid., p. 183.

5 ibid.

6 ibid., p. 184.

7 ibid.

8 ibid.

9 Jean-François Lyotard, 'After the Sublime, the State of Aesthetics', in *The Inhuman*, trans. G. Bennington and R. Bowlby (Stanford, CA: Stanford University Press, 1991), p. 136. For further critiques of this general position, see C. Norris, *The Truth about Postmodernism* (Oxford: Blackwell, 1993), particularly the chapter 'Kant Disfigured: Ethics, Deconstruction and the Textual Sublime' (pp. 182–256); and G. Madison, 'The Practice of Theory, the Theory of Practice', *Critical Review* (Spring 1991): 179–202, where the author argues that a postmodern rejection of foundationalism (recognizing the unavoidability of interpretation) need not entail the rejection of theory altogether – a point argued on the basis of a tradition of rational hermeneutic critique, ranging from Aristotle's theory of *phronesis* (practical judgment) to Richard Bernstein's recent thesis that a poetics of reading does not mean that we can no longer distinguish 'better from worse reasons', i.e. dispense with a hermeneutics of values (see R. J. Bernstein, *The New Constellation: The Ethical-Political Horizons of Modernity/Postmodernity* [Oxford: Polity Press, 1991], pp. 281, 276–7). Another interesting gloss on this debate is in Philippe Lacoue-Labarthe's *La fiction du Politique* (Paris: Ed. Bourgois, 1988)

where the author claims that the interrelationship between fiction and politics can constitute a certain discourse of 'mythopoesis' governed by a 'logic of aesthetic-political immanentism' that, at worst, degenerates into a politics of nationalist aestheticism of which National Socialism is the most poisonous historical example. Including in this 'mythopoesis', or self-fashioning *techné*, such figures as Nietzsche, Junger, and Heidegger (as reader of Trakl), Lacoue-Labarthe identifies it as a tendency to see the 'political as the sphere of the fictioning of beings and communities' (p. 71). See also Lacoue-Labarthe's *Heidegger, Art and Politics* (Oxford: Blackwell, 1990).

10 Ricoeur, *Time and Narrative*, Vol. 3, p. 185.

11 ibid.

12 ibid., p. 186.

13 ibid.

14 Primo Levi, *Si c'est un Homme?* (Paris: Julliard, 1987). For further discussion of this ethical role of narrative memory see my *Poetics of Imagining* (London: Routledge, 1991), pp. 220–8.

15 Ricoeur, *Time and Narrative*, Vol. 3, p. 187.

16 Cited by R. Wolin in *The Heidegger Controversy: A Critical Reader* (Cambridge, MA: MIT Press, 1993).

17 ibid., p. 188.

18 ibid.

19 ibid., p. 189.

20 ibid., p. 246.

21 ibid.

22 ibid.

23 Seyla Benhabib, *Situating the Self: Gender, Community and Postmodernism in Contemporary Ethics* (New York: Routledge, 1992), p. 5. See also Charles Taylor, *Sources of the Self* (Cambridge, MA: Harvard University Press, 1990); Hannah Arendt, *Between Past and Future* (Harmondsworth, Mx: Penguin, 1977); Alasdair MacIntyre, *After Virtue* (London: Duckworth Press, 1981); and the recent work by Martha Nussbaum on the role of 'literary imagination' in ethical judgment, *Love's Knowledge: Essays on Philosophy and Literature* (Oxford: Oxford University Press, 1990), especially the chapters 'Flawed Crystals: James's *The Golden Bowl* and Literature as Moral Philosophy', 'Finely Aware and Richly Responsible: Literature and Moral Imagination', 'Perceptive Equilibrium: Literary Theory and Ethical Theory', 'Reading for Life' (a review essay on Wayne Booth's *The Company we Keep: An Ethics of Fiction* [Berkeley: University of California Press, 1988], 'Fiction of the Soul', and 'Narrative Emotions: Beckett's Genealogy of Love'.

24 Ricoeur, *Time and Narrative*, Vol. 3, p. 247.

25 ibid., p. 248.

26 ibid.

27 ibid., p. 249; emphasis added.

28 ibid.

29 See James Miller, *The Passion of Michel Foucault* (New York: Simon & Schuster, 1993), p. 377. Foucault himself never hesitated to subordinate an ethics of responsibility to an 'aesthetics of existence', whose primary fidelity is to the 'care of the self'. See, for example, 'On the Genealogy of Ethics' in *The Foucault Reader*, ed. P. Rabinow (New York: Pantheon, 1984), p. 343. The above critique of Foucault distinguishes between the ethics of his personal life – which does not concern my argument – and the ethical implications of his 'aesthetic' readings of, for example, political violence or popular tribunals. It is also worth considering here the argument of a practicing artist like David Putnam, that contemporary art (in this case film) has profound ethical and political consequences for authors and the public alike. See *The Moral Imagination* (Coleraine: University of Ulster, 1992) for example, his belief that 'to have become a non-combatant in the battle for the world's "moral imagination" will, in my opinion, eventually be seen as something of an historical tragedy' (p. 10); or, his two conclusions: 'I have to believe in the possibility of a morally responsible community, one in which the artist, the communicator, can both function and be encouraged to find the very best within him or herself' (p. 19); and 'Artists, and those who work with them, have a considerable moral responsibility to carefully select projects which attune themselves to the needs of their audience, projects which at the very least offer them a sense of values' (p. 23).

30 See R. Wolin in his preface to *The Heidegger Controversy* (Cambridge, MA: MIT Press, 1993), where he accuses Derrida of rendering (no doubt in spite of himself) the ethical difference between Nazism and non-Nazism undecidable (p. xvi). See also Derrida's response to the charge of 'indifference' in 'Deconstruction and the Other', in my *Dialogues with Contemporary Continental Thinkers* (Manchester: Manchester University Press, 1984), pp. 107–24.

31 Hannah Arendt, 'The Crisis of Culture', in *Between Past and Future* (Harmondsworth, Mx: Penguin, 1977), pp. 220–1. For a lucid discussion of this theme see Jeffrey Isaac, *Arendt, Camus and Modern Rebellion* (New Haven, CT: Yale University Press, 1992), pp. 167–70.

32 ibid. Crucial ethical and political aspects of this intersubjective 'social' mode of 'representative' judgment are explored by Ricoeur in such texts as *Hermeneutics and the Human Sciences, Lectures on Ideology and Utopia* (New York: Columbia University Press, 1986); *Du texte à*

l'action: essais d'herméneutique, Vol. II (Paris: Editions du Seuil, 1986); *Lectures 1* and *Lectures 2* (Paris: Editions du Seuil, 1991–2); *Amour et Justice* (Tübingen: J. Mohr, 1990); *The Self as Another*, trans. K. Blamey (Chicago, IL: University of Chicago Press, 1992), especially Studies 7–9, and 'Quel éthos nouveau pour l'Europe?', in *Imaginer l'Europe*, ed. P. Koslowski (Paris: Cerf, 1992), pp. 107–18, where Ricoeur argues for a 'political imagination' capable of reconciling the dual narrative needs of identity and alterity at the level of collective memories and histories (see opening essay above, pp. 3–13). For further secondary glosses on the ethical and historical implications of narrative imagination see Kevin Vanhoozer's *Biblical Narrative in the Philosophy of Paul Ricoeur* (Cambridge: Cambridge University Press, 1990), pp. 224–39, and my own essay, 'L'Imagination herméneutique et le postmoderne', in *Paul Ricoeur: Les métamorphoses de la raison herméneutique*, ed. R. Kearney and J. Greisch (Paris: Cerf, 1991), pp. 357–72.

33 Edmund Husserl, *Cartesian Meditations*, trans. D. Cairns (The Hague: Martinus Nijhoff, 1960). It is debatable, indeed, whether Husserl's phenomenological disciples, from Heidegger to Sartre, ever fully succeeded in resolving the solipsistic implications of the Fifth Meditation on the other as 'alter ego'. The attempt to escape the self-revolving circle of Husserl's concern of Ricoeur's hermeneutics, from the critical seminal studies of Husserl published in *Husserl: An Analysis of his Phenomenology* (Evanston, IL: Northwestern University Press, 1967) and *A l'école de la phénoménologie* (Paris: Vrin, 1986), to the readings of Husserl's phenomenology of time in *Time and Narrative*, Vol. 3 (Chicago, IL: University of Chicago Press, 1988), and his phenomenology of self in *Oneself as Another*.

34 For a critique of the disjunction between the ethical and the aesthetic see Charles Taylor, *The Ethics of Authenticity* (Cambridge, MA: Harvard University Press, 1991), pp. 62–4; Peter Kemp, 'L'Irremplaçable', in his *Det Opersattliga* (Copenhagen: Symposium, 1992), where he argues that ethics implies narrative and narrative implies ethics (pp. 336 et seq.); and my own conclusion to *The Wake of Imagination* (London: Hutchinson, 1987; and St Paul: Minnesota University Press, 1988), pp. 359–97.

Gary Madison

Review essay

Ricoeur and the political

Paul Ricoeur, *Lectures I: Autour du politique* (Paris: Editions du Seuil, 1991)

In addition to his work in basic philosophical issues over the last several decades, work which has earned for him a foremost place among the leading thinkers of our time, and in addition, as well, to his generally less well known but nevertheless extensive and highly influential writings on religious and theological topics, Paul Ricoeur has also pursued a lifelong interest in political issues. The essays gathered together in *Lectures I: Autour du politique* amply testify to this enduring interest on his part.

This is the first of three volumes of Ricoeur's collected papers. Befitting the hermeneut of facticity that Ricoeur is, these 'readings' are indeed *interpretations*, interpretations of many of the prominent figures and central themes of recent times. Hannah Arendt, Jan Patočka, Eric Weil, Karl Jaspers and John Rawls are five such figures, with Rawls himself (and, to a lesser degree, Michael Waltzer) figuring prominently in a number of the thematic essays. In the keenly analytical and conceptually rigorous style which his readers have long since come to expect from him, Ricoeur seeks to come to grips in these essays with a number of the vexing aporias of our times. In one way or another, ours is, as Ricoeur says at one point, 'une époque tourmentée', one marked by a veritable 'Conflict of Interpretations' (to allude to the title of one of his earlier works). How could it be otherwise? In what we have come to call postmodernity, the problems confronting humanity are of an unprecedented magnitude and urgency; 'for the first time in the history of humanity, the latter is capable of actions whose dangerous effects are of a cosmic dimension' (p. 217). At the same time, however, many of the core values that we might want to fall back upon in tackling these problems have had their legitimacy called into question. In an era of global civilization humanity stands in need of an ethic of universal scope, yet the very notion of universality – perhaps the key notion of the philosophical enterprise, inseparable from that of humanity itself – has been denounced as 'Eurocentric' and hostile to numerous 'local' values. Ours is a time when, as Ricoeur says, 'ethics has become problematic as to its ultimate justification' (p. 278). The various essays gathered together here, which address the ecological challenge, the technological challenge, and other such pressing challenges, are so many attempts to stake out the ground on which an *ethics of responsibility* – a 'practical wisdom', as Ricoeur refers to it – might be built.

The common thread running throughout the essays is furnished by Ricoeur's ongoing attempt to work out the various implications of 'a philosophy of action of a hermeneutical sort', the ultimate goal being 'a moral theory of action'. What gives special urgency to this task is the qualitative changes that human action has undergone in our times due to the qualitative changes in our (technological) power to act. And what confers a special appeal on Ricoeur's meditations is the way in which he effectively realizes that what is called for is a distinct alternative to the way in which the ethical question has generally been approached, i.e. as if it were a matter of choosing between the mutually exclusive options of deontology and consequentialism. As Ricoeur recognizes, what is called for is an alternative to a stringent, but empty, formalism, a rigorous 'apriorism' of a Kantian sort, on the one hand, and an arbitrary and relativistic juridical positivism, on the other (see pp. 183, 185). An alternative, so to speak, to a rigid universalism (intolerant of cultural differences), on the one hand, and a ruinous relativism of particularist 'incommensurabilities', on the other. This is an extremely important issue at the present time, for if the 'ethics of human rights' (p. 266) is not in some way universal in scope and validity but is, instead, outweighed by cultural differences, then the very notion of human rights becomes philosophically meaningless, and, more importantly (or ominously) still, any appeals to such rights on the part of oppressed peoples lose greatly in practical efficacy as a tool for achieving freedom and democracy.

If a concern for the ethical and political dimensions of human action forms the general theme of these essays, what animates this concern, one is tempted to say, is the philosopher's faith in the supremacy of discourse over violence. There can be no philosophical *science* of ethics, Ricoeur freely acknowledges, but through argumentation in the rhetorical sense of the term people are – hopefully – capable of dealing in a humane and peaceful manner with their various *différends*. A universality sufficient for human coexistence is perhaps attainable in this way. Such a universality would not amount to a homogeneity of beliefs and convictions as to what constitutes the 'good life', and would certainly not be such as to eliminate the 'conflict of interpretations'. But why should consensus of a substantialist sort be held to be an ethical good in any event? Are not the virtues of pluralism and tolerance that underwrite the modern, secular liberal state – what Ricoeur often refers to as the Rule of Law (*l'Etat de droit*) – sufficient for a genuinely ethical praxis, if not an ethical science? In any event, as Ricoeur says, '*l'Etat de droit* expresses a deep transformation in *mentalités*, a *cultural mutation*' (p. 302). This 'mutation', Ricoeur recognizes, is a product of the Enlightenment, but, as he also seeks to show, it can be argued for on theological grounds. One thing that we have learned through the practice of liberal democracy is that an ethics of respect must respect difference. The only ethically acceptable consensus is a '*conflictual consensus*'. Alluding to Claude Lefort, Ricoeur recognizes that democracy is that 'regime which accepts its contradictions to the point of institutionalizing conflict' (p. 174).

Thus, in one sense the final message of these various essays taken together is that there is in fact only one regime, one mode of human coexistence, that is capable of responding to the ethical crisis of our time: democracy. Even though – or, precisely, because – democracy is that 'regime for which the process of its own legitimation is always in process and always in crisis' (p. 277), it is the only means by which various *différends* can confront one another in a morally acceptable manner; that is, with respect for human freedom and dignity. 'Democracy', Ricoeur asserts, 'is the political space in which this conflict [of interpretations] can be pursued with a respect for differences' (p. 293). The only ethics that is possible today is one which recognizes that the realm of human coexistence, i.e. the 'political', cannot, should not, be founded on *truth* in any quasi-absolutist or scientist sense (this would be a recipe for tyranny of either 'a fascist or Stalinist type') but, rather, on *justice*, i.e. the democratic, dialogical arbitration of rival claims (see p. 300). Summing all of this up, one is tempted to say that there is in fact only one truth today, and that is democracy.

McMaster University, Ont., Canada

Robert D. Sweeney

Review essay

Lectures II and a survey of recent Ricoeur publications

Paul Ricoeur, *Lectures II: La Contrée des philosophes* (Paris: Editions du Seuil, 1992). Also under consideration are recent publications by Lewis E. Hahn (ed.), Steven Clark, Pamela Sue Anderson, William J. Ellos and Calvin Schrag.

The purpose of this survey is to examine some recently published writings by Ricoeur and essays by others about his thought.

Lectures II

Lectures II: La Contrée des philosophes 'Readings II: The Region of the Philosophers' is valuable for its rich assemblage of articles and reviews from early stages to quite recent ones – from 1948 to 1992. The writings are grouped thematically under two headings: Part 1, 'Thinkers of Existence', and Part 2, 'Poetics, Semiotics, Rhetoric'. This lush pot-pourri gives us an opportunity to revisit the existentialist enterprise with a very discerning, intelligent and engaged tour-guide. We find here what are still original interpretations of Sartre, Camus, Kierkegaard and Marcel (for example, in 'Kierkegaard and Evil', where he describes the reader's 'astonishment, uneasiness, admiration and irritation at this incessant oscillation between the most acute imaginary experimentation and the most artificial conceptual dialectic'). Beyond the early dialogues with Jean Wahl and Marcel, we find Ricoeur taking up again in 1988 the latter's theme of 'disponibilité' and (himself an intense practitioner of it) situating it between ethics and ontology by way of the middle ground between attestation and mystery as they intersect in the gift. Here the reflective witness combines with the critical challenger of easy sentimentalities to actually advance our current understanding.

Another early essay, 'Return to Hegel (Jean Hyppolite)', from 1955, warily endorses Hyppolite's Hegelian enthusiasm and sits, somewhat uncomfortably, with the (much later) chapter of *Time and Narrative*, 'Renouncing Hegel'. We also find here studies on Nabert which impress us not only by their filial dedication, but also by their revelation of the Fichtean foundations of Ricoeur's own thought. The early review of Merleau-Ponty's *Humanism and Terror* is updated by the 'Homage to Merleau-Ponty' of 1961 and the more recent (1989) 'Merleau-Ponty beyond Husserl and Heidegger'. This last essay is an incisive rethinking of the position of Merleau-Ponty, which, having lost its relevance because of the irrelevance of its opponents, can be rethought in terms of its contribution to the theory of time. That is, we can see how Merleau-Ponty goes beyond both Husserl and Heidegger as he utilizes them, namely, by reason of the priority given to the aspect of time as 'being a whole' in contrast to the 'game of intentionalities' (p. 168). Heidegger initially prevails over Husserl in terms of the cohesion of a life as an 'ecstasy of time' that endures in such a way that it even can be personified in myth. But then the primacy given to the present (to the point of giving us the illusion of eternity) (p. 169) returns Merleau-Ponty to Husserl – the Husserl of the *fungierende* intentionality and the 'passive synthesis' (p. 170) that actually brings Husserl close to the transcendence of *Dasein* and points to a convergence of Husserl and Heidegger (p. 172).

The recent (1983) essay, 'Personalism Is Dead but the Person Has Returned' ('Meurt le personalism, revient la personne . . . '), gives us a vivid reminder of the quandaries of the Christian intellectual in the 1930s and 1940s. To try to encapsulate the person in Mounier's formulas was an effort futile for its difficulty and doomed to be wiped away by changed conditions and loyalties – by crisis (Scheler) in values to which the only effective response is conviction and engagement. The discussion of Dufrenne's *Poetics* (1960) gives a thorough review of the most recent version of this phenomenological aesthetics (one of Ricoeur's few sorties into this area) and then argues against its approach to language as expressivity, that is, the claim of its emergence from nature à la Spinoza. The review and discussion of Michel Henry's *Marx* gives us another incisive essay in which Ricoeur credits Henry with the definitive refutation of Althusser's 'scientific' Marx, as well as with demonstrating the centrality of the *German Ideology* over against the *1844 Manuscripts* as a focus on praxis versus idealism. But Ricoeur also finds that the circumstantial passivity endorsed here and elsewhere by Henry overly segregates life from representation; action requires articulation in symbolic systems.

But perhaps the major contribution of the book is in the culminating structuralist and hermeneutical studies. The discussion of Greimas is enlightening for several reasons: it reinforces the validity of Ricoeur's utilization of structuralism as he criticizes its over-ambition; it challenges the atemporality of structuralism even as it recognizes its later prioritizing of narrative understanding; and it delineates the inchoative value-system that Greimas has illuminated with his semiotic square.

Recent Ricoeur publications

A very recent volume is the *Philosophy of Paul Ricoeur* (Chicago, IL: Open Court, 1995; The Library of Living Philosphers, Vol. XXII) edited by Lewis E. Hahn (Hahn is the successor of Paul Schillp in this prestigious series). Most salient here is the intellectual autobiography (of 52 pages) that begins the volume, in which Ricoeur interweaves the milestones of his life (including the suicide of his fourth child – their 'Good Friday in life and thought') with the major philosophical themes (the theological dimensions of his thought being maintained, as he says, in complete separation). Particularly valuable here are reflections on the early works and their comparison with later ones; for example, on the difference between myth and narrative. Another is the focus on metaphor ('metaphoricity') and its analogical relation to narrative ('narrativity'). Both the risk and the inevitability of this parallel are underscored, especially in terms of the issue of reference both in metaphor ('split reference') and in narrative, where its supersession by 'refiguration' is explicated and clarified. Here Ricoeur explains how the role of the reader in completing the meaning of a text became an 'active reorganization of our being-in-the-world . . . following the invitation of the text . . . to become the reader of oneself'. The differences here involve comparisons not just between *The Rule of Metaphor* and *Time and Narrative*, but also between Volumes 1 and 3 of the latter wherein the 'realism' of the first position is both refined and altered by the strict hermeneutics of the second. There are many other such comments relating to differences between early and later work, as, for example, why value declined in centrality in his ethical theory and had to be replaced by Aristotle's teleology and a greater emphasis on Kant's deontology.

Most of these themes return, but in much more detail, in Ricoeur's 24 responses to his critics – individual essays that are masterpieces of generous summation and deft riposte. Complete accuracy would require a fuller discussion than is possible here, but a few of the more striking might be mentioned. For example, to the charge (repeated but refuted by Mary Gerhart) that he has misjudged the role of metaphor in philosophy, Ricoeur responds that his focus on the live metaphor entails the listening to it in its proper place in poetics; it plays only a secondary role in philosophy. In answer to Thelma Lavine's charge that he has ignored the value of natural science in his hermeneutic treatment of Freud, he recalls his emphasis on explanation in concert with understanding (and not in conflict). Somewhat conversely, to John Smith's complaint that the value of restoration is subordinated to that of suspicion, he points out that the putative asymmetricality is really balanced out in favor of hermeneutic understanding as the passion for truth.

To Peter Kemp's essay bringing out the role of narrativity in ethics by way of exemplarity, Ricoeur responds that the ethical intention must be added to the narrative structure of the self to reach its moral imputability. Charles Reagan takes us through key issues in *Time and Narrative* and outlines Ricoeur's theory of history in terms of the dialectic of understanding and explanation that navigates between the scientistic extremes of the 'covering law model' and the *annalistes*, on the one hand, and narrative history and Gallie's 'followability' on the other. But Reagan does not bring out the ingenuity of Ricoeur's theory of the historical plot understood as 'singular causal imputation' featuring quasi-events and quasi-characters as first-order referents. To Dabney Townsend's effort to replace metaphorical reference with a version of situation semantics, Ricoeur replies that such a realist semantics still presupposes interpretation.

In her 'From the Ego to the Self', Kathleen Blamey gives us an extensive and thorough treatment of subject throughout the Ricoeur corpus with a generous explication of narrative identity from *Oneself as Another*. It might be noted that Ricoeur offers only a token response here, evidently because his overall strategy is the frequent reference to *Oneself as Another* as answering many of the puzzles left hanging by his critics, since, apparently because of editorial constraints, they give the more recent writings relatively less attention. For further research, this volume also contains the latest version of Franz Vansina's invaluable bibliography with entries in a variety of languages (resulting in a few understandable misspellings.)

Robert D. Sweeney

A recent study by Steven Clark, *Paul Ricoeur* (London: Routledge, 1990), presents a perspective that is primarily literary, but still well informed by philosophical background. This enables him to argue the case for Ricoeur's hermeneutics on several fronts, including both deconstruction and analytical philosophy, in a very thorough exposition of *Time and Narrative* (up to but not including Volume 3). But it is a rather critical defense that is intermixed with the exposition – sometimes to the confusion of the reader albeit with a sure sense for the text. Clark is perhaps most helpful in the section comparing Ricoeur and Lacan, and in his explication of the *Rule of Metaphor*, especially Study 8, where he critiques Heidegger's etymological reduction of metaphor and Derrida's resurrection of dead metaphor as part of the 'collusion of metaphor and metaphysics', at the same time that he finds Ricoeur's view of philosophical language too controlling. Clark's explanation of metaphorical reference relies too much, perhaps, on the (Fregean) redescription notion of reference to allow for Ricoeur's modifications in terms of refiguration.

Among other recent works that deal with Ricoeur's oeuvre, one written from a religious and postmodern perspective is Pamela Sue Anderson's *Ricoeur and Kant: Philosophy of the Will* (Atlanta: Scholars Press, 1993). This features a fine-grained, if overly compact, treatment of the early works, claiming to detect a persistent transcendental idealism. It does attempt to bring the issue up to date in terms of *Oneself as Another*, but the treatment of this material is quite sketchy, focusing, as it does, on the 'mysterious functioning' of the imagination, but ignoring Ricoeur's utilization of the *Critique of Judgement*. The crucial distinction between *ipse* and *idem* is not discussed even though this would have helped to resolve the tension she finds – one of the main critical points of the book – between the transcendental and empirical ego in Ricoeur's thought. 'The Weavings of Narrative', in *Narrative Ethics* by William J. Ellos (Aldershot: Avebury Series in Philosophy, 1994) explores the possibility of utilizing Ricoeur's theory to do practical ethics, especially in terms of the three meanings of 'tradition' in *Time and Narrative*, whereby we can learn both to accept and to struggle with ethical traditions. Finally, mention should be made here of the continuing sensitive and creative reference to Ricoeur's thought found in the work of Calvin Schrag, including his latest, *The Resources of Rationality: a Response to the Postmodern Challenge* (Bloomington: University of Indiana Press, 1992). Ricoeur's narrativized temporality, he explains, gives us superior access to the 'chronotopal field of tranversality' – the closest approximation to space–time universality available to us in a postmodern world.

John Carroll University, University Heights, OH, USA

David Tracy

Review essay

Ricoeur's philosophical journey: its import for religion

Paul Ricoeur, *Lectures III: Aux frontières de la philosophie*
(Paris: Editions du Seuil, 1994)

Lectures III includes essays with an extraordinary chronological range
(1952–93) but with a singular consistency. These essays show Paul
Ricoeur's exceptional contributions directly to the philosophy of
religion and the hermeneutics of religions, and, more indirectly, to
Jewish and Christian theology.

That philosophical consistency is best seen initially in the essays
constituting Part 1 of this volume ('Philosophie et non-philosophie').
In a philosophical self-portrait worthy of a sketch by Rembrandt
(which Ricoeur honors with the first suggestive essay of this volume)
Paul Ricoeur once described his philosophical journey as a return to
Kant through Hegel. Many of us have admired Ricoeur's long
philosophical journey over the years – a journey notably singleminded
and straightforward despite the many important developments and
changes and, at times, almost labyrinthine detours. Ricoeur's self-
description – to Kant through Hegel – is, in my judgment, an entirely
accurate description of the basic Ricoeurian journey.

The reader of *Lectures III* soon learns that Ricoeur, in philosophy
of religion, maintains the contours of a Kantian philosophy of limits

that has journeyed widely and deeply through the multifaceted forms, both figurative and conceptual, of history, culture and religion. Thus can Ricoeur show how Kant, too, in *Religion within the Limits of Reason Alone* is a surprisingly hermeneutical thinker of religion, just as he can show, with equal care, that Hegel, by his concentration on the mutually dialectical relationships of *Vorstellung* and *Begriff*, still defines the kind of hermeneutical journey needed by any contemporary philosophy of religion faithful to, without ever confusing, figurative and conceptual thought. Hence the Kantian theme of 'limits' yields a surprisingly *hermeneutical* turn to philosophy of religion just as the Hegelian *Aufhebung* of figurative by conceptual forms yields a surprising attention to the *limits* of each form in the fuller range of historical, cultural, religious and philosophical forms.

This return to Kant through Hegel also allows Ricoeur, with characteristic generosity united to full-fledged critique, to engage in serious conversation with 20th-century philosophers of religion: as in his brilliant reading of the notorious complexities in Rosenzweig's project as philosophy, and his critical conversation with his own philosophical contemporaries Emmanuel Lévinas and Stanislas Breton. In a surprising move, the earliest essay (1972) of Part 1 ('L'herméneutique du témoignage') might just as well have been the most recent. Indeed, this early essay provides an admirable summary of where Ricoeur's conversations with such contemporaries as Lévinas have led him in his own Ricoeurian return to his beloved, modest, cautious, rigorous philosopher of limits, Kant, in and through an immersion in all the signs and symbols, both figurative and conceptual, in the methods and disciplines of our post-Kantian era. Like Kant, Ricoeur always keeps the genres clear in order not only to allow figurative and conceptual forms their distinct but dialectically related roles but also to keep properly distinct religion, philosophy and theology. Ricoeur's impact on contemporary Christian theology has been enormous, of course. However, that influence has always been, from Ricoeur's side, intended as a strictly philosophical contribution to theological self-understanding. Unlike some of his admirers, Ricoeur himself never allows philosophy or theology to be confused or conflated.

This care with distinctions, boundaries, limits (all nicely suggested by the subtitle for this volume, 'Aux frontières de la philosophie') allows Ricoeur the freedom he needs and wants in order to study, with hermeneutical care, certain non-philosophical phenomena in relationship to philosophy. This care (again like Kant's) allows one to see the characteristically Reformed sensibility of Ricoeur's choice of phenomena for study: propheticism, tragedy and, above all (in an extraordinarily careful, complex, indeed dense essay, a fine study), evil as a challenge to both philosophy and theology.

Moreover, Ricoeur's Kantian care with distinctions and limits frees him, in so much of his work (as the explicit hermeneutics of religion essays of Part 3 display), to show how the polarity between conceptual and figurative thinking has not been superimposed from without upon some Jewish and early Christian sayings but is already adumbrated *within* these sayings and forms themselves. The fruitfulness of Ricoeur's hermeneutics for interpreting religion shows in these essays of Part 3, especially the ambitious because wide-ranging study of the major genres of the Hebrew Bible, the brilliant hermeneutical essay on naming God. Moreover, a religious sensibility, united to the philosophical rigor in Ricoeur's philosophy of religion, shows itself more clearly in the essays of Part 3. That sensibility, not surprisingly, is classically Reformed: at home in the whole Bible (not only the New Testament); insistent on the power but, above all, the necessary limits of thought; careful, rigorous and consistent without over-systematization; always aware of the finitude, the tragedy and evil even in the midst of moments of transcendental truth, goodness and beauty.

Even those philosophers whose philosophical and religious sensibilities (the two are most clearly linked in the essays of Part 3) are other than Ricoeur's – the Lutheran Hegel, the Jewish Lévinas, the Catholics Marcel and Marion, the Orthodox Eliade – would not but stand back and admire with deepfelt thanks the remarkable achievement of Paul Ricoeur. He possesses all the virtues of the classical Reformed tradition (as did Kant!): rigorous in philosophical method; generous, but straightforward in criticism; aware and honest about distinctions and the need for limits. In a word, beautiful in the Reformed sense: as Rembrandt's Reformed self-portraits are; as Calvin's finely wrought distinctions within the *Institutes* are; as Kant's philosophical integrity always is. This is a finely selected volume of essays that illuminates Ricoeur's larger philosophical corpus as nicely and as clearly as some of Kant's later essays on religion, history and art so clearly illuminate Kant's three Critiques. *Lectures III* is a worthy companion not only to *Lectures I* and *II* but to the full range of the distinctive, indeed extraordinary, philosophical achievement of Paul Ricoeur's whole oeuvre.

University of Chicago, IL, USA

William Richardson

Review essay

Olivier Mongin, *Paul Ricoeur* (Paris: Editions du Seuil, 1994)

'God writes straight in crooked lines', and so does Paul Ricoeur. This is the thesis that emerges from Olivier Mongin's exhaustive study of this major thinker of the late 20th century. The shifts of focus in Ricoeur's thinking from a phenomenology of the will to the symbolism of evil to the hermeneutics of symbolism to the mysteries of hermeneutics to the unfolding of these mysteries in time and history to the nature of the self that does it all (or where it all takes place) – these appear coherent to the reader who can come to appreciate the singleness of purpose that permeates the prolific vitality and indefatigable curiosity of this true explorer of the mind in his undaunted effort to confront the diverse philosophical challenges of contemporary culture.

Mongin, former student of Ricoeur and (at the time of this writing), editor of the review *Esprit*, has offered us an exhaustive study of the workings of that mind. He has done so by maintaining a dynamic tension between two principles of exposition, difficult to reconcile in the concrete: an insistence on the coherent unity that underlies the entire enterprise; a willingness to tarry along the way in the sinuousness of Ricoeur's ongoing dialogues with his contemporaries in the context of the entire Western philosophical tradition. This Mongin achieves by an organization of his own exposition that chooses to be more thematic than chronological, concerned rather with discerning the continuity of the evolving problematic than tracing the intellectual biography of its author.

The development falls into five segments that Mongin conceives as self-contained, but mutually integrated, parts of a five-act play. The first act deals with Ricoeur's basic philosophical concern: the relationship between anthropology and ontology as concretized in the ontological structure of the human act. The philosophy of action that emerges from these considerations leads naturally to questions concerning politics and law, which become the substance of Chapter 2. The third act centers its attention on the problem of time and history, emphasizing the role of reflection in the generation of a narrative identity. Such reflection allows for the integration of a 'descriptive' approach (characteristic of phenomenology and analytical philosophy) with a more 'prescriptive' (ethical) one that makes a critique of historical narratives possible. Act 4 is devoted to *Oneself as Another*, Ricoeur's latest book (as of 1990), with all the resonances it contains of the major themes that have been previously articulated. Here Ricoeur's own approach to ethics becomes discernible, distinguished as it is from the 'ontology without ethics' of Heidegger and the 'ethics without ontology' of Lévinas. The final act of this drama (Chapter 5) deals with what Ricoeur himself calls 'non-philosophy', i.e. philosophical issues (especially the problem of evil) that are presented under a non-philosophical template, such as in Greek tragedy or the Great Code of biblical history. This material forms a kind of coda, however, and leaves the focus on *Oneself as Another* as the clear centerpiece, in Mongin's view, of Ricoeur's entire achievement. As the work unfolds, each of these five sections in turn is preceded by a concise résumé of the detailed analysis to follow.

Mongin writes well, and his expositions of complex issues are generally lucid. If one were to find fault with the presentation, it would be, perhaps, the apparent lack of critical distance between Mongin and his subject-matter. To be sure, there is much more here than sheer exposition, for the selection and arrangement of the material is synthetically creative, but one gets the feeling that the author conceives his task as that of Ricoeur's lawyer rather than his critic. However, Ricoeur himself is so careful and Mongin's account of his controversies with critics so detailed that the general atmosphere of the work is one of open-minded honesty.

The book is a rich resource for any student of Ricoeur at whatever level, though Anglo-Saxons will find its usefulness severely limited. Despite a detailed table of contents and a full bibliography, there is no adequate instrument available to mine its considerable wealth. As the book stands, it is sorely in need of adequate indexing, i.e. at least indexes of authors cited and of subject-matter. Hopefully, an eventual English translation, highly desirable in itself, will fill such a need. That said, the book makes an important contribution to the understanding of this major philosopher of the 20th century – reason to rejoice and be glad.

Boston College, MA, USA

Index